D0331155

BREAK

THESE

CHAINS

BREAK
THESE
CHAINS

The Battle for

School Choice

**DANIEL
McGROARTY**

Published in Association with ICS Press

An Imprint of Prima Publishing

© 1996 BY DANIEL McGROARTY

All rights reserved. No part of this book may be reproduced or transmitted in any form or by any means, electronic or mechanical, including photocopying, recording, or by any information storage or retrieval system, without written permission from Prima Publishing, except for the inclusion of quotations in a review.

PRIMA PUBLISHING, FORUM, and colophons are trademarks of Prima Communications, Inc.

Library of Congress Cataloging-in-Publication Data

McGroarty, Daniel.
Break these chains: the battle for school choice / Daniel McGroarty
p.   cm.
Includes bibliographical references and index.
ISBN 0-7615-0507-5
1. School choice—United States—Case studies. 2. Educational vouchers—United States—Case studies. 3. School choice—Wisconsin—Milwaukee. 4. Educational vouchers—Wisconsin—Milwaukee. I. Title.
LB1027.9.M395 1996
379.1'1—dc20   96-280
                                                                                              CIP

96 97 98 99 00 DD 10 9 8 7 6 5 4 3 2 1
Printed in the United States of America

PRIMA PUBLISHING

ICS PRESS

HOW TO ORDER

Single copies may be ordered from Prima Publishing, P.O. Box 1260BK, Rocklin, CA 95677; telephone (916) 632-4400. Quantity discounts are also available. On your letterhead, include information concerning the intended use of the books and the number of books you wish to purchase.

To my family:
Jacky,
Michele, Erik, and Corey

We've got to break these chains before the system turns our children into slaves.

—POLLY WILLIAMS

Contents

I

The Education Plantation

II

Emancipation

III

Church, State, and Choice

IV

Report Card

Foreword

Vouchers. The word invites controversy. To the education establishment, vouchers are a dagger at the throat of the public school; in conservative circles, vouchers are often the equivalent of the Unified Field Theory, a one-size-fits-all solution to our educational shortcomings. The school choice argument has long since become formulaic: The same arguments, for and against, espoused to the same audiences, somehow hermetically sealed so as to prevent any possibility of creating conversion or consensus. And each side has too often been content to engage in theory mongering, at the expense of taking a close look at real schools and real experiments. But there is one publicly funded school choice program in existence today. And *Break These Chains* takes a look at it.

This book is one part battlefield account of Milwaukee's pioneering Parental Choice program, one part policy discussion of education, race relations, and urban policy. *Break These Chains* gets beyond the stale certitudes of the existing voucher discussion because it gets inside—inside the schools, the homes, and the lives both of the political players who fought for and against Milwaukee's choice program, and of the parents and the students who have so much at stake in our schools. That combination elevates *Break These Chains* above the freeze-dried analysis that all too often passes for policy debate.

Consider the key question of publicly funded vouchers to students at religious schools: Consult any number of law-review treatises on First Amendment establishment-clause case law; no one who relives the ordeal of Brother Bob Smith described in this book will see church-state issues in quite the same light. Likewise, listen to the typical "ed conference" jabbering on ways to generate more educational options—then look through parents' eyes at the miracles of Messmer High School and the educational implosion at North Division High within the same square mile of Milwaukee's Near North Side.

As in any carefully drawn portrait, Milwaukee's story contains features many people familiar with the subject will not have noticed before. For conservatives, whose celebration of vouchers often derives from their attraction to free markets, *Break These Chains* makes clear how much education is primarily not a market issue but a moral issue—indeed, for many minority Americans, an extension of the long civil rights crusade. For others used to championing school choice and in the same breath flaying the "multicultural" fads popular with many public education experts, it may come as a shock to see that parents may use vouchers to choose schools with a multicultural curriculum. For liberals, the book brings home the sense of betrayal Polly Williams and her African-American allies experience when they find themselves opposite the NAACP and the liberal establishment in their anti-voucher lawsuit. Finally, in an age when we have all learned to decry gridlock in government, Williams's odd-bedfellow alliance between urban liberal Democrats and conservative Republicans demonstrates political savvy and offers a blueprint for political action, not simply on education but on other policy issues as well.

Readers of *Break These Chains* will come away from the experience armed with a new understanding of the challenges of the American classroom: A heightened sense of the pressures for change simmering beneath the surface of the American education system, the educational possibilities that exist in every city, and the new coalition that may be emerging in support of the most provocative—and promising—education reform of our time.

WILLIAM KRISTOL

Introduction:
Milwaukee As Microcosm

Principal Faces Drug Charges," blares the front-page headline. ". . . Accused of possessing crack cocaine," runs the subhead of the story, an account of the arrest of an urban school principal with a $200-a-week cocaine habit.[1] The principal's defense attorney hastens to assure the public that his client never used drugs on the premises of his school or in the presence of his students at 95th Street Elementary.

". . . Dropout Rate Hits 17.4%."[2] The 1994 number is "the highest since the district began reporting the statistic more than a decade ago." African-American and Hispanic students led the list of those most likely to drop out.

The district's schools reported 79,513 incidents of "classroom disruption" and "refuses instruction" in 1992–93—this for a student population of approximately 100,000 children.[3] During this school year, two shootings occurred on school grounds (neither fatal, the school district's Office of School Safety reported); 66 guns were discovered in students' possession, out of a total of 599 weapons of all types. Several of the city's high schools are equipped with permanent metal detectors; all high schools and middle schools possess hand-held Garrett scanners of the kind used to prevent airplane hijackings.[4]

Principals on crack. A lost generation of students. Prisonlike schools bristling with weapons. Stories and statistics like these are so familiar in urban school systems across America that readers in New York, Chicago, or Los Angeles might take these anecdotes as their own. Yet each concerns the same public school system—in Milwaukee, Wisconsin.

What these anecdotes illustrate is the pervasiveness of pathologies we once took to be the special province of our mega-cities. The blackboard jungle is no longer a cluster of schools in Bedford-Stuyvesant or Cabrini Green or South Central L.A. Milwaukee suggests that it has spread across this country's urban education system.

And Milwaukee is in many respects close to the unfortunate average. The twenty-third-largest public school system in the United States,[5] Milwaukee stands near the statistical center in terms of per-pupil spending: $5,867, a scant $7 off the average among large city school districts nationwide.[6]

Yet in key educational indicators, Milwaukee manifests an advanced state of educational decay.

- Milwaukee falls below the big-city school district average in students in the top quartile for reading and math tests, and exceeds the big-city average for students in the bottom quartile on math.[7]

- Milwaukee ranks first among the forty-seven Great City districts in dropouts. Milwaukee's dropout rate is double the Great City average, four times the national rate—and rising.[8] Chicago, often branded the worst public school system in America, ranks third in dropout percentage, behind Milwaukee and Los Angeles.

- Prospects are worse still for the city's minority students. At North Division High School, whose student population is 99 percent African-American, fewer than one in five students, just 17 percent, graduated on time. More than 53 percent of North Division's 1987 freshman class dropped out before graduation in 1991. Most of them never set foot in an eleventh-grade classroom.[9]

None of this is to suggest that Milwaukee is the new poster child illustrating the plight of urban public education. The Milwaukee Public Schools (MPS) district is, if anything, somewhat more responsive and innovative than many public systems of similar size. There are sought-after public schools in the city; parents strive and scheme to get their children into specialty schools like Milwaukee Tech and Rufus King High School.

In the end, what distinguishes Milwaukee is not its public school pathologies but an experiment unique in the annals of education reform: the Milwaukee Parental Choice Program—the first-ever "voucher" plan, providing public funds for private school choice.

REFORM AND REALITY

The failure of our schools cannot be attributed to a paucity of school reforms. Thanks to the alarm bell of the U.S. Department of Education's 1983 study, *A Nation at Risk*, America's schools have been on the receiving end of an enormous outpouring of reformist zeal. Many states and school districts have gone "back to basics," lengthened the school day or extended the school year, reemphasized discipline, strengthened testing, raised teacher pay, and assigned students more homework. Yet this flurry of reform—more symptomatic than systemic—has produced little in the way of results.

As this first wave of reform recedes, battlelines are being drawn around a radical measure that has been more talked about than tried: school choice.

Few education reforms have aroused more heated debate. To critics, choice vouchers are a dagger aimed at the very heart of the public schools. "Voucher pushers," National Education Association president Keith Geiger calls school choice backers, with a venom usually reserved for purveyors of an altogether different sort. To its champions, school choice is part lever, part lash to be used to move a public system resistant to real reform.

But after a decade-long war of words about vouchers, apocalyptic warnings and extravagant praise, Milwaukee remains the one city in the United States where rhetoric has given way to reality. If the problems of the Milwaukee public schools represent the plight of urban education in general, the premise of this book is that Milwaukee's voucher experiment may well represent a solution to a national problem.

For all their diametrical differences, both sides in the voucher debate share an odd addiction to theory. For most school choice supporters, advocacy takes the form of abstractions—"competition v. centralized bureaucracy"—theoretical models that borrow from free-market economics. Voucher opponents, for their part, believe in the myth of the "common school" imparting a democratic culture to a harmonious melting pot of students. Few on either side of the voucher divide care to test their theories—what choice looks like, who it hurts, who it helps—against the reality of the one city where it exists.

The impetus behind school choice in Milwaukee is anything but abstract. It was born less of ideology than of intimate frustration with failure: the persistent failure of inner-city public schools to educate children. Yet its radicalism should not disguise the traditional tenet at its core: a dogged belief in education as a passport to opportunity.

What follows is a battlefield account, a street-level view of the schools, the parents, the children, the politicians and public officials on both sides of the barricades. It is a story of failed reforms and false hopes, of the smoldering frustration that lit the fuse of what advocates and opponents alike agree is the most radical reform ever to thrust its way into the education debate. It is a discourse on the meaning of education and opportunity in American society, with implications far beyond the narrow confines of Milwaukee's Near North Side.

BREAK
THESE
CHAINS

PART I

The Education Plantation

Room 207

The film is a bit blurry, out of focus. At the front of Room 207 stands a teacher, slight, white, bespectacled. As he steps to the side, his legs alone are visible in the odd angle of the lens.

TEACHER [to students]: Can you act like you're reading? At least pretend you're reading?

In the first row of seats, little more than an arm's length from the teacher, a girl stands, reaches into a pocket. Ignoring the teacher, she begins bantering with the boy slumped in the chair next to her.

STUDENT: We don't have no book.
TEACHER: I know you have no books.

The videotape rolls. The teacher abandons his wan attempt to lead the class; no one seems in the mood to pretend, about books or anything else. Two students exchange stylized slaps, the kind favored by sports heroes and hip celebrities mugging for television. Unbeknownst to them, on a Sunday night several months later, millions of television viewers across the country will witness the scene in Room 207, North Division High School, on Milwaukee's Near North Side.

The videotape rolls. Students chatter, roam the room. At the edge of the picture, a wrist flicks forward; a ball of crumpled paper arcs through the frame. The teacher sits at the front of the class, flipping the pages of a magazine. He could be a patient waiting in a doctor's office. He glances at his watch, and back down at the magazine. He does not look up at the class. Minutes pass before he speaks again: "Well, what are we doing here today?"

Beyond the camera's eye, a challenging voice, male, brays back: "Nothing."

For eight hours over the course of two weeks, the hidden camera—jammed into a student's open book bag—captured daily life at North Division High School from an unflattering angle. Like the work of an avant-garde film student, the worm's-eye view, the tilted frame, the skewed shots of often headless bodies suit the anomie that pervades each class.

In one classroom, a jumble of chair legs does not conceal students shooting dice on a carpeted classroom floor; no teacher interrupts them. On and on the images roll. Students sleeping in class, slumped chin in hand. A bearded teacher, also chin in hand, sits staring ahead. Five feet in front of him, a student in the first row rolls to the rhythms of a pop song playing in his head, singing a few falsetto snatches. To no one in particular, the boy delivers a personal progress report: "I went to high school and I flunked every class." He punctuates his declaration with laughter. The teacher, still in a trance, shows no response. "I pass your class, buddy," taunts the student.

Between classes, the camera takes in chaotic hallway scenes. The conversation of the students booms and echoes: trash talk, laced with obscenities and casual threats of violence. In the raucous halls, no teachers or administrators are in sight.

NORTH DIVISION

North Division High School sits at the center of a half-dozen square blocks of some of Milwaukee's most grinding poverty. According to census data, in the neighborhood around North, as the school is known, just 48 percent of all adults have jobs.[1] To know an adult with a regular job is outside the experience of many North students.

Statistics give a snapshot of the depth of poverty around North. Average household income is $11,216; according to the census, there are 475 people with jobs in 584 households. Forty-three percent of the neighborhood's residents live below the poverty level; 80 percent of households with children are headed by single parents; 60 percent of all households are headed by a female. One in every eight homes is vacant, a magnet for vagrants and crackheads.

Births to unmarried women are epidemic, at 90 percent. In 1990, just seven children born in the North Division neighborhood were born to married couples.[2]

The story of this neighborhood is common enough in the history of urban America. Once home to the stolid immigrants who made Milwaukee the most German city in the United States, the Near North Side has long since seen the migration of those early inhabitants to suburban enclaves such as Brown Deer, Wauwatosa, and West Allis. Today, the North Division neighborhood is 98 percent African-American. In the streets around North, the grand monuments to Lutheran worship have given way to congregations like the Church of Our Father's Business, little more than a house-front ministry. On Teutonia Avenue (pronounced Tie-tonia by local residents) stands Union Cemetery, the favored antebellum burial ground of the Near North Side's German community, where the tombstones record the final resting place of immigrants born in Black Forest villages; at the cemetery's south end stands Calvary Baptist Church, modernist brick and rust-red I-beams, designed in the shape of two African huts.

South of the school, Schlitz Park, at the turn of the century the brewery's grand beer garden and site of open-air speeches by Presidents McKinley, Cleveland, and Teddy Roosevelt, is now Carver Park, spliced at its northern end by the I-94 expressway to

Chicago. At night, after the baseball diamonds empty out, Carver is off-limits to the law-abiding, a shadow world where young men who meet at the park periphery retreat and reemerge. In 1993, more than half the murders in Milwaukee were committed within a three-mile radius of North Division High School.[3]

In the 1960s and '70s, much of the housing below North Avenue was razed, with the area slated for urban renewal. More than twenty years later, vacant lots remain for sale, in spite of incentives to promote homeowner investment. In time, the urge to bring the wonders of urban renewal to the area ebbed; the Near North Side has been left to its own devices. For many Milwaukeeans, it is the frame house on a forgotten street where their grandparents lived, an exit they won't take on the highway to the skyscrapers rising on the rim of Lake Michigan.

But North Division's ruddy red-orange brick building is by all appearances an imposing structure. Completed in 1978 and taking up a full city block, the school boasts the solid if uninspired architecture common to so many public buildings built in the past two decades. Replacing the original North Division, a decrepit seventy-year-old building that was demolished once the new school was ready, the new North was to be a flagship school.

It is difficult to recapture the sense of hope that surged as the new North rose up alongside the old, but the construction of a new school in a long-neglected neighborhood seemed naturally to take on a symbolic meaning. From the first, this school was to belong to the neighborhood. During construction, parents demonstrated to prevent the new North from being designated a citywide magnet school, a decision that would have limited the number of seats available for neighborhood students by holding spaces open to children from other parts of the city—especially white children whose attendance would help meet desegregation targets. "The Committee to Save North," neighborhood parents called themselves.

The parents prevailed; North was zoned as a neighborhood school. Their high hopes for the new North, however, never materialized. In a way, their very victory had ensured disappointment; with the school district so heavily committed to the success of its magnet school venture, North had positioned itself on the periphery of the system's field of vision. Today, North is known as the worst high school in Milwaukee.

On average, a full three-quarters of the students who enter ninth grade at North Division fail to graduate four years later. Most of those who drop out disappear before ever attending even a single day of eleventh grade. Two-thirds of the students who do attend North maintain a D average—in classes where, students contend, simply showing up warrants a C.

North is a school where keeping students in and strangers out is a constant challenge. Security personnel clad in blue nylon jackets communicate with the principal by walkie-talkie. At one entrance, the task of door monitor is shouldered by a slight, grandmotherly woman, her stiff graying hair pinned into a bun. Walkie-talkie crackling at her belt, she doesn't hesitate to tell two boys, latecomers muffled under fur-trimmed parka hoods, to stop shuffling and step along to class. Surprisingly, the boys pick up their pace. A moment later, two undercover cops, dressed casually in denim but with giveaway cadet-school razor-cut hair, poke their heads into the main office. They want to see whether a student wanted for dealing drugs has come to school that day; no one in the office seems to know.

CANDID CAMERA

Eric Ransom, the young man whose hidden camera captured the surreal classroom scenes, is a survivor, an exception to the rule.[4] An honor student and senior class president at North Division, he had picked his way across an academic no man's land. He was one of the students the school officials boasted about, a bright spot of educational achievement in a school known citywide for its failures. He will, several months after shooting his film—his secret still unknown to anyone at North Division—cross the stage in the school gym, receive his diploma, and be acclaimed to his fellow graduates as recipient of a four-year, $60,000 scholarship to Marquette University, a dozen blocks and a world away from North Division High.

The reasons that led Eric Ransom to pack a camera into his black nylon bag and turn a videotape over to a national news organization are complex and even contradictory. They included anger and a desire for revenge against his school and "the system"; there was also the hope that the tape would help and not hurt his school, that it would reach people who could truly change things. He has no sense of regret.

Ransom had always been a bit different from the other kids who went to North, an outsider in a world where outsiders could find themselves in dangerous situations. Born in Milwaukee, he was raised in rural Mississippi from the age of nine months by his grandmother, who was certain a farm was a better place for a boy than a city, with all its dangers and distractions.

At fourteen, a ninth grader headed for high school, Eric Ransom came north to live with his mother in her house on Burleigh Street, eight blocks from North Division. A new arrival, he was captivated by the hard-edged boys who belonged to the "street organizations," who feared nothing and no one. The pull of the gangs, however, was countered by the far more wholesome influence of the Keystone Boys and Girls Club, on Center Street between his mother's house and North Division. There, he met older boys who won honors and awards, who traveled to other cities and states and, one summer, even to Europe. To his mother's relief, Eric became a regular at Keystone.

His transformation into a model member of the club was almost immediate. When he first joined, he dreamed of going with the club when they got free tickets to Brewers' games at County Stadium. A few years later, honored as Keystone's Young Man of the Year, Eric Ransom stood on the pitcher's mound at County Stadium and threw out the first ball.

Eric proved a natural ambassador for his school, in demand as student representative at innumerable conferences and symposia. One evening, at a charity dinner, he was introduced to Howard Fuller, then the incoming superintendent of Milwaukee Public Schools, himself a graduate of North Division. Eric wondered whether North could have possibly been the same when Fuller was a student.

Failure was tolerated—that everyone knew; but what distressed Eric was that success was greeted with equal indifference. All around him, students faltered and fell prey to the streets; it was as though they were invisible. Still, Eric thought, at some level these kids brought things on themselves; you couldn't hold teachers or the school responsible. Yet Eric soon learned that even the better students were invisible. He could cut a class, without consequences. He could work hard or slide by; it was all the same. In the end, it was the wall of official indifference to academic achievement that angered him; he was more celebrated than educated. "When I left North, I had the grades," Eric recalls, "but I was empty as a hollow tree."

In the spring of his senior year, a producer from a television show called Eric, by then better known for his string of leadership honors than some of the best high school athletes in inner-city Milwaukee. The producer wanted to talk about urban schools and the shocking things he'd heard went on in the classrooms. He asked Eric whether the stories were true. Eric said they were. Would he take a camera into the school? He would.

Depending on one's point of view, the tape Eric Ransom left behind is a smoking gun, Exhibit A in an indictment of public education, or a media-manufactured fraud, a hatchet job on unsuspecting teachers. Yet, like the Rodney King tape that seared itself into public consciousness, the tape resists interpretation, insistently speaking for itself.

The fact that few can penetrate the system to see what really happens at unguarded moments is what makes the tape so compelling. Like a strange signal from a distant planet, the tape forces us to confront the prospect that there is a world we didn't know existed—that our schools may in fact be entirely alien to us. Into a debate that focuses on the familiar if lamentable reasons our children do not learn—a fermenting stew of fractured families, poverty, joblessness, crack, crime, guns, and gangs that spills over into the classroom and intrudes on urban schools' educational mission—the tape thrusts the raw and unwelcome possibility that, somewhere along the line, the war against the odds that characterizes all urban public education resolved itself into surrender.

What we see on the tape is a reality that surpasses the fevered imaginings of even the harshest critics of urban public schools—a reality far more damning, and far more damnable. Absent is the heroic picture of teachers struggling to educate children in the face of poverty and family breakdown. Guards and inmates populate this place where teachers and students should be.

What if students do not learn because teachers do not teach? What if there is no order because administrators are not around? What if classrooms resemble holding tanks and the school day is reduced to so much time-serving? Should it surprise if students fed such a steady diet of cynicism—inner-city students already schooled in the indifference of the world around them—meet that cynicism with a sullen hostility of their own?

What if this is what really goes on in our city schools?

Exposé

Word of the tape travels through the school like a hand grenade rolled down a hallway. Reporters from NBC, the national network that will broadcast Eric Ransom's hidden video on the Sunday be-fore Labor Day 1991—the traditional start of the school year—are invited into the school. Cameras rolling, they receive a Potemkin Village tour of happy North students and orderly classrooms.

The tour arrives at Room 207 to find its teacher mid-lesson, drilling an attentive class on the intricacies of public finance.

TEACHER: . . . and what policy is set by the Federal Reserve?
STUDENTS [in unison]: Monetary policy!

Yet the staged visit cannot compete with the raw reality captured on Eric's tape. His teachers won't talk, but the superintendent of the Milwaukee Public Schools, North Division's principal, and an offi-cial from the teachers' union agree to watch the tape with an NBC reporter from its investigative show *Exposé*.

Superintendent Howard Fuller, on the job for a mere month, la-bels the display unacceptable; three days after seeing the tape, he suspends the teacher in Room 207 and two of the other teachers who appear on it. North Division's principal, too, offers no excuse. While defending the 100 other teachers at North, he confesses em-barrassment. "There is no time during the school day," he says, "where what we observed is acceptable teacher behavior."

A representative from the Milwaukee Teachers Education Asso-ciation (MTEA), the city's teachers' union, is not so willing to don sackcloth and ashes. "I know if I taught in a building 180 days," Don Ernest begins, "and the students didn't want to do the work, and I tried everything I did throughout the year, I may have to give up, too—if I couldn't think of anything else to do with those stu-dents to get them motivated to learn."

In the union official's response is a hint of a countercharge meant to cast the teachers' performance in a different light. Indeed, the MTEA appealed the superintendent's disciplinary action. In the end, to the superintendent's chagrin, all three teachers on Eric Ransom's tape would be reinstated—with back pay.

Ineptitude, far from being a punishable offense, was in the appeals process treated as an extenuating circumstance. In overturning the suspension of one teacher, the arbitrator's report "made a distinction between the *lack* of effort . . . and the *ineptness* of the effort" made by the teacher: "The former may have warranted a disciplinary response but the latter did not."[5] The fact that teachers who can't teach and teachers who can but don't try leave students equally uneducated was of no consequence in the proceedings. Indeed, the teachers' behavior was hardly at issue; in the words of the arbitrator, "the real culprit in this case [is] NBC, who had sought to sensationalize the conditions at the school."[6]

SURRENDER

In Room 207, the teacher sits with his back to the class, working in a notebook. One by one, the students are leaving the room. No one asks permission; no one offers an excuse.

STUDENT: I'll see you tomorrow, teach.
TEACHER: Kevin, you really shouldn't go skipping out.

A trace of a smile crosses his face. They're sharing a joke, he and Kevin. Going through the motions.

TEACHER: Why don't you do the work and pass the course?
STUDENT: I'll see you tomorrow.
TEACHER: It wouldn't be easy, but you could still pass the course.
STUDENT: I'll see you tomorrow about that.
TEACHER: I'll be here. Bye.

Surrender. With a shake of the head and a sigh, the teacher busies himself in his notebook.

Next, a girl shouldering her backpack stands to leave.

TEACHER: Did you want to copy down any of that stuff off the board before you leave?
STUDENT: I've already got it.

TEACHER: You couldn't have got those five questions. I just added them today. . . .
STUDENT: I'll be back tomorrow.

A big grin this time, as he looks at the girl. It is as if the teacher is waiting for her to acknowledge the joke. Out of camera range, the girl is silent. For a moment the camera lens fills with the blurred form of a torso, then a backpack. She is leaving. The teacher shakes his head, goes back to his notebook. He'll be there tomorrow.

STUDENT [off camera]: Why's everybody leaving?
TEACHER [his back still turned to the class]: Who knows.

CHAPTER TWO

Autopsy Report

In the acrimonious debate on public education, it was an event unmarked: the death of the last defender of urban public schools. Yet at some point in the past decade, an entire species of argument silently became extinct; institutions charged with educating tens of millions of children in scores of America's largest cities had squandered whatever tattered bits of public confidence that had once allowed advocates to defend their cause. No less than Keith Geiger, president of the National Education Association, waves the white flag. Inner-city public schools, Geiger says, "are absolutely terrible—they ought to be blown up."[1]

For public school advocates, a new line of defense has been built up; as is sometimes the case in desperate battlefield retreats, the new position uses the corpse of urban public education to shield itself against its enemies. In this argument, the educational implosion of urban public schools is not disputed, but offered into evidence as Exhibit A: the inescapable consequence of insufficient funding.

This claim that schools need more money is, of course, a public school perennial. Of all the many who have made this claim, none has been as highly praised as Jonathan Kozol, whose 1991 book *Savage Inequalities* made him the Upton Sinclair of inner-city public schools in the eyes of the education establishment.[2] What ails urban public schools? Kozol hammers home his answer page after page: funding, or, more precisely, the lack of it.[3]

Indeed, *Savage Inequalities* paints a vivid portrait of extreme neglect: schools where rainwater cascades down decrepit stairwells, where plastic trash bags patch rotted walls, where heroic teachers buy lab equipment out of their own pockets.

Yet for all that, if what Kozol reports is true—and who doubts that such schools exist, or that frustrated administrators would open their doors to a writer well known for arguing that public schools are painfully underfunded—the scandal goes far beyond Kozol's imaginings. For the crisis Kozol chronicles might make sense if public education funding was indeed drying up; the truth is, however, that public schools are soaking up resources like a sponge.

THE HIGH COST OF FAILURE

By nearly every indicator, and from any reference point, spending on public education in the past three decades has risen well in excess of the rate of inflation. And going backward in time, at any given point lower costs coincide with superior student achievement. Moving forward, the gap between funding and achievement is widening. Dollar for dollar, in urban public schools especially, we are quite literally paying a premium for failure.

Nationwide, all indicators chart the steady rise in what the public education establishment antiseptically terms "inputs." Between 1960 and 1991:

- Public school student enrollment increased slightly, from 36.1 million to 41.2 million.

- The number of teachers increased even more rapidly, from 1.4 million in 1960 to 2.4 million in 1991—an infusion of 1 million additional teachers into the classroom ranks.

- As a result, the pupil–teacher ratio steadily declined, from 25.8:1 in 1960 to 17.3:1 in 1991.[4] In urban public schools—routinely depicted as consigning students to overcrowded classrooms—the ratio is 17.9:1.[5] In a school of 500 students, the slim urban-to-national average variance translates into 28 teachers in an urban school versus 29 in the average public school.

During the same three decades, expenditures on public education rose even more rapidly:

- In current dollars, overall spending on public elementary and secondary education mushroomed from $15.6 billion in 1960 to $228.9 billion in 1991.[6] Factoring out inflation, that is a real increase of 202 percent in a thirty-year span.[7]

- Teachers' salaries, adjusted for inflation, increased 45.5 percent, from $24,229 to $35,243.[8] In the nation's larger urban school systems, average teacher pay reached $36,650 in 1990–91, up from $20,475 in 1980–81. Nationwide, urban public school teachers actually outearn the all-teacher average of $33,015—by about 11 percent.[9]

- Per-pupil expenditure more than doubled—again, after adjusting for inflation—from $2,147 to $5,872.[10]

Nor was the spike in public education spending limited to the 1960s and '70s; nationwide, the 1980s—the "Reagan era" during which, Kozol asserts, "public schooling social policy [was] turned back almost one hundred years"—saw a rapid rise in education expenditures.[11] Per-pupil expenditures rose by a full 40 percent, after adjusting for inflation.[12]

Even on the federal level—the one level, given the Reagan administration's alleged animus against education spending, where cuts might have been expected—education spending rose, in current dollars, from $13.9 billion in 1980 to $20.1 billion in 1988, the final year of the Reagan administration. In constant, inflation-adjusted dollars, federal spending on education did indeed decline: from $13.92 billion in 1980 to $13.47 in 1988—a decline from the pre-Reagan era of 3.25 percent, more a shaving nick than the bloodletting lamented by the education establishment.[13] In fact, the Reagan administration's final budget request, for fiscal 1990, contained $20.9 billion for education, erasing even the 3.25 percent cut. After one month in office, the Bush administration boosted the final Reagan request by another $441 million.[14]

What emerges is a reality that does not square with the image of cash-starved public schools. Higher expenditures per pupil, lower pupil–teacher ratios, more teachers paid higher salaries: All of this is precisely what the public education establishment assures will produce superior student performance. Instead, student achievement is stagnant at best and measurably poorer in important areas.

From 1966–67 to 1990–91, verbal and math scores on the Scholastic Aptitude Test (SAT) dropped a combined 62 points, impervious to the billions of dollars in new "inputs" pumped into America's public schools.[15] According to economist Robert J. Samuelson, claims by education apologists that lower SATs are a result of a vastly expanded pool of test-takers are statistically unfounded. Between 1951 and 1963, the number of test-takers exploded from 81,000 to more than 1 million—and test scores rose slightly.[16] The so-called democratization of the SAT, often cited as the cause for lower scores, actually *preceded* the steady decline in test scores.

The decline of American education is evident in international comparisons that pit U.S. students against their foreign counterparts. While the United States ranked third among the world's industrialized democracies in 1990–91 (and, notably, ahead of economic powerhouses Japan and Germany) in percentage of gross domestic product (GDP) spent on elementary and secondary education, in the 1991 International Assessment of Educational Progress,

U.S. thirteen-year-olds ranked twelfth of fourteen countries in math, tied with Spain and besting last-place Jordan, and twelfth in science.[17] Student interviews conducted with each test identified just one area where American students excelled: 90 percent had a "positive attitude" toward math (Korean students, who scored highest, had the lowest "positive attitude" ranking).

Whether American students can even comprehend their lamentable international status is arguable: In a much-reported Gallup geography survey, the average U.S. high school student could identify fewer than seven of fifteen countries or oceans on a blank map—a performance that placed the United States sixth out of the six nations whose students took the test.[18] To put it charitably, the billions of dollars in new educational inputs have produced embarrassingly little in the way of results.

Yet the lack of connection between dollars and scholarship simply reflects the research community's findings. In spite of the insistence of public education advocates, the claimed causal link between increased spending and improved achievement has been notoriously difficult to document. While common sense tells us spending differentials have to affect education, that a hypothetical school spending $1 million per student will produce more achievement than a school spending $1 per student, there is little to indicate that the incremental differences that separate existing schools in actual fact calibrate to degrees of educational achievement. Researcher Douglas Munro finds that "in statistical terms only 0.014 percent of the variation between the schools' mean scores can be explained in terms of funding." Likewise, on a funding-related measure, Munro has determined that class size accounts for only 2.8 percent of the variance in states' education results.[19] Not surprisingly, according to a study by the American Legislative Exchange Council (ALEC) published in 1993, of the five states with the highest average SAT scores, none were in the top half of states in per-pupil spending.

The ALEC study is no anomaly; it merely ratifies the findings of Eric Hanushek, an economist at the University of Rochester, who reviewed almost 200 studies to examine the relationship of education "inputs" to "outcomes." His finding: There is no significant relationship between money spent and student achievement.[20]

Criminally Underfunded?

What about *urban* public schools, places like North Division High School, whose students are more likely to score lower than the U.S. average? Are critics like Kozol correct when they charge that public schools in our inner cities are chronically, if not criminally, underfunded?

North Division, at least, is no scene from Kozol's nightmare. It is a clean school, well kept, with no trash in the hallways and no graffiti on the walls. As "physical plant," North is first-rate. It is the students who pass through North's doors who lack the furnishings of a functional education. Indeed, a case can be made that the school's poor educational performance is its meal ticket: Regularly ranked lowest of all Milwaukee city high schools in student grade point average, North Division receives the highest per-pupil funding.[21]

Nationwide, urban schools do tend to spend less than their suburban public school counterparts. Even so, twenty of the forty-five biggest city school districts are funded at or above their state average.[22]

How much less do the low-spending systems spend? Where critics like Kozol resort to hyperbole, the Council of the Great City Schools, a traditional advocate for urban public education, puts a number on what it calls "the shortfall in support for urban schools": "Urban school students, once need is taken into account, are being funded at a level about 7% below the national average."[23]

But 7 percent can be significant only if one assumes the present public school system allocates every dollar wisely and for maximum educational effect. Even granting the statistically unfounded hypothesis that greater spending produces increased achievement, any degree of inefficiency greater than 7 percent severs the alleged link—and raises the prospect that it is not *how much*, but rather *how* public education funds are spent that matters.

And there is ample reason to suspect that public schools spend a significant portion of their funds with no educational result. A 1990 study prepared for the Chicago public schools by economist Robert Genetski compared the productivity of the city's public schools with that of its Catholic schools. Unlike many commentators who glibly equate private school tuition with the full per-student cost of private education, Genetski carefully controlled for costs. Not only did he build books and transportation costs into the private school total, but he controlled for the large public–private school wage differential, doubling Catholic school teachers' salaries to equal wages paid public school teachers. Even so, Genetski estimated the "cost of private school in Chicago at anywhere from 45 to 77 percent of the cost of public education."[24] For a class of twenty-five children, that puts the cost per classroom of Catholic education anywhere from $30,000 to $72,000 lower than for an equivalent classroom in Chicago's public schools—an amount sufficient to buy each class one to two additional teachers.[25]

Surprisingly few states subject their public schools to a systematic audit; what evidence there is suggests that a generation of rapidly rising public education expenditures has bought plenty of bureaucracy.

TRICKLE-DOWN BUREAUCRACY

Public school systems' growth has come in ancillary, outside-the-classroom services and support staff. Statistics on the percentage of teachers among total public school staff convey a sense of this growth: In 1949–50, 70 percent of all public elementary and secondary school employees were teachers; in 1969–70, 60 percent; by 1991, the percentage had dropped to 53 percent of the total.[26]

Public school districts nationwide report that administrative costs consume anywhere from 32 to 58 percent of their overall budget. If anything, this probably overstates the percentage of funds that reach the classroom; a number of studies of public school systems show that they routinely devote less than 40 cents of each dollar they spend to classroom instruction.[27] The difference comes from the loose way the systems themselves define instructional spending.

Milwaukee Public Schools provides a case study in statistical sleight-of-hand. According to the system's own figures, 45 percent of Milwaukee Public Schools' total budget went to what it terms "instructional" spending.[28]

The reality is far worse. On closer examination, researcher Michael Fischer discovered the system includes in its total *for instructional spending* the costs and salaries of running eight central office bureaus, overhead and capital costs for building and maintaining the district superintendent's office, the expenses for Milwaukee's busing program, 60 percent of the district's consultants' fees—and even catering and hotel costs for administrative meetings. Fischer's own tabulations indicate that in the city's public elementary schools as little as 25.7 percent of total funding reaches the classroom.[29]

Stripping away the layers of bureaucracy exposes the true perversities of public education's priorities. In 1988–89, for instance, per-pupil spending for reading materials in Milwaukee's public elementary schools was $9.87; on art books and supplies, spending per student was a relatively robust $1.66. Per-pupil spending on science materials, however, was a paltry 21 cents.

To put this in perspective, Milwaukee allotted approximately four times as much for the superintendent's travel budget as for science materials for a population of more than 50,000 elementary school children. Simply holding the superintendent's travel budget to the rate of inflation from its 1979 level would have freed up enough funds in the 1988–89 school year for an immediate infusion of 300 percent more science materials into the city's elementary schools— all without a single new dollar from hard-pressed taxpayers.

Researcher Douglas Munro, citing a Fordham University study of New York City's public schools, speculates that when "instructional" spending can be accurately isolated, researchers may indeed find some correlation between *classroom* spending and student achievement.[30] What they will also find is that it takes, on average, between three and four additional dollars in the budget to produce one extra dollar of classroom spending.

The portrait that emerges puts the lie to the carefully tended image of cash-starved public schools. Instead, we see a shrinking fiscal commitment to classroom activities at the expense of a massive administrative apparatus, having little or nothing to do with the basic educational mission of the system or the students it is intended to serve. Yet critics like Kozol, who point indignantly to science labs where gas jets are broken and fulminate against the affluent Americans who have fled the cities for the suburbs, seem never to question the "trickle-down" budgeting that leaves so little funding for the classroom.

DOCUMENTING A CRISIS

Milwaukee's public schools mirror the national trend toward bigger education expenditures and lower educational achievement. Between 1976 and 1988, per-pupil spending rose 190 percent in the city school system, nearly double the rate of inflation. "State aid to the system," reported public education critic Charles Sykes, "leapt by 278%, more than twice the rate of inflation." During the same period, administrative spending increased a stratospheric 1,011 percent. By 1989–90, the city spent nearly $6,000 per student, a 22 percent boost in just three years. "None of this," Sykes observes, "brought even modest improvement in educational achievement."[31]

The impetus behind the cash infusion was a report, released in the fall of 1985, that documented the perilous state of MPS in incontrovertible detail. Commissioned by Wisconsin governor Anthony S. Earl and Department of Public Instruction (DPI) superintendent Herbert Grover, "Better Public Schools" undertook an elaborate statistical survey of Milwaukee and twenty-one surrounding school districts.

The report's candor marked a sharp break with the past. During the tenure of Milwaukee superintendent Lee McMurrin, the slipping performance of public school students had been masked by the official fiction that most students performed at or above the national average—which didn't explain that the "average" being cited was the median for *urban* public school students: the 23rd percentile.[32]

"Better Public Schools" exploded the myth behind McMurrin's happy talk, exposing the glaring gap between Milwaukee's public schools and the suburban systems surrounding them. Ten years later, it remains the most exhaustive attempt to examine and document the state of crisis in the city's schools.

With a "sense of urgency" and in a manner reminiscent of the 1983 national study, *A Nation at Risk*, "Better Public Schools" reported the following:

- By the fifth grade (perhaps earlier), a significant majority of poor and/or minority children are performing below the national average on achievement tests.

- There is a significant gap in math scores between boys and girls, with longitudinal data showing large drops in math scores from grade 7 to grade 10 for girls of all races, but particularly for Hispanic and black girls.

- The average grade point average in thirteen of the city's fifteen public high schools is less than 2.0 or C.

- Over one-quarter of the courses taken in public high schools end in a recorded grade of F or U for unsatisfactory. In seven of the MPS high schools, the percentage of F's was above 30.

- MPS has a dropout rate more than double both the state average or the highest rate of any suburban school, with most dropouts occurring before the eleventh grade.

- For the grades tested—2, 5, 7, and 10—the percentages of Milwaukee Public Schools students below the national median ranged from 45.2 percent in grade 2 to 58.3 percent in grade 10. Of all suburban students tested, the percentage below the national median ranged from 17.6 percent in grade 2 to 29 percent in grade 10.

- In schools with significantly lower achievement scores, there was *less parent involvement.*[33]

- Fifty-eight percent of MPS dropouts were never enrolled in eleventh grade.[34]

The reality behind the statistics was even worse. While MPS did an admirable job in resisting the temptation toward grade inflation that allowed other districts to disguise declining student achievement, it seems clear there was a great deal of what might be termed "expectation deflation." Teachers repeatedly told the team of Better Schools examiners that "students could pass courses by being present, doing most of the work, and generally putting forward some effort."[35] That alone would warrant a C. Even then, an astonishingly large number got F's.

In contrast to the dispassionate tone of "Better Public Schools," team leader John Witte's interpretation was scathing. Speaking a year after the report's publication, Witte summarized its findings to the National Conference on School Desegregation Research as demonstrating that "a number of the MPS schools are . . . essentially bankrupt institutions."[36]

The system itself remained remarkably impervious to the educational implosion. In the five years between 1985 and 1990, not a single MPS teacher was fired for incompetence, and not one of the approximately 1,000 new teachers hired by the Milwaukee Public Schools during that period was denied tenure.[37] At most, ineffective teachers were shuffled from one school to another, in a ritual known within the system as the "annual dance of the lemons."[38]

Still, the system understood that the news was too bad for it simply to adopt a head-in-the-sand response. MPS appeared to accelerate its reform agenda; over time, however, "reform" translated into little more than a public relations offensive.

From year to year, goals were set, reset, abandoned, and re-adopted. In 1986–87, for instance, the system declared itself dedicated to eliminating the test-score gap between minority and white students in ten years; four years later, in the system's new five-year plan, MPS declared itself resolved to halve the gap by 1996.

By 1993–94, two years short of the initial ten-year timetable, MPS once again revised its goals. Now the hope is simply to narrow the achievement gap, rather than eliminate it. Also, there is a new target date: the year 2000.[39]

Lost in all the goal-setting and five-year planning is the actual achievement gap itself. In the nine years since the initial goal, the achievement gap between African-American students and white students stands at 38 percent—down a scant two points from 40 percent in 1983–84.[40]

The difference, in the parlance of education researchers, is statistically insignificant. Yet for the first grader in 1983 who spent the next ten long years at the bottom of his class before dropping out in 1993, the significance is scarring. That student has become a statistic of a different sort.

As an exercise in reform, MPS's many attempts must be judged a failure; as an exercise in public relations, however, each new plan bought time for a failing system. Judged from this standpoint,

"Operation Rolling Reform" appears a rousing success. As Charles Sykes reports, the media were complicit in MPS's mediocrity; each reform was invariably greeted by a wave of favorable reaction in Milwaukee's mainstream press. The system, according to education expert Susan Mitchell, was so publicity-conscious that it faithfully measured the number of negative and positive column inches of press it had received during each school year.[41]

PATHS NOT TAKEN

Looking back ten years later, one sees in "Better Public Schools" the glimmers of paths not taken. Among its largely undifferentiated mass of thirty-five "action ideas," the report uncovered convincing evidence of the importance of parental involvement in education. Even after adjustment for school characteristics and statistical control in regression analysis, the "Better Public Schools" researchers found a link between high student achievement and strong parental involvement. As a result, the document set as its second goal "increas[ing] parental involvement in the educational process."[42]

How the system planned to bring parents into the schools is instructive. In the manner of King Midas, every issue the report touched was transformed into another gold-plated bureaucracy, and parental involvement proved no exception. From the statistical link between parental involvement and student achievement, "Better Public Schools" deduced a need for "the position of *parent advocate* and an *Office of Parents*." These new offices "should be created in the Milwaukee Public School System to stimulate greater parent access, input, and involvement in the MPS system."[43]

Nor was the creation of new administrative functions limited to the city school district; the Wisconsin Department of Public Instruction was itself instructed to develop a policy statement and guidelines on parent involvement—to be implemented, of course, in a new "state office of parent involvement."[44] The Better Public

Schools Commission advised each district to draft its own policies on parental involvement (with due diligence to avoid conflict with the state's legislative or administrative guidelines), to be distributed to parents of all pupils. Whether parents would in fact find schools more responsive might prove arguable; at any rate, their children would bring home the paper to show that the schools wanted to be.

Indeed, the focus on parent involvement quickly translated into a new funding imperative, replete with ample new employment opportunities. The Commission's recommendations bristle with "in-service programs," "staff development," and "design programs." Districts were counseled to create "parent education programs," and "select" teachers were to be relieved of their classroom duties to become Parent Community Educators, adept in "utilizing parent involvement techniques" to spread the gospel of parental involvement.[45] Lest anyone reading "Better Public Schools" wonder about the fiscal impact of these innovations, the Commission gave assurance that financial and personnel resources would be part of any implementation package.

Buried beneath all of this bureaucratic empire-building and its accompanying avalanche of paper is a good idea gone awry. Had anyone asked parents, their solution to increasing parental involvement would have entailed not a new oversight office in the state capital, but an open door at their child's school, a phone call from a teacher, an invitation to help at lunchtime or on the playground.

The authors of "Better Public Schools" were not about to experiment with such radical reforms. It is hard to escape the sense that parents, for all their potential impact on their children's achievement, were meant to be "managed," with any increased involvement in the schools carefully choreographed by the system. According to "Better Public Schools," surveys showed that "principals viewed the effectiveness of parent involvement more positively than did teachers, particularly the effectiveness of having parents in the classrooms and using parent volunteers." Put simply, parents were the last people teachers wanted to see peering in the classroom door.

From the distance of a decade, one notion in the report stands out, an idea at odds with all the others. In a single paragraph, the report recommended considering the possibility that increased parental involvement take the form of allowing parents to choose which public school their children would attend. Yet no sooner had the door opened than it closed; any public school choice program, the report hastened to add, "must not be allowed to upset current school desegregation policies. . . ."[46] The idea was never acted on.

To even hint at school choice was incendiary. At the city's least successful public schools, the idea opened up visions of a new exodus, one that would dwarf the desegregation-driven white flight to the suburbs. Already, "checkbook choice" among the remaining middle-class city-dwellers—the power of more affluent and even middle-income families to enroll their children in private school—was epidemic. Most telling, however, was the number of public school teachers who sent their own children outside the public system.

TEACHER KNOWS BEST

Milwaukee, which has a residency requirement for all city employees hired after 1978, is one city where being public school teachers with school-age children carries special implications. For obvious reasons, public teachers' unions have been less than receptive to requests to poll their members on their own children's private school enrollment. Milwaukee's MTEA—half of whose officers live outside the city limits—reports that public–private school enrollment patterns of their membership or officers "is information we do not track."[47]

What evidence there is, derived from U.S. census data, suggests that public school teachers in urban systems favor private schools for their own children in numbers far beyond the population as a whole; according to one study, urban public school teachers are "two and three times as likely as the public at-large to use private schools."[48]

In Milwaukee, the preference of public school teachers for private schooling for their own children was confirmed in a study conducted by the University of Wisconsin's Applied Population Laboratory. Looking at the 1990 U.S. Census Public Use Microsample File, researchers discovered that for public school teachers with children ages five to eighteen, the percentage with children enrolled in private school was 29.2 (weighted; raw count: 32.1 percent); for public school teachers with children ages four to eighteen (to capture children in K–4 programs), 31.4 percent (weighted; raw count: 34.5 percent).[49]

In either case, the percentage was two to two and a half times the 1990 national rate of private school enrollment of 13.1 percent—a resounding "no confidence" vote in urban public education, by the very people who know it best.

The study showed the tendency to be most pronounced for public school teachers who resided in Milwaukee's Central City neighborhoods, including the Near North Side. In the two Central City census areas, the percentage of public school teachers enrolling their children in private school rises to 42.1–44.5 (weighted; 47.6–50 percent raw count).[50]

Poorer parents, whose children populated the public schools through lack of any alternative, could only speculate what it meant that so many of the very people who taught their children sought private education for their own.

SYMPTOMS OF DECLINE

Six years after the "Better Public Schools" report, and one month before Eric Ransom's tape shocked the system, incoming MPS superintendent Howard Fuller—the Near North Side native who had so impressed Ransom—pronounced MPS "a failing system."[51] Fuller's statistical indictment showed the degree of decline since the 1985 study:

- Citywide, only 40 percent of freshmen graduated from high school.

- In 1990, the average grade point average for MPS high schoolers had dropped to D+.

- African-American students fared even worse. Just 32 percent of African-American students graduated from high school—down from 45 percent a decade earlier.

- At some schools, the average grade point average for African-American students was F+ or below; more than half of black students flunked core academic courses.

- Only 23 percent of the city's African-American students read at or above the national average, as compared to 61 percent of white students.

- Just 22 percent of African-Americans scored at or above the national average on math tests, compared to 59 percent of whites.[52]

The *Milwaukee Sentinel* captured the complacency pervading MPS: "Many Black Freshmen at Less Than 'D,'" read a headline sharing a page with a second article titled "Teachers Say MPS Passing," in which a survey reported that teachers gave their school system a job performance score of 60 positive to 39 negative.[53]

By 1993, scores on the Iowa Test of Basic Skills fell below the national average for fifth and seventh graders in both reading and math, with African-American students trailing 10 to 12 points behind the already lower-than-average districtwide scores. Scores on the tenth grade Test of Achievement and Proficiency (TAP) weren't much different, although the gap between African-American students and the national average broadened from the 10 to 12 points separating seventh graders to 15 points for tenth graders taking the TAP. Compounding poor test scores was a dropout rate of near epidemic proportions: By 1993, the dropout rate had reached 17.4 percent—

"the highest since the district began reporting the statistic more than a decade ago"—and up sharply from the rate that had rung alarm bells in the 1985 "Better Public Schools" report: 10.7 percent.[54]

Given these statistics, a return to the dire days of 1985 would have been hailed as progress of near-miraculous proportions. The system John Witte had pronounced "essentially bankrupt" in 1985 had in the ensuing eight years seen the onset of rigor mortis.

PROSPERING FROM FAILURE

Critics of the public schools—especially critics taken with a free-market orientation—often charge that the problem with the public school system is that it does not respond to incentives. Such statements are sloppy. The iron law of incentives does not stop operating simply because a system achieves an effective monopoly over families too poor to secure other educational alternatives for their children.

In fact, the problem is that such systems are all too responsive: Not only is there no penalty for failure, the objective fact is that *poor schools prosper.* When funding follows failure, bringing underachieving schools more social workers and school psychologists, special "stay-in-school" programs, an army of "at-risk" coordinators and early-intervention experts, schools faithfully produce the failure that begets funding. Failure, in this Orwellian inversion, *is* success. Schools, predictably, sink to the challenge. Meanwhile, for parents locked in to Milwaukee's public schools, apathy was giving way to anger.

Time after time, beleaguered parents were told that education in the inner city was all but impossible. The education establishment and its apologists generated hundreds of reasons successful education could not happen there, reasons ranging from single-parent families, crime, crack, gangs, and guns to lead-based paint in public housing projects. Sometimes the problems were pinned on parents; at other times, as when the teachers' union representative was asked to explain Eric Ransom's tape, the problem was said to be students who just didn't want to do the work. Each excuse, plausible in itself, rose into a brick wall of reasons that proved that it was simply impossible to educate children in an urban environment.

There was only one problem: Parents knew it wasn't true.

They knew of schools educating children every day; not the ones wealthier, white children went to out in the distant suburbs, but schools right in their own inner-city neighborhoods, flourishing amid the same urban squalor, succeeding against the same long odds.

These schools were private schools, whose tuition, though modest, was far beyond poor parents' means.

CHAPTER THREE

The Lessons of Urban Day

The children sit in rows, shoulder to shoulder on the staircase, waiting for the story to begin.

"When is the first day of Kwanza?" The thick-set woman with close-cropped hair surveys sixty first graders from her place on the first-floor landing. She is Zakiya Courtney, executive director of Urban Day, a private school on Milwaukee's Near North Side, about a dozen blocks south of North Division High.

Courtney's question echoes in the stairwell. Hesitation, until a round-faced boy in white shirt and shiny blue pants ventures an answer.

"December 26," he says warily into the silence.

Chin up, eyes fixed on the child, Courtney bobs her head violently. "That's right."

"1993," adds a little girl a few rows back, eager to share Miss Zakiya's approbation.

"That's right. And it goes on how long?"

"Until January 1st." A few voices this time.

"And so that's how many days?"

"Seven days" comes the shout from a dozen or more voices on the staircase.

"Seven days of a holiday that comes right after what?"

"Christmas!"

"Well, today we're going to have our own mini Kwanza celebration. We're going to tell a story and sing some Kwanza songs. What about that?"

The cry is unanimous, echoing in the stairwell.

A PRODUCT OF COMPROMISE

Zakiya Courtney is not a quiet woman and Urban Day is not a quiet school. Restless energy propels her down the hallway, in and out of classrooms, touching base with teachers, exchanging greetings with students. The children are everywhere—exuberant, active, alive. Spilling out onto the playground for recess, they seem the only spark of color against the smudgy monochrome of a bleak Milwaukee winter.

Housed in a soot-grimed brick building at the back end of a church parking lot, Urban Day is one of a dozen private elementary and grade schools scattered across the city that participate in the Milwaukee Parental Choice Program. Among the children listening to the Kwanza story are some who attend Urban Day not because their parents have paid the annual $2,200 tuition, but because the state of Wisconsin sends Urban Day a check in the amount of the per-pupil share of state funds allotted for public education.

Passed by the Wisconsin state legislature in March 1990, the Parental Choice program is, in spite of its small scale, one of the most argued-about education experiments in America. A decade after the concepts of school choice, tuition tax credits, and vouchers elbowed their way into the national education debate, Milwaukee's program remains the only existing *publicly* financed *private* school choice experiment in the United States.[1]

Beyond the core concept that parents choose their child's school with public funds following the child, there is no one-size-fits-all approach to school choice. Some proposed programs would extend vouchers to all students, regardless of family income or present enrollment in private and even religious schools. Other voucher plans are more tightly focused, targeted to help low-income families, with eligibility of students whose private school enrollment predates the plan phased in over several years.

Milwaukee's Parental Choice program falls on the targeted end of the spectrum. It is means-tested: Eligible families can have incomes no higher than 175 percent of the poverty level—in 1995–96, $22,033 for a family of three[2]—a condition met by as many as 70 percent of all families with children in the Milwaukee Public Schools, and an even higher percentage of the households in the Urban Day neighborhood.

While voucher efforts in other states have foundered on the issue of whether and when to include presently enrolled private school students, Milwaukee's Parental Choice sidestepped the issue entirely: Only children enrolled in public schools or entering kindergarten can receive vouchers; children already enrolled in private schools are not eligible. Each voucher—for 1994–95, worth $3,245, the state's share of Milwaukee's per-pupil expenditure[3]—must be accepted as tuition in full at Urban Day or one of the eleven other private nonsectarian grade schools located within Milwaukee city limits that have registered for the program.

This "payment in full" proviso renders the Milwaukee program immune to the criticism aimed at other choice proposals that the voucher amount will not be enough in itself to enable poorer families to enroll their children in private schools, but will supplement or "top off" the resources of more well-to-do parents. For some private schools, the Parental Choice voucher meets the true cost of educating a pupil; at others, the shortfall must be made up from the school's other sources of funds.

The product of compromise, Milwaukee Parental Choice bears signs of the political push and pull that preceded its passage. From

the beginning, the program has labored under significant constraints: For its first four years, despite the fact that the vast majority
of city school children met the program's low-income eligibility requirements, Parental Choice was capped at 1 percent of the nearly
100,000 school-age children in Milwaukee. Beginning September
1994, the state legislature authorized the cap to rise to 1.5 percent,
or 1,500 students.

In practice, however, the number of actual private classroom seats
available has never kept up with the caps. The reason has to do with
a second constraint, this one placed on individual private schools
taking part in Parental Choice. Under the 1990 statute, Choice
schools had to limit voucher students to 49 percent of their student
body. A school at the 49 percent limit could add its next Choice student only by "twinning" him or her with a tuition-paying student—
commodities not in infinite supply for even the best inner-city
school. In reality, the problem is compounded by the practical im-
peratives in staffing a school; to add an additional class, assign a
room, and hire a teacher, a school needs not one or two new students but ten to fifteen paying students in the proper grade, twinned
with ten to fifteen more in that grade from the Choice waiting list.[4]

Not surprisingly, these constraints discouraged some private
schools from taking such a gamble.[5] As a result, in the four years
since Parental Choice's inception, the lack of space has resulted in
more children being turned away than have been accepted into the
program. Available spaces have been apportioned by lottery. Still,
the number of children in Parental Choice has grown each year,
from 341 in September 1990 to 846 in 1994–95.[6]

WHATEVER IT TAKES

While a smattering of elderly residents can still be heard speaking German at the bus stops and corner stores, the Urban Day
neighborhood is now nearly 80 percent African-American. Also

among the polyglot population are significant numbers of Hispanics, Native Americans, and Laotians.[7] There is even a tiny, tight-knit Hmong community, transplanted ten thousand miles from the jungles of Southeast Asia to an alien North American ghetto; they live on the blocks adjacent to the social service center that occupies a corner of the property housing Urban Day.

The closest public school to Urban Day is 27th Street Elementary, at 27th and Vliet, just a short walk from Urban Day. By a quirk in school zoning, however, the neighborhood in which Urban Day sits is part of the Siefert Elementary district. At 13th and Cherry, Siefert is a full dozen blocks away, down streets lined with drifting trash, past King Park and a gauntlet of corner stores that attract street people and young toughs—a walk many parents deem too dangerous for their children. Parents in this part of the city are wary. They still remember the grisly goings-on in the Oxford Apartments (since razed), just three blocks south of Urban Day, where serial killer Jeffrey Dahmer lived.

But even attendance at Siefert is by no means guaranteed. Many public school children from the Urban Day neighborhood are bused to another public school across town for reasons of racial balance. Ask children playing on the sidewalk where the neighborhood school is, and none mention 27th Street or Siefert. They point past the rooftops to the spire of old St. Michael's that marks Urban Day.

Before Choice, some parents would visit Urban Day late in the summer, while the pace was still slow for the office staff. Over the hum of the electric fan, they would request a moment of the principal's time. These were the parents who, too poor to pay the school's tuition, pleaded that their children simply had to be allowed to attend Urban Day.

"We've had parents who are unemployed. They come in and do janitorial work, secretarial work, paint the halls in summer—something to make up the difference," says Zakiya Courtney. "Whatever it takes to keep their kids here." There is a limit, however, to how much Urban Day or any school can accept in-kind contributions in place of cash. "When payday comes, it doesn't matter how many people you have painting the walls for free."

Parental Choice meant that for some families, particularly families in the immediate Urban Day neighborhood, money would no longer be a barrier. In the streets around the school, welfare is ubiquitous, work intermittent, crime and drugs a clear and present danger. Just 40 percent of adults have jobs, a figure even lower than the 48 percent in the struggling North Division neighborhood. More than half of those who are employed work in the service sector or as unskilled labor. In 1990, the average household income stood at $8,792 for a household of three people; almost 60 percent live below the poverty level.[8]

Predictably, poverty hits women and children hardest. Two-thirds of all households in the neighborhood are female-headed; 78 percent of households with children are single-parent. Behind the numbers is a profile in childhood poverty; nearly half the residents of the Urban Day neighborhood are seventeen or younger. As in the North Division area, out-of-wedlock births in the Urban Day neighborhood stand at nearly 90 percent.

Yet these are not the statistics you will learn on a visit to Urban Day. There, only one number matters: The high school graduation rate for Urban Day alumni is 98 percent.

When other private schools in the Parental Choice program opened up a dozen or two dozen seats to voucher students, Urban Day offered 103 positions in that first year, a number that has grown four years later to 254.[9] In the 1994–95 school year, 57 percent of Urban Day's K–8 students enrolled via the voucher program.

"We just jumped in, because we're about kids and we're about families," Zakiya Courtney recalls. Urban Day was a thriving school with a twenty-year history prior to Parental Choice. "Ideally, we want to get kids into Montessori," Urban Day's K–4 program, "and keep them through eighth grade. That's where our graduation rate comes from." An influx of Choice students, some of whom had serious problems in public school, would prove a challenge. Still, Urban Day's administrators saw vouchers as a natural extension of their philosophy of parental involvement and their role as a neighborhood school.

Courtney herself was Urban Day's PIC, its parent involvement coordinator, when Parental Choice began.[10] It fell to her to oversee and enforce the "parent contract" that commits parents, whether on welfare or working two jobs, to volunteer eight hours a month at Urban Day. She was a natural at the task: "Before I was anything at Urban Day, I started out as a parent." Indeed, at one point after becoming executive director, Courtney had children of her own in kindergarten, fourth, sixth, and eighth grades at the school. "They're the ones you see running the other way when I come down the hall."

Indeed, at Urban Day the lines blur between family, community, and the classroom. "We don't have a nepotism clause," Courtney reflects, "and it's a good thing we don't, because it would kill the school." One Urban Day teacher has been associated with the school since 1975. "The woman graduated from Urban Day. She went to college, earned her degree, and came back to teach here. Her mother is a Head Start teacher here, her father is one of our maintenance engineers. And now her children go here."

WHEN CHOICE MEANS KWANZA

On this day a few weeks before Christmas and Kwanza, the metal fire doors that lead out to Urban Day's playground are wedged wide open, and the school's parking lot is blocked by a semi truck. Along the first-floor hallway, parents pass single file with boxes for the annual fruit sale to raise money for the school's summer camp fund. By early afternoon, the parent volunteers will unload 1,000 cases of fruit.

Urban Day is almost self-consciously nonsectarian, in keeping with one of the statutory requirements of the 1990 law establishing the Parental Choice program. At the mention of a Christmas sale, Zakiya Courtney issues a gentle correction: "A *holiday* sale. At Urban Day, we take a multicultural approach. The emphasis is not on one holiday more than any other."

Courtney gestures down the hallway, which at this moment is uncharacteristically quiet. "When you go about the school you'll probably see as much red, black, and green"—the colors of Kwanza—"as Santa Clauses."

Today is "picture day." There are a few more ribbons in the girls' hair, and more boys squeaking uncomfortably on the polished floors in dress shoes than in sneakers, but the corridors are still a sea of navy blue and white, the colors of Urban Day's school uniform. "We made the decision to go to uniforms long before you started seeing all these 'crimes of fashion,'" Courtney says, referring to the robberies and even shootings occasioned by designer shoes, coats, and caps. "We were ahead of the game—and we're glad we were."

And the students? What do they think about the uniforms?

"Oh, they hate them," Courtney laughs. "The parents love it."

There's another advantage in the dress code. "With the uniforms, you can't tell how much money a family has or doesn't have from the way a kid dresses," Courtney explains. "Everyone looks the same. Everyone's on the same level." Even the teachers don't know which children are on Choice vouchers and which ones are "tuition" students.

Mr. Turtle

The children on the staircase are silent now, ready for the story to begin.

"This story is about an animal called Mr. Turtle, and it's one of my favorites. How many of you know how a turtle moves?"

Children shift and slide on the polished stairs, delighted with this license to move.

"Very, very slowly, right? One . . . step . . . at a time." Courtney crouches, hands on hips, swinging each leg forward in a slow arc. "But turtles didn't always move so slow. In fact, the turtle in this story never moved slowly. He even talked fast. And he always had his nose in everybody's business.

"You see, Mr. Turtle thought he was *fine*. He would sit around all day long, shining his shell. He had a nice, pretty, shiny shell, and he'd walk around all day long shining his shell, shining his shell. He'd say: 'Nobodyhasashell asshinyastheshell asIdo.' That's what he'd say."

Courtney reaches one arm high and the other low, shining an imaginary cloth across her back; she struts in a small circle. Laughter peals from the children.

"Now, one day he walked by the pond and looked down, and he saw Mrs. Fish. And Mrs. Fish was doing the kind of thing that fish do. What do fish do?"

"Swim," the children shout.

"Well, Mr. Turtle said, 'Icandiveasdeepasyou, Mizz Fish! Takeme-onadiveandyou'llsee. MizzFishMizzFish, comeoncomeoncomeon, pleasepleaseplease.' And Mrs. Fish told Mr. Turtle to grab on to her fin, and she dove deep.

"When Mr. Turtle got out of the lake, he saw Mr. Fox. 'MisterFoxMisterFox, Icanrunasfastasyou! Takemeonyourbackand-you'llsee!' And Mr. Fox took the turtle on his back and he ran fast.

"Then Mr. Turtle saw Mr. Eagle, sitting on a tree branch. 'Mister-EagleMisterEagle, Icanflyashighasyou! Takemeonyourbackandyou'll-see!' And Mr. Eagle flew him high into the sky, higher than Mr. Turtle had ever, ever seen.

"Then, something happened. Mr. Turtle let go.

"And he fell from high in the sky, down to the ground, with a crash.

"And his shiny shell—his beautiful shiny shell—was shattered, into a hundred pieces.

"Now, all the animals came out from miles around, and they picked up all the pieces and glued his shell back together."

Courtney motions to the children on the first step, who come forward and pretend to pick up pieces of shell and pat them on the back of a boy in the middle. "But to this day, you can see the cracks on a turtle's shell.

"Just then, they heard an old voice. It was Mr. Owl, and he was the wisest animal in the woods. 'You are not an eagle, and you are not a fox, and you are not a fish. Do you know whhhhooooo you are?' asked Mr. Owl. 'Do you know wwhhhhhooooooo?'"

A few whhhoooos echo back from the stairwell as Courtney leans toward the children.

"A turtle!" comes the shout.

"That's right. And Mr. Owl said, 'You can swim in the lake like a fish and walk on the shore like a fox. You can't fly like an eagle, but you carry your house on your back wherever you go. That is something only turtles can do.'"

As Courtney speaks, she directs the children who encircle her. Some imitate a swimmer's stroke, some crouch and pantomime a crawl, others pat the imaginary shells on their backs. On the stairs, thirty children who learn never to talk to strangers or walk the grim streets of Urban Day alone after dark smile and laugh with Miss Zakiya.

"Be proud of who you are. Be proud of where you come from. Be proud of the things that you can do.

"And that is the lesson of Kwanza."

Theory versus Practice

For some conservative supporters of school choice, the Kwanza celebrations will come as a shock, a case in point of the way practice collides with theory. At an abstract, theoretical level, the tension can be obscured; one can champion freedom of choice and condemn, for instance, the faddish focus on multicultural curricula, without confronting a simple fact: Some parents, given a choice, will choose multicultural schools.

In the case of Urban Day as well as another Choice private school on Milwaukee's Near North Side, Harambee, the Afrocentric focus does not diminish or detract from an essentially traditional approach to the teaching of math, English, geography, and science. In fact, the Afrocentric elements present a parallel to the kind of ethnic pride evident in urban schools located in neighborhoods where Italian or Irish or Hispanic families predominate. As such, the elevating effect this focus on heritage and history can have on students constitutes an overwhelmingly positive part of the school culture.

For voucher advocates, the challenge is clear: Defenders of choice in theory must have the courage of their convictions to accept choice in practice.

VOUCHER PARENTS

What is the one thing different about Urban Day? Courtney's answer comes without hesitation. "Parent involvement."

"If you find something you like or don't like, you don't have to wait a year for change. The bureaucracy is not there. Parents see me here. If they don't, they call me at home.

"Do we do everything parents want? That's not what I'm saying. But we work it out. We don't hide from the people with complaints or the people with questions. We work it out."

Courtney has noticed a difference among voucher parents. "Choice parents are more active than our tuition parents are. Choice parents want the opportunity to get involved with their child's education. They don't take us for granted the way parents might who've been here for a while, and know what it is we're doing."

Alma Walton, a Near North Side parent with two older children in public school and two younger children attending private school on Choice vouchers, recalls her own attempts to bring her concerns to the attention of her sons' public school teachers and principal. "I went to the teacher first. She sent me to the principal," Mrs. Walton recalls. "We talked, and he told me he agreed with a lot of what I was saying, and that the school board ought to hear what I had to say." Almost imperceptibly, Mrs. Walton found herself being steered further and further from the classroom. "[The principal] told me I should go to the school board to 'vent my concerns' the next time they had a hearing. I didn't want to 'vent my concerns'; I wanted to work things out with my son and his teacher.

"They can say whatever they want about bringing parents into the process; the last person they really want to see in that school is a parent."

Gloria Collins agrees.

In an empty first-floor classroom at the end of a school day, Mrs. Collins and her daughter Natasha, a fifth grader, talk about the difference between her old school and Urban Day. Natasha, ebony-skinned, with her hair in a long braid, is shy and reserved, soft-spoken, like her mother. Yes, she misses her friends at her old public school; no, she likes her teachers here better: "They don't let me slip." She grows animated only when I ask whether there's anything she doesn't like at Urban Day.

"We want to wear our own clothes," she says, glancing with scorn at her navy blue uniform. "Ask anyone."

Mrs. Collins laughs. Disappointed that I do not make an immediate promise to intercede with Miss Zakiya to abolish the school uniform policy, Natasha sits silent and listens to her mother talk, then asks to be excused. Her friends are waiting for her in the hallway.

"I wish I could show you her report card," says Gloria Collins, as her daughter leaves the room. "Not the grades so much, but the teacher comments."

Before Parental Choice existed and not long after moving to Milwaukee from East St. Louis, Illinois, Mrs. Collins enrolled Natasha in public school. At first, school seemed fine, and Natasha was bringing home all A's and B's.

Then one evening near the end of her daughter's second-grade year, Gloria Collins handed the storybook she was reading to her daughter. "Now, you read it to me," she told her. Natasha haltingly picked her way through, stumbling over the simplest words. Midway through a sentence, she stopped. "She looked so helpless," Natasha's mother remembers.

The next morning, Mrs. Collins called the school. "I told them I wanted to talk to Natasha's teacher. When they asked me why, I said, 'Tell her my daughter doesn't know how to read.'"

Natasha's school didn't see a problem. Natasha's marks were fine, better than most, in fact. Mrs. Collins disagreed. Her daughter, she insisted, should be able to read by now.

That night, Gloria Collins made the most difficult decision she had ever faced as a parent. She would demand that the school fail her daughter so Natasha could repeat second grade and learn to read.

Amazingly, the school refused. Natasha, they said, was on track for promotion to third grade.

Gloria Collins surprised herself; refusing to give up, she fought back against the school authorities. In the end, she prevailed. "I was the mother who wanted her child held back." That fall, Natasha entered second grade for the second time—and entered public school for her last year.

That summer, Mrs. Collins heard about Parental Choice. She made it her mission to get Natasha into Urban Day, half a mile from their home. At Urban Day, Natasha is "on grade level," earning A's and B's—but now, Mrs. Collins sees a confidence in Natasha and a willingness to demonstrate that she knows her lessons well. "This is the right place for her. I think even as young as she is, she knows it."

At the end of our talk, I ask Mrs. Collins whether she knows how many other cities in America have a program like Parental Choice; she doesn't. I tell her Milwaukee is the only place.

"Well, I'm glad they got it here."

A skeptical look crosses her face, as if I must be wrong about a program whose value is so obvious and premise so simple.

The interview over, I am at the doorway when Mrs. Collins speaks.

"They can't go to court again," said Mrs. Collins, referring to the state supreme court decision upholding Parental Choice. "I mean, the court decided."

The tone in her voice suggests what she says is more a question than a statement. Suddenly, she appears worried by this outsider in her daughter's school, taking notes, asking questions.

The court's decision, I assure her, is final.

Mrs. Collins nods. Pulling her coat on, she calls out to her daughter that it's time to go home.

REGIS

Critics of school choice often charge that voucher programs will allow private schools to steal away the best and brightest students. Siphoning off the "cream of the crop," they say, will make the public schools' job even harder.

With entry by lottery, however, Milwaukee Parental Choice schools have no say in which students arrive at their door. Evidence indicates that the program draws a fair share of students with academic and behavioral deficiencies.[11] Dennis Alexander, principal of Harambee Community School, a private school a half-dozen blocks east of North Division High, scoffs at suggestions that Parental Choice's lottery system allows private schools to hand-pick their new students. "How can we pick and choose," Alexander asks about students who use vouchers to transfer from MPS to his school, "when we get the students in September and their files in October?"[12]

"We don't bother with labels like LD [learning-disabled] and so on," Urban Day's Courtney says, waving a hand. "We don't have all those special tracks and resources MPS has. Why bother with LD when all our kids end up in the same classroom anyway? We've got to teach them all the same."

Regis Chesir is one student who came to Urban Day to escape a label. Yet, labeled or not, when the sixth grader arrived at Urban Day, he was, in the words of administrator Robb Rauh, "totally irresponsible."

Regis went to a city public school until third grade, when his mother shifted him to the 220 Program, which buses students—the vast majority African-American students from inner-city Milwaukee—to outlying suburban schools for racial balance. Mrs. Chesir had no complaints, until Regis reached fifth grade, when school officials suggested that he be "M-Teamed" (the system's label for an array of behavioral and achievement tests). Unsure what this meant, Mrs. Chesir asked other parents with children bused to white suburban schools. What emerged was a pattern: at some schools, including her son's, minority students in the 220 Program were subjected to the battery of M-Team tests—and then shunted into LD programs. "To me, it wasn't testing," recalls Mrs. Chesir. "It was more like branding." She feared her son's school was preparing to push him into a slower or lower track, or perhaps out of the school altogether.

Indeed, Mrs. Chesir had noticed a change in her son. Regis's father, an intermittent factor in the boy's life, was around again; Regis was acting a bit wild and his schoolwork was suffering. Other times, he was so sensitive even a small remark could send him sulking. Mrs. Chesir did something she'd never done before: She went to see a child psychologist. The psychologist thought that given the new influences in Regis's life, his behavior was not surprising; subjecting him to a battery of school tests seemed excessive and premature.

Mrs. Chesir refused the test and, with no other options, re-enrolled Regis in a Milwaukee public elementary school. It was September 1990. One day she happened to pass Harambee School, where "some sort of Parental Choice rally was going on." She came away with a phone number for Urban Day; that afternoon, she registered Regis for the Choice program.

For Regis to go to a private school was a dream his mother could literally never afford to have. Yet two weeks later, she was told a seat was open at Urban Day. Mrs. Chesir, who had already scrimped to outfit Regis with new clothes at the start of the school year, had to scramble simply to buy the white shirts and navy pants for his Urban Day uniform.

Regis changed schools, but his C's and D's continued. Yet, while his work habits and his classroom behavior may have remained deplorable, his leadership potential was beyond dispute. Within a month at Urban Day, Regis was elected sixth-grade class president by his classmates. Mrs. Chesir remembers the way Regis's teachers took note of his popularity among his peers. "Either [Regis] was going to 'get with the program,' or he was going to be a problem with the other kids."

Regis became a reclamation project. When he finished seventh grade at Urban Day with a grade point average closer to a D than a C, Mrs. Chesir and the school's administrators sat down one day in the office. Someone, Mrs. Chesir can't recall who, mentioned that perhaps Regis should repeat seventh grade. Mrs. Chesir went home realizing the decision would be hers.

As she wrestled with what to do, a scene kept playing through her mind. One afternoon, riding down Center Street on the bus past North Division High School, Mrs. Chesir and the other passengers had watched three girls, armed with baseball bats, swinging wildly at a fourth girl, chasing her from the front door of the school out into Center Street. Traffic stopped; a crowd formed. What Mrs. Chesir remembers most was that through the entire melee, not one adult ever emerged from the school.

In two years' time, with no high schools eligible for the nonsectarian Choice program and no chance of paying his way at a private religious high school, Regis would be out of Urban Day and back in MPS. As a transfer student, he would have no claim to a seat in any particular high school; there was no telling where he might be assigned. Mrs. Chesir knew that students held back in high school might simply refuse to go to school at all. "Better to hold him back now," she decided.

Regis repeated seventh grade at Urban Day. When grades came home, he had earned all A's and B's. For the next two years, Regis Chesir's name, previously a regular entry on the office's detention schedule, turned up on a different list: Urban Day's honor roll.

Today, with grade school a long summer behind him, Regis, already 6 feet 1, has his eye on high school basketball. "My feet are size 13," he volunteers. Having spent the summer engineering Regis's enrollment in Rufus King, a public school well known for having Milwaukee's lowest dropout rate, his mother discerns a growth of a different sort. "I see a strong sense of identity, character, that he didn't have before.

"He used to come home from [Urban Day] and complain," Mrs. Chesir recalls. "The teachers were on his back. 'Mom, they nag at me so much.' But you know, when he turned things around, he started getting that pat on the back. You could see he liked that.

"Sometimes a kid needs that: to have a whole lot of people pulling for him."

In two days, Regis starts school at Rufus King.

"I just have to hope we can get him through."

PART II

Emancipation

CHAPTER FOUR

White Lies

Bertelle E. remembers the day with almost preternatural clarity. She stood on the steps of the MPS Administrative Building in the waning light of an autumn afternoon. She remembers talking to herself, remembers the passersby steering a path around her—this distracted black woman, standing alone in the middle of the sidewalk, talking to no one.

Nothing was going according to plan. Bertelle thought back to the day, less than a month before, that she and her son, Ellis,[1] had moved in to their new home in Northwest Milwaukee just a few blocks below the point at which 60th Street becomes Brown Deer. When her friends had asked why she was moving from their apartment in Brown Deer back into the city, her answer was simple. To Bertelle, she wasn't moving back to the city, she was buying a home of her own.

She'd chosen the neighborhood so that Ellis, who would start third grade that September, would go to Thoreau School, just three blocks down 60th Street. Bertelle knew the Milwaukee Public Schools well. She had worked in them for a dozen years. She'd bought her condo in a respectable neighborhood, and Thoreau was a good school. It was so close Ellis could walk there with his friends.

A few days later, problems began. The mail brought an assignment slip listing Ellis's school not as Thoreau, but as a school far beyond their neighborhood. Ellis would be bused there, in compliance with the Milwaukee Public Schools' citywide desegregation plan.

MPS had transferred Bertelle herself to a job at a school on Milwaukee's Far South Side, fourteen miles away. It meant their morning routine would start at 5 o'clock, and it would mean Ellis coming home to an empty house every afternoon. This was not at all what Bertelle had wanted.

When the first day of school arrived, Bertelle's mind was made up. She would hold Ellis back. She asked her mother to babysit him. For the first week of school, her son stayed home.

Each morning, Ellis walked his friends to Thoreau, then turned around and walked home. Some days he came back at lunchtime, for recess. One of those times, he even spoke to the principal. "He asked me 'What's your name?'" he told his mother when she got home from work. " 'Why aren't you in school?' I told him my mom wants me to go to school here. He said, 'You have to have that piece of paper with permission.'"

Bertelle called the central office and asked how she could have her son's assignment changed. They told her she could not; no transfers were being approved at the beginning of the year. She asked the woman on the phone why they weren't sending her son to the public school three blocks away. "That's Thoreau, right? They have enough black kids there," she was told.

Yet as the week wore on, Bertelle noticed the number of new students she was processing in at her own school on the South Side. She checked the date on a transfer slip, and asked the girl who'd handed it to her when she'd received it. "It came in the mail this morning," the girl told Bertelle.

That day, Bertelle went from work directly to the MPS central office. "I know you're making changes," she told the woman behind the desk. "I've been processing new kids at my school all day long. I want to move my son to Thoreau."

"You have to have a reason," the woman said.

"I do. I want my son to go to school in his own neighborhood."

"That's not good enough. He won't enhance racial balance."

"What do you mean?"

"He's black. They have more than enough black children at Thoreau."

"He's not black."

The school official blinked. Bertelle's ebony skin announced her own race unmistakably.

"My son is white."

Bertelle was greeted with silence.

"I am his mother and I know my son's race and I say he's white, not black."

After the rush of words there was an absence of sound so pure that it seemed to Bertelle all the air in the office had been siphoned out. Her words seemed to hang in the air, a lie so large and desperate that it was improper—no, impossible—to contest it.

Bertelle remembers becoming agitated. An administrator came out to quiet her down. He made a show of asking the woman at the counter whether she had Bertelle's file and, talking in exaggeratedly soothing tones, began to walk her toward the door. Bertelle relented. She went home.

The next day, Bertelle's mother called her at work. A letter had come in the mail; inside it, a transfer notice.

Ellis E., Caucasian, was assigned to Thoreau Elementary.

It was late morning. Three blocks away, Thoreau's children spilled onto its playground; recess was under way. Bertelle told her mother to walk Ellis down to Thoreau.

That day, when all the kids went in from recess, Ellis E. went in, too.

"MY NAME IS POLLY WILLIAMS"

Polly Williams knows Bertelle E. and other parents who waged guerrilla war against MPS. "The system is the system. It doesn't care. It doesn't feel. If you're a parent, what do you do?"

For Williams, the question answers itself.

"You do what you have to do."

Polly Williams did what she had to do. A single mother with four children to raise, Williams knew the strains and stress of living near the poverty line. At one point, medical problems and a long period of home recovery cost Williams her job; reluctantly, she went on welfare. "I remember my father talking about people going 'on the dole,'" Williams recalls. "I was embarrassed. But with children, you can't let your pride get in the way of what's right for them." Polly Williams is careful to add that she was on welfare less than a year.

As her children grew, Williams worked for a mail order company, for an inner-city employment project, and as a medical assistant in a mental-health program. Even though money was tight, she nevertheless enrolled each of her children at Urban Day School.

Tuition was figured according to parents' ability to pay; for Williams, tuition for all four children was reduced to $75 a month. Still, there were times when she missed a payment. "I was always active at the school, helping out," she recalls. "So when I missed a month, they didn't put us out." Years after her children had graduated from Urban Day, Williams would send occasional checks to the school, remembering the days when she could not pay.

But Urban Day stopped with eighth grade, and parochial high schools were beyond Williams's reach. Reluctantly, she sent her children to public school.

"But not just any public school," Williams recalls. When her daughter was slated for busing to a high school she thought inferior, Polly Williams called MPS to see how she could have the assignment changed.

She petitioned in writing, as she was told to do, and was refused. She appealed, as they told her she could. Her daughter in tow—"I intended to make sure she saw just how hard I was fighting for her"—Polly Williams went down to the MPS building.

She was ushered into a small room. Seated in front of her were three women, her appeals panel. One of the women Williams recognized as an old high school classmate who worked at MPS. She wasn't an administrator, just a clerk or secretary. "I guess they rounded up anyone they could to hear those appeals," Williams recalls.

Her case made, the panel told her to wait in the hall. Ten minutes went by. The door opened, and a woman leaned out to speak to Williams. "Your appeal has been denied."

She was furious. Striding down the hall, she stopped suddenly. She asked a woman where she could find the superintendent's office. Half-prepared for confrontation, Williams found the office empty. Spotting a legal pad on the superintendent's desk, she wrote: "My name is Polly Williams. I live at 1437 Burleigh Street. I will not send my child to the school you've assigned.

You may come and arrest me."

"Then," Williams recalls, holding her wrists together as if ready for handcuffs, "I went home to wait."

Three hours passed, and then the phone rang. Williams's daughter sat watching at the kitchen table as her mother answered. The conversation was short and, uncharacteristically, Williams did most of the listening.

Hanging up, she turned to her daughter.

"It was the superintendent's office. You start at Riverside on Monday."

In her sparsely furnished conference room in a basement suite of offices on Capitol Street in Milwaukee, Polly Williams—State Representative Annette "Polly" Williams, Democrat of Milwaukee—reflects on how far she has traveled from the days when she struggled to find work and raise her family. Seven times since 1980 she has run for, and won, the right to represent her Near North Side neighborhood in the Wisconsin Assembly. Her children are grown and have children of their own; her hard years are long behind her, yet she considers that chapter of her life "job training" for her role as representative.

Her tenacious style has made her enemies in Madison but has won her respect on the Near North Side of Milwaukee. For years now, neighbor boys have rushed to help "Miss Polly" carry grocery bags into her kitchen, while their parents wave and call out, "Polly, we saw you on the TV!" But Williams has known nothing like the national notoriety that came when she pushed through Milwaukee's Parental Choice program in the waning moments of the legislative session in March 1990.

While the voucher debate stirred ideological winds in Washington, Wisconsin's landmark law had its origins in Williams's own experience as a parent. Recalling her own run-ins with the system, Williams knew that not every parent was willing to seek out the superintendent and invite arrest. In Parental Choice, she institutionalized the right she'd won for herself a dozen years before.

In the years following the Second World War, tens of thousands of blacks migrated north to Milwaukee. Drawn by work in the tanneries and breweries, and serving as metal benders in the city's heavy industries, they filled boardinghouses on the Near North Side, accumulated savings, and sent word for their families to join them. Polly Williams, born in Belzoni, Mississippi, on the banks of the Yazoo River, was sent for in 1946. Her father, a former sharecropper, had come north with his brother the year before and found work in a tannery. Nine-year-old Polly enrolled in public school; nine years later, she graduated from North Division High School.

Mississippi faded into memory. In the half-century since she left Belzoni, Williams has lived on Milwaukee's North Side; within the same one-mile radius of her first home, she married, divorced, raised a family, and ran for public office. "Somewhere along the line, I realized that this is where I belong."

A Walking Philosophical Jigsaw Puzzle

Polly Williams is a politician who courts controversy.

"I am not someone who is good at compromise. If there's a fight, you'll find me in the middle," she says. "I like to win, and I don't cry if I lose.

"I've had a lot of people tell me, 'Polly, you'd get along better if you shook hands and smiled and met people halfway.' Here's what I see: This mess we got into—there were smiles and handshakes all along the way."

Not surprisingly, Williams has a reputation for being prickly and unpredictable. "Being in the 'in crowd' in Madison doesn't interest me," she asserts, recalling her days as a rookie representative and the blandishments of Madison's old hands. "My attitude is: I'm not here to make friends. I'm here to make a difference."

Williams herself professes not to understand the charge that she is unpredictable. To her mind, the positions she takes should be no surprise to anyone.

"I *am* beholden to a special interest," Williams divulges, eyes flashing behind her tinted glasses. "The black children of this city."

If there is one constant in the political career of Polly Williams, it is her aversion to alliances of any sort. Nominally a Democrat, with a voting record on many issues indistinguishable from those of her party counterparts, Williams nonetheless delights in recounting instances when she has thumbed her nose at the Democratic hierarchy. In the final weeks of the 1992 presidential campaign, with Bill Clinton making one last stop in Milwaukee, Williams was recruited to endorse the Clinton candidacy by adding her name to a paid advertisement. Alone among Wisconsin's African-American state officeholders, Williams refused. "I am not a Republican, I am not a conservative, I am not a backer of President Bush," Williams told her Democratic colleagues who sought in vain to persuade her, "but President Bush is right on parental choice, and Bill Clinton is wrong."

A self-described "Jesse-crat" who chaired Jesse Jackson's Wisconsin presidential campaign in 1988, Williams nevertheless criticizes Jackson for his opposition to school choice: "He's wrong. He's in the wrong place on vouchers," Williams declares. "Did I tell him that? No. But I will. Look at him and Clinton, sending their children to [private] school. He gets a piece of my mind on that, no question."

In the aftermath of the passage of Milwaukee's voucher program in 1990, Williams became the darling of conservative circles not simply in Wisconsin, but nationwide. The woman who had never lived more than a mile from Burleigh Street after leaving Belzoni, Mississippi, received invitations to travel to the White House to meet with President Bush and his staff, to speak at Harvard, the Heritage Foundation, and scores of conferences on education reform across the country. Her picture often adorned editorials in the *Wall Street Journal* that lionized her as the champion of school choice.

Happy to be recognized, Williams quickly became wary of being taken for granted. Within months of the passage of the Milwaukee Parental Choice Program, Williams appeared with Mike McGee, a Milwaukee alderman who had formed a militia dedicated to the cause of African-American separatism; McGee spoke of reparations from the white ruling structure, and sympathized with Saddam Hussein in the run-up to the Gulf War. At one point, Williams donned camouflage fatigues and posed as McGee's "minister of education." As Williams later explained her dalliance with McGee's militia to the *Chicago Tribune*, "He's an old friend. . . . He needed a 'minister of education' for his group and I said: 'Why not?'" As the *Tribune*'s Ron Grossman concludes, "Williams is a kind of walking philosophical jigsaw puzzle, a role she obviously relishes."[2]

"You think it's tough having Polly for an enemy?" says one Milwaukee Democrat. "Try having her for a friend."

Allies

Williams's battle for Parental Choice was by no means a one-woman war. Allies in the effort made painful personal choices of their own and broke ranks to back the black woman whose newest friends came from Milwaukee's predominantly white establishment.

Still, having friends at the White House and on the *Wall Street Journal* editorial board is no match for having enemies at MPS headquarters on Vliet Street, across the table on the Urban Education Committee, and on the editorial pages of the *Milwaukee Sentinel* and *Milwaukee Journal*. Even a force as formidable as Williams needed allies close to home, a counterweight in her own community against the powers arrayed against her.

"You see, I never worried what the *Sentinel* or the *Journal* had to say. Let them attack. Walk into the beauty salon, take a look at what's on the magazine table," Williams counsels. "The *Community Journal*. With an article telling you where the next Choice rally will be."

THE REVOLUTION'S PAMPHLETEER

For a twenty-block stretch through the Near North Side, Third Avenue becomes Martin Luther King Jr. Drive. As in so many Northern cities, the name change came along as a gesture of atonement after the murder of the charismatic civil rights activist. The new nameplates went up on the lampposts, but the street itself, like the neighborhood around it, continued its shamble toward squalor.

Third Avenue's proud past exists largely as a matter of urban archaeology. In turn-of-the-century Milwaukee, Third Avenue was the commercial center of the Near North Side, a promenade for the well-to-do among the German burghers who made their home in the neighborhood. Today, all that remains are hints of the grandeur, evident in the upper stories of the facades along Martin Luther King Jr. Drive. The first floors have long since been covered over with slabs of tarpaper siding, factory stamped with a wood-grain pattern. Shuttered buildings alternate with corner markets, their heavy iron grate doors propped open to passersby.

At 3612 Martin Luther King Jr. Drive stands a one-story brick building, baking in the summer sun; a small sign proclaims it the home of the *Milwaukee Community Journal*. Within, the *Community Journal*'s offices are a warren of rooms behind a smoked-glass receptionist station that seems a relic from a previous tenant, a dentist's office perhaps, done up in vintage 1970s decor. Along a plywood-lined hallway, a labyrinth of half-completed construction gives no clue of its date of origin and no sign that it will ever be finished. It is here, from his back-room office, that Mikel Holt, editor of the *Community Journal*, wages his war of words for African-American equity.

Holt's dark office is a jumble of confusion. Egyptian posters, their corners curling, adorn the walls, a tribute to Holt's interest in Africanist scholarship. Papers and coffee cups litter his desk, competing for space with stacks of old issues of the *Community Journal*. Holt has been the weekly paper's editor since 1978.

Holt is someone whose face may go unrecognized but whose name is known, and whose words can sometimes rouse the community to anger and to action. In the revolution Polly Williams was preparing in 1989, Mikel Holt would play the role of pamphleteer. In his hands, Williams's revolution became a revelation—a new political primer for African-Americans, in which friend and foe changed places.

Holt's paper was the only one to endorse Parental Choice; the mainstream Milwaukee dailies, the *Journal* and the *Sentinel*, remained obdurately opposed. To Holt, the editorial stance of what he dismissively calls the "majority media" came as no surprise; the fact of their opposition merely confirmed his conviction that his cause was right.

The editor of the *Community Journal* was not simply indulging a desire to play David to the system's Goliath. For Holt, conspiracy—a grand scheme to hold poor and particularly black people down—is never far away. In an odd way, it is a comfort to think that somewhere, perhaps atop the glass and steel high-rises along the lake, a group of corporate titans and their handmaids in a compliant press orchestrate the oppression of Milwaukee's less fortunate. A comfort, because an implacable enemy with a devious plan is preferable to the alternative that no one cares; that the plight of the urban poor is a matter of monumental indifference. Without a conspiracy, without false prophets to betray the people and hidden agendas to confound them, lies the fear that there are no forces that can be fought. Conspiracy, in these circumstances, is less a theory than a fighting faith.

And Holt is by no means a man without faith. A gut full of grievances has not diminished his conviction in the power of education.

"The black parents I know are believers," Holt observes. "Ask the average black parent—regardless of economic or social status—what he wants most for his children, and he'll say education. It is universally accepted that education is the passport out of poverty."

This is the shining certainty that fueled the great desegregation battles, the belief that led people to chain themselves to buses, to endure arrest, and to donate, as Holt puts it, "their dollars, dimes, and pennies" to fund a lawsuit to desegregate public schools.

In those days, education and desegregation came to be synonymous. Holt recalls the parents and members of the Milwaukeeans United for School Integration Committee (MUSIC), who in 1964 chained themselves to school buses to protest the double standard inherent in the doctrine of "separate but equal." Holt himself was in high school then; civil rights activists were his first heroes, from CORE, SNCC, and of course, first among equals, the NAACP.

On the subject of public education, Holt speaks from authority. He is an alumnus of North Division High Scool—"but not," he is careful to specify, "a graduate."

The North of the 1960s, the old North, was filled to overflowing. Classes were held in the cafeteria, in the auditorium, in storage closets. The building, built in 1907, was in a state of rampant disrepair. Cracked windows were patched with duct tape, broken bulbs protruded from light sockets. In the early morning, as students arrived, rats sometimes skittered across dark hallways.

Textbooks at North Division had not been replaced for more than a decade. Holt recalls the standing joke from those days. "Ask a student how many states there were. If he told you forty-eight, then you knew he was from North."

The notion that the schools set aside for blacks or other minorities were in any way equal to white public schools was known by all to be a fraud. Black schools got hand-me-down texts and firetrap facilities—and these were not the least of the outrages. Holt remembers the days of "intact busing," a Milwaukee practice whereby entire classrooms of black children and their black teachers were bused to white schools. Once there, they entered self-contained classrooms and took recess only after the white children had gone back in from the playground. In many cases, these children were bused back to their original school for lunch, instead of eating in the cafeteria at the white school. Lunch over, they returned by bus for afternoon classes, never once coming in contact with white children.

Holt also remembers the protests in February 1964, with CORE and the NAACP organizing pickets against intact busing. In March of that year, MUSIC formed, an umbrella organization with members drawn from NAACP, CORE, and SNCC. Its first action was the boycott in May 1964. Seventy-one MUSIC supporters were arrested for blocking buses; as many as 16,000 students abjured their public schools in favor of "freedom schools" held in churches and taught by student activists from Marquette University. While MUSIC's methods—human chains, sit-ins at the superintendent's office, and the like—were the model of nonviolence, its rhetoric occasionally verged on the violent. MUSIC officials threatened at one point to destroy McDowell, Parkman, and Meineke Avenue Schools, new facilities under construction in black neighborhoods at the time.

MUSIC's threat, though never acted on, was very much a sign of the times: Black groups were not against busing—they were for integration. Their goal was not to keep black children in their own neighborhoods, but to see them seated next to white children. In this scheme, each new black school was nothing more than a gilded cage, built to keep blacks out of white schools.

Black activists and enlightened whites fought the system for fifteen years, with enormous courage and unshakable conviction, refusing to rest until the schools were integrated.

Finally, Holt recalls, a horrible thing happened.

They won.

Bus Ride to Nowhere

"They sold us desegregation as a panacea, a placebo," Holt declares. "It was supposed to be our educational Emancipation Proclamation, leading us out to educational equality." He shakes his head. "For fifteen years, we've been on a bus ride to nowhere."

Holt thumbs through a copy of a report by the U.S. Commission on Civil Rights, "The Impact of Desegregation in Milwaukee Public Schools on Quality Education for Minorities 15 Years Later." The editor has quoted its key findings in his column in the *Community Journal*:

> Some believed that desegregation would improve education for Black Americans, provide equal educational resources and services, moderate racial views and prepare students for living in a pluralistic society. Instead, grades and test scores of Black students have declined, disciplinary actions and dropout rates have increased and racial attitudes have polarized.[3]

"If MPS were a business," Holt declares, waving the report for emphasis, "it would have filed for bankruptcy long ago—that is, if it survived the product liability suits it would have faced along the way." Animated now, he shifts in his seat and ticks off his indictment:

- Only one in five black MPS students exceeds national test averages.

- Black students fail more than one-fourth of their classes.

- At North Division, 30 percent of the students are absent on any given day. Not surprisingly, North's schoolwide grade point average is a D–.

- The gap between black and white students remains wide in MPS. Where it has narrowed, it is due not to black improvement, but to dwindling white achievement scores.

"The only way MPS makes sense, the only way you can say the system works," Holt states, "is if you think of what it does as transportation, not education."

A Multimillion-Dollar Business

Mikel Holt calls it the one question every African-American wants to ask: "Before you ask me to hand over my children, tell me: What is there for them at the end of the bus ride?" And busing—the hopes it raised and the harm it did—is key to understanding the pull of school choice.

Twenty-five years would pass from the segregation protests of 1964 to the day Polly Williams would introduce her voucher plan. In that quarter-century span, 1979 proved a watershed year for public schooling in Milwaukee. First, it was the year Milwaukee Public Schools became a "minority majority" district, when white enrollment dropped below 50 percent.[4] It was also the year MPS authori-

ties and the NAACP reached agreement on a consent decree to desegregate, after an arduous fifteen-year journey through the courts.
Coupled with the voluntary 220 Program,[5] created in 1976, the decision made Milwaukee one of very few areas in the country where
busing broke the barrier between the predominantly black Central
City and the predominantly white suburban systems ringing the city.[6]

In 1976, the system had adopted a "specialty" schools program, a
magnet scheme that employed specialized academic tracks to attract
voluntary student transfers, a program that by 1979 offered obvious
opportunities to spur desegregation.[7]

While the agreement was neutral on its face, in reality, African-
American students bore the brunt of the busing. As schools were
designated "specialty," seats were reserved for white students volun-
tarily enrolling; displaced black students were bused elsewhere. In
some cases, predominantly black elementary schools were simply
closed, their student population bused to outlying, majority white
schools where they provided the requisite racial balance.

Larry Harwell, chief administrative assistant to Polly Williams
and her tactician in the Wisconsin Assembly, saw in this practice a
pattern of deliberate discrimination. In the mostly black Central City,
MPS lacks space in neighborhood schools for 14,000 children, even
after others have chosen specialty schools elsewhere in Milwaukee
or in suburban schools through the 220 Program. As a result, these
inner-city children must be bused to outlying areas.[8]

The effect on Central City neighborhoods was the educational
equivalent of a neutron bomb: Neighborhood schools in many cases
remained standing, but neighborhood children were dispersed
across the city. Some children boarded buses as early as 5:30 A.M.
and didn't return home until 6 P.M. Not all parents had the nerve or
the know-how of Bertelle E. or the young Polly Williams to confront the system.

The statistics reveal the scope of busing and its impact on Milwaukee's African-American children. As of 1988, across Milwaukee

there were nineteen neighborhoods (school attendance areas) in which 60 percent of the students were bused to an average of 86 different elementary schools. For instance, in the Clark Elementary School attendance area—96 percent black—481 children attended school in the neighborhood, while 1,652 more were bused to 104 different schools in all corners of the city.[9] In the Siefert Elementary attendance area (the neighborhood in which many of Urban Day's children live), 505 neighborhood children went to Siefert, while 768 were bused to 91 different schools. As late as 1991, busing from one attendance area to 80 or more occurred in sixteen areas.[10]

Observers like Polly Williams trace a number of pathologies to busing's role in furthering the breakdown of neighborhood bonds. Foremost was the way busing provided recruitment opportunities for gangs. "Children that young, sent off to neighborhoods they don't know full of people who don't want them there—those children are ripe for the picking for any gangbanger who promises to protect them," Williams notes.

Yet in the years after 1979, busing evolved into a multimillion-dollar business. MPS buses a full two-thirds of its students—more than 65,000 children—at an annual cost of $45 million.[11]

Finance formulas created incentives for the school system to keep the buses filled. As Mikel Holt sees it, "Busing money is like cocaine. School systems got hooked." Transfers within the district are encouraged by a state funding formula that gives the system 1.2 times the per-pupil allotment whenever a minority student transfers from a school that is more than 30 percent minority to one where minority enrollment is 30 percent or less. In this way, each transferring student yields a 20 percent "busing bonus" for the system.

For transfers between districts under the 220 Program, the incentive to bus was even greater. The receiving district would get 100 percent of the funding to cover the incoming student, and the sending district would be "held harmless," receiving its full allotment for the student's empty seat. In addition, receiving districts got a 20 percent bonus when the number of transfers exceeded 5 percent of their resident enrollment—all on top of funds to cover the cost of transportation.[12] At a time when declining white birthrates made it difficult for some suburban schools to fill classrooms, 220 was a significant source of students and funding.

Not surprisingly, although 220 was designed for two-way transfers, few suburban whites opted to send their children to city schools. The first year, 330 minority children were bused to suburban schools, while 11 suburban children came to Milwaukee. A decade later, in 1986–87, the numbers were 3,074 and 769. By 1990, 5,000 blacks were being bused to forty schools in twenty-three Milwaukee suburbs; 1,300 white suburban children traveled to the city, most to magnet programs that allowed only a certain number of black students in order to reserve seats for whites.[13]

Cynics suspect 220 is also a way for suburban schools to siphon away Central City athletes. Editor Mikel Holt tells of a tall and talented African-American high school student ferried each day from his inner-city home to his suburban school and back not by a school bus, but by taxicab. Taxpayers, apparently, picked up the fare.

Despite the phalanx of yellow buses crisscrossing the city, busing's impact on desegregation was, in the end, negligible. Fifteen years after the consent decree, North Division, 99.2 percent black in 1975, is 98 percent black in 1994–95; North's 842 students include 4 whites.[14] While there are no solid statistics to measure "white flight," from 1975 to 1986 the percentage of minorities in the Milwaukee Public Schools rose from 39.9 to 65.6 percent.[15]

In one respect, busing's impact was undeniable, if unintended: It utterly demolished the reality of the neighborhood school, a devastating blow to parents who sought to keep their children close to home where watchful eyes might counter the increasing lure of gangs and violence.

"The only neighborhood schools that were left," Polly Williams notes, "were private schools."

• • •

In front of Mikel Holt's offices, sweltering on a June afternoon between thundershowers, Martin Luther King Jr. Drive is almost silent. Across the street stands a down-at-the-heels building; carved into its stone facade is the oddly out-of-place word "Hollywood," a clue from a forgotten past as remote as a message from a distant star.

Three young toughs glide by, sneaking a sideways glance at Holt. They display no recognition, but they seem momentarily curious at this compact coil of a man holding forth on their sidewalk about history and hopes and conspiracies to keep people down, a man obviously at ease—a kind of mayor of black Milwaukee, or at least of Martin Luther King Jr. Drive.

SECESSION: THE NORTH DIVISION PLAN

Mikel Holt and others began to view the impact of busing on the educational opportunities of black children with increasing alarm. By 1988, the black community had formulated a new strategy. Building on a proposal put forward by Robert Peterkin, then MPS superintendent, to subdivide the system into six smaller, independent districts, black leaders seized the opening to push for more autonomy. Crafting a plan around five racially balanced subdistricts, they proposed for the sixth an overwhelmingly black district in the heart of the Central City.

The idea was to free this district from MPS central management and build a system within the system, with North Division High School as the flagship and almost two dozen elementary and middle schools as feeders. The backers of this effort were Polly Williams and Howard Fuller, the activist who had years before led the "Committee to Save North" and would several years later assume the superintendency of the Milwaukee Public Schools.

Williams and Fuller sought nothing short of full autonomy: power to elect their own school board, site-based management, complete control over teacher hiring and firing. The "North

Division Plan," as it was called, passed the Wisconsin Assembly, only to stall in the State Senate.

The failure of the effort seared its lessons into the Central City activists' minds. Community leaders had tried to work within the system. The next effort would strike at the system itself.

Reflecting on the rejection of the North Division Plan, Holt described it in one of his newspaper columns as "a scenario straight out of South Africa: A system of educational apartheid, keeping Black parents powerless pawns in a game based more on financial considerations than educational needs." On the sidewalk of Martin Luther King Jr. Drive, Holt offers a simpler description: "It was like spitting into a hurricane.

"Black parents look at the suburban schools, white schools, in Whitefish Bay, Bayside, Mequon. They see them working. The 220 Program says, 'We'll bus you there,'" Holt recounts. "And for some people, that's positive.

"But there's something else going on. We see schools right here in the Central City—Messmer High, Urban Day, Harambee—teaching black children. These schools are working—and they're right here, in our own neighborhoods."

To Holt, these private schools defined precisely what black parents wanted from MPS: talented teachers, an atmosphere of high expectations, a culturally attuned curriculum, and a premium on parent involvement. On the last ingredient, Holt is insistent. The proof, he says, is whether parents are paid lip service, as in MPS, or whether they help run the school—influencing curriculum, teacher hiring, questions of expansion and upkeep.

A TROJAN HORSE

Polly Williams is matter-of-fact: "I came up with choice outside of the public school system because I couldn't get choice inside it."[16]

A 1989 article in the *Milwaukee Times* illustrates the evolution. Detailing yet another of Williams's plans for public school reform, the news story's last line provides what in retrospect is a clear portent of the coming battle: "Williams also said she plans to begin pushing Gov. Tommy Thompson's parental choice plan allowing students to obtain vouchers to attend private schools."[17]

Governor Tommy Thompson, an advocate of vouchers, had tested the waters several times, only to see the Wisconsin legislature divide for and against vouchers along predictable party lines. By 1989, however, Thompson's support for school choice and the concept's persistent popularity had sparked a counterproposal from MPS. The MPS bill was meant to build upon the existing "Children at Risk" statute, an "alternative education" vehicle established in the mid-1980s to permit placing in private schools children designated "at risk"—a catchall category for behavior ranging from drug use, chronic truancy, violence, teen pregnancy or parenthood to academic performance two grade levels behind their age group. MPS's idea was to extend the "at risk" label—used primarily for middle and high school students—to elementary-level students beginning as early as kindergarten.[18]

The choice concept came in as a reference to parents' ability, once confronted with the designation of their children as "at risk," to select one or another alternative private school. Those schools, which would agree to hold open certain slots for public school transfers, would be compensated with "at least 80 percent of average cost" not simply of the state per-pupil allotment, but of the school district's cost of education.[19]

The MPS alternative set off alarm bells for Polly Williams. She learned that administrators at Urban Day, the school her own children had attended, were interested in the MPS bill; compared to the always-tenuous process of tuition collection, with parents on a month-by-month payment schedule, the stability of state funding for slots—whether filled or empty—was a tempting proposition. For precisely that reason, Williams worried that the bill would turn Urban Day and other schools like it into a dumping ground for the public schools' problem children.

More than that, Williams aide Larry Harwell feared that MPS could use this new financial foothold as a way to pressure private schools to follow state licensing guidelines for all new hires. The "at risk" law mandated placement of MPS teachers in the receiving private schools, alongside the private school staff. Harwell, who made it his business to learn the economics of the issue, also suspected the plan, which promised the "sending system" a 10 percent payment, would allow MPS to turn a profit on every student shifted out of the public system.

For Williams, the conclusion was inescapable: The MPS alternative was a Trojan horse. "I had to fight it," she recalls. "But I knew you can never fight something with nothing."

By October, Williams had introduced her own voucher alternative: Parental Choice vouchers in the amount of $3,100—at the time, close to the average per-pupil cost of education for the city's private schools—for 3,000 low-income Milwaukee students. Aware that Governor Thompson's efforts to win vouchers for religious schools had generated controversy, and knowing that many of the community private schools in Milwaukee were nonsectarian, Williams sidestepped the issue by limiting participation to the city's nonsectarian private schools.

UNDERGROUND RAILROAD

The battle for Parental Choice began in the church basements and meeting halls of the Near North Side. From the start, the Milwaukee proponents' language was appropriated from the civil rights movement. Their rhetoric was more redolent of Martin Luther King than the free-market pronouncements favored by conservative voucher proponents—against which the other side deployed their own tried-and-true assault on the consumerization of education. As a result, the ensuing debate often involved arguments that failed in any meaningful way to engage the other side.

The public education establishment took their cue from the national voucher debate, which revolved around free-market models and vouchers as vehicles creating competition for change. Meanwhile, Polly Williams pitched vouchers as a ticket on an educational Underground Railroad out of an oppressive public system.

"The way I saw it," Williams recalls, "the system is preparing our children for slavery. Look at the situation: Drop out by tenth grade, get into the street life—when you should be walking across that stage getting a diploma, you're standing in front of a judge wearing chains."

Parental Choice "is the difference between empowerment and enslavement," Williams told a gathering of the group Black and White Men Together, in February 1990, in what was fast becoming a stump speech. "We gotta fight. I'll be the one leading the revolt to destroy the system."[20]

Early in the effort, Williams recalls, she looked around one public meeting and assessed her troops, many of them mothers or even grandmothers scraping along on AFDC. "This is my army," she thought; as a group, they were not the kind of people adept at fighting City Hall. Yet as she moved from meeting to meeting, Williams began to see her audience differently. These mothers were animated by a simple and strong desire to do right by their children. The fact that they had little, that the system treated them as outcasts, simply served to highlight the righteousness of their cause. There was a power, Williams came to see, in their very powerlessness. "I've always said there is quality in poverty—people with heart and character.

"If you have a million dollars, is it hard for you to give some away?" Williams poses her rhetorical question. "I know people, they don't have a dollar—but they'll find a way to give you what you need."

Williams and her aide Larry Harwell sized up the situation in the State Assembly, and realized a back-room strategy would get nowhere. Their only chance was to raise the visibility by pressing for a public hearing. "My idea was," Williams says, "if you want to tell us no, then you're going to have to tell us to our face."

Williams and MPS agreed on one thing. Parental Choice was revolutionary.

According to MPS superintendent Peterkin, Williams's "bill would threaten public education by leaving the city schools with the hardest-to-educate students and with fewer resources."[21] For Williams, it was eerie confirmation of precisely which children the MPS "choice" bill sought to rid the district of.

Still, the State Assembly was only one half of the political equation. With her campaign under way to pressure the Assembly's Urban Education Committee to put Parental Choice to a vote, Williams began to confront the realities of getting her program through the State Senate. Like the rest of the representatives in the Assembly, Williams was dependent on State Senator Gary George, head of the powerful Joint Finance Committee. Williams's aim was to add Parental Choice to the Senate's must-pass mini-budget. George, with the power to make or break other legislators' pet projects, was accustomed to the deference due a kingmaker.

In Williams's case, however, standard deference didn't begin to address the problem. George, whose Senate district included Williams's Assembly seat, could under other circumstances have been Williams's powerful Senate patron. Instead, the two politicians, elected together in 1980, barely spoke to each other.

The rift was personal. In a hard-fought campaign, George had won his seat by defeating Monroe Swann, Williams's cousin and the state's first elected black senator. For ten years, George had delighted in never lifting a finger to help Williams, who, for her part, refused to reach across the divide. In her frequent diatribes against the unnamed powers-that-be, listeners could make out a person with more than a passing resemblance to Gary George.

Parental Choice changed the equation. Realizing there was no way to succeed without George's blessing, Williams went to see the chairman of Joint Finance. "I told him, 'Pass this bill, and you will never hear a cross word from me. I will go out in the street and shout that Gary George is the greatest state senator Wisconsin has ever seen. I will say it loud, and I will say it with conviction, and I will tell my constituents what a wonderful thing you have done for our children.'"

Williams shifts back in her seat.

"Then I told him, 'If you sink this bill, I will never, ever get off of your backside. You will never have a moment's rest from Polly Williams.'"

On February 21, 1990, the *Milwaukee Community Journal* carried the story: "Board Director, Senator Endorse Choice Bill." It began: "State Senator Gary George and School Board Director Jared Johnson have added their names to the growing chorus of political leaders endorsing a proposed parental choice bill."

Williams's strategy had worked. Under pressure, Barbara Notestein, chair of the Urban Education Committee, scheduled a single public hearing, for Friday, February 23, 1990, at 9:30 A.M. Mikel Holt, in an editorial announcing the hearing date, scored Notestein, "the 'liberal Democrat,'" for the timing of the hearing: "[S]cheduling such an important hearing on a weekday morning is tantamount to insuring a small audience (unless Notestein is assuming most low-income people don't work and thus should be available)."[22]

More troubling to Holt was the choice of venue: Incredibly, the hearing was to be held at MPS administrative headquarters. For readers of the *Community Journal*, it had the impact of a slap in the face; coming to the hearing was nothing less than a matter of self-respect.

Two hundred parents and children attended the hearing, which, running three full hours, resembled a religious revival more than something governed by Robert's Rules of Order.

Like a good general, Williams built the core of her attack around a superior knowledge of her enemy. "When you've been around like I have, you get to get inside the liberal's mind." She determined to strike at her opponents' ideological Achilles' heel. "Guilt," Williams says matter-of-factly. "They think they know better. You've got to call them on it." As she later told the *Wall Street Journal*, "They say they're liberal, but whenever it comes to empowering black people, they stab us in the back. We want self-determination, not handouts and dependency."[23]

Williams zeroed in at the hearing. "I've heard that excuse," she told the committee, her audience of parents and children at her back: "If you're poor, you're stupid. Until you have parents as part of everything, until you incorporate them [into the decision-making process], nothing will change."[24]

Her pitch to the committee members often met with a chorus of "amens" from the parents in attendance. When the hearing concluded, Williams sensed they had turned a corner.

On March 8, the Urban Education Committee assembled. The bill backed by MPS fell short, 6–7. Harwell and Williams's head count put the tally for their bill at 7–6. Yet, as the votes were cast, one of the supporters Harwell had counted as being for Parental Choice, Kim Plache—a white, single, childless first-term Democrat from Racine with the same liberal voting record as the leadership—abstained; the vote was deadlocked, 6–6.

Neither Williams nor Harwell had lobbied Plache, concentrating their efforts on minority members from Milwaukee. Now their fate was in her hands. Williams was numb. She looked around the small committee room, at the lobbyists for the teachers' unions in attendance; not a parent was in sight. In a few moments, it would all be over.

Plache was queried again; she voted aye, with Williams. The bill was reported out of committee to the Assembly floor.

Afterward, Williams sought out the representative from Racine to thank her for her support, and to find out something more. "I had to know. I had to ask her for myself, Why'd you do it?" Plache explained her vote, her most difficult then or since as a self-described supporter of public education, as the right thing to do given the condition of Milwaukee's public schools.[25] Williams recalls a slightly different, personal angle to Plache's decision: "She told me she had a niece who had trouble in public school. From what she said, I think she was the one paying her niece's private school tuition. I think it helped her see sometimes you've got to reach out when children need help."

When the time came for the floor vote, Williams and the Milwaukee parents she had mobilized for Choice rented a bus and made the journey up I-94 to Madison. In committee, Barbara Notestein and a fellow Democrat had succeeded in attaching a sunset provision, under which the program expired automatically in five years, unless reenacted; Governor Thompson, using his broad item-veto authority, would later strike this language from the bill. Other amendments capped the program at 1 percent of the population of MPS, effectively ratcheting down the number of Choice vouchers from Williams's hoped-for 3,000 to approximately 1,000, and mandated a random lottery selection process for schools with more student applicants than open seats.[26]

The most dangerous amendment, however, was offered by liberal Democrat and Speaker of the Assembly Tom Loftus. It moved to strip the funding from the program—potentially fatal for a measure built into the budget bill. Williams watched as one of her key sponsors defected to the liberal leadership. With the vote deadlocked at 48–48, once again the decisive vote came from Representative Plache.

"A VICTORY FOR AFRICAN AMERICAN PARENTS," bannered Holt's *Community Journal;* "ASSEMBLY PASSES CHOICE BILL." "To the applause of nearly 50 African American parents and children," Holt wrote, "the Assembly approved the parental choice initiative after nine separate votes to either amend or limit funding for the measure."[27]

Holt devoted his signature "Signifyin'" column to the Assembly victory:

> If nothing else, the debate, deception and dogma which highlighted the parental choice scenario should leave every African American in the state with a new definition of "Democratic liberal."
>
> ... The average liberal is nothing more than a missionary without a collar. And we should never forget that right before soldiers unboarded the ship in Africa, they first sent in the missionaries to soften us up.
>
> Control people of color with a smile, keep them impoverished, enslaved by welfare programs (which are run by other missionaries) and unwilling or unable to make a decision without our approval.[28]

Holt noted in his column that the celebration spilled over into Polly Williams's birthday party, at which "there were even a couple of Republicans in attendance."

The last hurdle was the State Senate, and the race against time before the session adjourned March 23. A last-minute compromise trimmed the value of each voucher from $3,100 to $2,500—but pegged the voucher's future value to 50 percent of the state per-pupil expenditure, a benchmark Williams (rightly) anticipated would rise every year. Most important, Senator Gary George kept his word. On March 22, the mini-budget passed; in it, amendment to the Wisconsin Statutes 119.23, "the Milwaukee Parental Choice Program."

In the days that followed, word began to ripple out about Polly Williams's victory. The battle for parental choice, until then played out within the confines of Milwaukee's Near North Side and the cloakrooms of the capitol in Madison, was now a national story, reported in the *New York Times* and the *Wall Street Journal*.

Williams, equipped with 20–20 peripheral political vision in the Wisconsin Assembly, was slow to see the looming legal threat triggered by her legislative victory. When Clint Bolick, attorney in the Washington, D.C., offices of the Landmark Legal Foundation, a conservative public-interest firm, finally succeeded in contacting Williams after several attempts to offer pro bono legal representation, she was still savoring her triumph. Accustomed to adulatory calls from constituents, her response to attorney Bolick was simple: "We don't need a lawyer. We won."

Bolick knew that a system with the resources of the public education establishment would never simply surrender; he also knew the national coverage would raise the stakes of Milwaukee's experiment, transforming Parental Choice from a mere program into a precedent. Still, Williams had worked hard to win something no one had ever won before. After years of being steamrollered by the system, she had earned the right to celebrate.

"You've got my number. Keep it handy," Bolick said, "just in case."

CHAPTER FIVE

The Empire Strikes Back

The celebration was short-lived. The formal enactment of Parental Choice took place on April 27, 1990; in mid-May Governor Thompson came to Milwaukee for a ceremonial signing of the bill.[1] At Harambee Community School, several blocks from Polly Williams's Near North Side home, Williams and Thompson presided over the event, dispensing signing pens to some of the dozens of parents on hand. It was the same ceremony Regis Chesir's mother wandered into.

Beneath the celebrations, however, ran an undercurrent of unease. Even before the governor's visit, Polly Williams was scrambling to find Clint Bolick's phone number at the Landmark Legal Foundation. Opposition to vouchers, ineffectual in the Wisconsin legislature, had found a champion in the person of State Superintendent Herbert J. Grover, the hulking, gravel-voiced former five-term Democratic State Assemblyman. Grover, whose responsibilities as the state's top education official included administering the new Parental Choice program, assumed the position of point man in the battle against vouchers.

Never shy about his opinions and always ready with a sharp quote, Grover put opposition to Parental Choice at the center of his stump speech. Traveling the state in the spring of 1990, he issued repeated public invitations for groups to sue to stop Parental Choice. On May 7, speaking to the Wisconsin Association of School District Administrators in La Crosse, Grover escalated the attack, coupling his public solicitation for a suit with a prediction: A complaint would result in an injunction to stop the program before the next school year.[2] The strategy was clear: The public education establishment could win in the courts the battle it had lost in the Wisconsin legislature.

Predictably, Grover's prayers were answered. On May 30, a suit was filed with the Wisconsin Supreme Court, seeking a permanent injunction against Parental Choice.[3]

Parties to the suit read like a Who's Who of the public education lobby and its allies. Heading the list: Felmers Chaney, president of Milwaukee's local NAACP chapter. Polly Williams admired the audacity of the gambit; enlisting the NAACP as plaintiff would imply opposition to vouchers in the African-American community. The other plaintiffs were predictable: the 55,000-member Wisconsin Education Association Council, the state's largest teachers' union; the state's PTA organization; the Wisconsin Congress of Parents and Teachers, a frequent fifth column for the public education establishment; the Wisconsin Federation of Teachers (the state's American Federation of Teachers affiliate); the Administrators and Supervisors Council of Milwaukee; and, of course, the Wisconsin Association of School District Administrators, the very group Grover had invited to sue him several weeks earlier.[4]

Given the heavy institutional firepower leveled against Parental Choice, someone in the public education apparatus sensed a need to enlist a parent as petitioner; George Williams of Milwaukee, father of Aronica Williams, appears as party to the suit. On the second to last page of the filing, the complaint lists Mr. Williams's employer: the Wisconsin Education Association Council.[5]

Grover's efforts had paid off; through his contrivance, anti-voucher forces would gain a legal platform to assault Parental

Choice. Better still, as superintendent, Bert Grover would be cast in the role of Parental Choice's defender. Despite the ostensibly adversarial nature of the proceedings, no one in the courtroom would want to see Parental Choice survive. Polly Williams's program was in trouble.

Grover's forces had attended as well to the public relations war against school choice. The day before the suit was filed, the Wisconsin Department of Public Instruction (DPI) complied with its statutory responsibility to implement Parental Choice, releasing a terse one-page public announcement notifying private schools in the city that they had until June 14 to petition for a place in the program.[6] Superintendent Grover's office then released a three-page statement, outlining the legal case that had been filed against Parental Choice. In it, Grover called Parental Choice "fundamentally flawed and very possibly unconstitutional," even as he repeated his pledge to fairly implement the law. Grover justified his comments as proper for "the only constitutional officer in the state specifically charged with the educational welfare of the state's children."[7]

ENTER THE NAACP

The political rift dividing the once-unified ranks of the North Side's civil rights warriors was amplified by the intimate physical proximity of the antagonists in the voucher debate. A dozen blocks south of Mikel Holt's office on Martin Luther King Jr. Drive, up a flight of worn linoleum stairs, a cluster of offices house the Milwaukee chapter of the National Association for the Advancement of Colored People. A secretary, speaking in stentorian tones to a caller, assures him of assistance, admonishing, "Don't you know you've reached the most powerful African-American organization in America?" Each morning on King Drive, children clad in blue and white school uniforms and shouldering book bags could be seen marching north toward Harambee Community School.

In the afternoon, knots of teenage boys filtered down from North Division High School to Carver Park, two blocks behind the NAACP. Yet despite the short distances involved, antagonists in the voucher debate were soon locked into their own separate worlds as surely as they would seat themselves on opposite sides of the courtroom.

Felmers O. Chaney, the head of the Milwaukee NAACP, asked by Mikel Holt's *Community Journal* why he had lent his name as lead plaintiff on the lawsuit challenging the program, responded: "Well, you know, choice is just a subterfuge for segregation, like it was in the South. If it's only for Blacks, it discriminates against Asians and Hispanics." When Holt asked Chaney whether he realized that an estimated 85 percent of the children eligible for Choice vouchers would be black, that eligibility for the program was determined by income and not race, and that a number of the schools interested in participating were integrated to a degree few MPS schools could match even after a dozen years of busing, the NAACP leader answered with a remarkable admission: he had yet to fully investigate the schools or read the legislation in its entirety.[8]

Milwaukee's African-American community grappled with the implications of the civil war between the NAACP and Polly Williams and her activist allies; for Clint Bolick, the white Washington lawyer as skilled in the use of symbols as in the letter of the law, the decision of antichoice forces to position Chaney as lead plaintiff was the kind of political masterstroke to be expected from a formidable opponent. In contrast to the long list of teachers' unions and other organs of the public education establishment, Chaney's name gave the antivoucher side a chance to portray the program as one opposed by the "civil rights community." Few would bother to go beyond the fact that the NAACP opposed the program. "No matter what the reality," Bolick notes, "what the NAACP says still has real resonance in the community."

The morning after Felmers Chaney and the teachers' unions filed their suit, both of Milwaukee's mainstream newspapers, the *Sentinel* and the *Journal*, editorialized against Parental Choice.[9] In her Near North Side community, Polly Williams began to worry about the cumulative effect of the constant barrage; would parents want to step forward to claim vouchers when the program was under a legal cloud?

Williams assessed her options. The court case Grover had instigated, with himself as Parental Choice's nominal defendant, meant the voucher plan could be struck down without any advocate of the program appearing in the courtroom. A series of phone calls from Williams to Bolick's Washington office led June 1 to an announcement of their own: The Landmark Legal Foundation would represent the low-income parents entitled to vouchers under Parental Choice.[10] Williams was determined, she recalls, "to get our day in court."

RED-TAPE WAR

For many proponents of school choice, it amounts to an article of faith: Vouchers will exert a healthy catalytic effect, forcing public schools to compete to keep students. That theoretical faith in the power of competition, however, could not withstand the ground-level realities of a public education system under siege. The education establishment's strategy was clear—and the rules of engagement were not to be some sort of Marquis of Queensberry quest for educational excellence. Rather than summon up the effort to outcompete Choice schools by serving students better, the Wisconsin public education establishment adopted a different strategy: It deployed its considerable powers to strangle the Choice experiment in its crib.

To this end, Superintendent Grover's legal case was just one weapon in the antivoucher arsenal. To be sure, the superintendent himself continued to beat the war drum against Parental Choice; June 6, during an appearance on Milwaukee's *Emphasis Wisconsin* TV program, Grover called Choice schools "souped-up day care centers."[11] Yet the rhetorical assault was peripheral to a parallel strategy, pursued just as cannily, to employ the state's administrative powers to encumber program participants.

At Grover's behest, his DPI promulgated an eight-page "compliance form." The DPI's one-page letter to prospective Choice schools, issued two weeks before the deadline, was accompanied by the compliance sheet, listing a spate of state and federal regulations ranging from handicapped education strictures mandating equal access to all facilities and activities to tailored "individualized education program" requirements.

The following passage is typical:

> Special Education and related services are provided to EEN [Exceptional Educational Needs] children with the following handicapping conditions or any combination thereof:
>
> - Physical or orthopedic disability
> - Mental retardation or other developmental disabilities
> - Hearing impairment
> - Visual disability
> - Speech or language disability
> - Emotional disturbance
> - Learning disability
>
> The following supportive and related services are provided as needed to assist an individual child to benefit from special education.
>
> - Transportation
> - Audiological services
> - Psychological services
> - Occupational therapy
> - Physical therapy
> - Recreation
> - Medical services for diagnosis and evaluation
> - Counseling and guidance
> - Social work services
> - Parent counseling and training
> - Others[12]

Beyond the requirements and statutes cited in the Milwaukee Parental Choice Program legislation itself, DPI's intent form required each private school to guarantee compliance with the following provisions:

- the Wisconsin Pupil Nondiscrimination Act, 118.13, Stats., and Wis. Adm. Code PI 9;

- Title IX of the Education Amendments of 1972, as amended, 20 USC 1681 et seq.;

- the Age Discrimination Act of 1975, as amended, 42 USC 6101 et seq.;

- 504 of the Rehabilitation Act of 1973, as amended, 29 USC 794;

- the Family Education Rights and Privacy Act, 20 USC 1232g;

- the Drug-Free School and Communities Act of 1986, 20 USC 3171;

- "all federal and state constitutional guarantees protecting the rights and liberties of individuals including freedom of religion, expression, association, against unreasonable search and seizure, equal protection and due process";

- "all regulations, guidelines, and standards lawfully adopted under the above statutes by the appropriate administrative agency";

- "all applicable federal and state laws" regarding the delivery of services to handicapped students under the Education for All Handicapped Children Act, 20 USC 1401 et seq., 115.76 et seq., Stats., and Wis. Adm. Code PI 11; and

- Public school district standards for staff licensure and development, ancillary services, curriculum, etc. under Wis. Adm. Code PI 8.[13]

At the bottom of each page was a box for the school administrator's signature.

For private schools desiring to participate in Parental Choice, the legal implication of signing the compliance forms was ominous: an open-ended and unfunded commitment to graft onto each existing school a special education apparatus of a scope the average MPS school itself could never hope to match. This, Polly Williams pointed out, while the public system allotted nearly three times the amount of per-pupil expenditure for special education students. Parental Choice vouchers were limited to the state share of per-pupil spending, itself just half the average MPS's per-pupil expenditure: in the first year of Parental Choice, $2,500. "We can't expect the private schools to do with $2,500 what the public schools do with $15,000," Williams argued.[14] "I call it MPS math. They wanted to give Choice schools all of the regulations and one-sixth of the money."

On the basis of the compliance forms—and despite public statements by Grover's deputy as early as May 30 that indicated six schools had expressed interest in participating in the Parental Choice program[15]—Grover was able to issue the promised press release on the June 15 deadline listing only two schools as eligible for Parental Choice vouchers.

One of the schools, SER–Jobs for Progress, was an alternative high school already participating in the "Children at Risk" program—the very program on which MPS had patterned the "choice" plan that had so alarmed Polly Williams. SER–Jobs would ultimately win approval to participate in Parental Choice, enrolling twenty-seven students in the program's first year. The second school, Lakeshore Montessori, a well-regarded kindergarten-only school for three-, four-, and five-year-olds with a total enrollment of around forty students, would in the fall of 1990 enroll four Parental Choice children.

Given how precarious the first days of Parental Choice were, the success of the Grover gambit was devastating. Low-income parents looking to Parental Choice to expand their educational alternatives suddenly found their options limited to a handful of seats in a kindergarten school and a "last-chance" high school for problem students. Then, having created an administrative mountain for prospective Parental Choice schools to scale, Grover delivered the coup de grâce; the final sentence of the DPI statement read: "A constitutional challenge of the Milwaukee Parental Choice Program has been filed with the Wisconsin Supreme Court."[16]

To Polly Williams, speaking daily to teachers and administrators of private schools readying seats for hundreds of voucher children, momentum for Choice was gathering steam. According to Wisconsin's state education authority, however, it looked as though there was little interest in school choice, and great likelihood the program would be derailed by the courts.

The skirmishing continued. Urban Day School had sent a letter to DPI expressing its intent to participate June 1, within days of DPI's announcement. It learned only on June 14—DPI's deadline day—that its failure to sign the "compliance assurance" forms would keep it off the published list of participating schools. According to Zakiya Courtney, Urban Day was preparing to open 135 seats to Parental Choice students.

Piqued by Grover's maneuvering, Governor Tommy Thompson directed his Milwaukee office to issue a press statement identifying nine schools as having "notified the Department of Public Instruction of their intent to participate in the program."[17] Grover immediately volleyed back, expressing "concern over possible confusion" caused by the governor's office, and reiterating that only two schools were cleared to participate. Again, Grover took the occasion to cite the constitutional challenge "filed by several Wisconsin citizens," by which he appears to have meant Chaney, Wisconsin Education Association Council president Richard Collins, and officials from the Wisconsin Federation of Teachers and Wisconsin Association of School District Administrators—the group Grover had urged to file suit to stop Parental Choice in May.[18]

Zakiya Courtney recalls the atmosphere of uncertainty at Urban Day: "I would take the calls and talk to parents, try to be positive and practical, too. But at the end of the day, I would sit back and ask myself, 'Is this still going to happen?'"

On June 26, the Wisconsin Supreme Court issued its ruling in *Felmers Chaney et al. v. Grover,* declining the invitation to assert original jurisdiction, a decision that effectively denied the request for permanent injunction. The vote was the narrowest possible, 4–3, with the court's chief justice providing the decisive vote on the procedural grounds that the case ought to be heard "as soon as practicable" in circuit court.[19]

Yet even as the Wisconsin Supreme Court issued its ruling, the legal battle had taken a different turn. Rather than stand by as Parental Choice opponents arrayed themselves on both sides of a lawsuit, and uncertain as to how the State Supreme Court would rule, Polly Williams and Landmark Legal's Bolick sought a way to bring parents and students into the equation. Their answer: a suit brought on behalf of a handful of prospective Choice parents and students, and the Choice schools they sought to attend. The defendant: Herbert Grover, state superintendent.

Bolick filed suit in Dane County Circuit Court less than twenty-four hours before the Supreme Court ruled against Chaney and his coplaintiffs. Two days later, Felmers Chaney, the teachers' unions, and the other parties who had responded to Grover's call petitioned to intervene in the new case—this time, on the side of the DPI.

CHAPTER SIX

Davis v. Grover

"Lonzetta Davis, in her own behalf and as natural guardian of her daughter, Sabrina Davis . . ." begins the cover page of Case No. 90CV2576, *Davis et al. v. Grover.*

Lonzetta Davis, plaintiff, seated on the plush, tropical-patterned sofa in her apartment in the Northlawn Projects in the winter of 1994, thinks back to the days when the suit was filed. "We've lived here two and a half years," Lonzetta recounts, "since the fall when heat went off on Second Street. That's where we were living when we went to court."

Davis gestures with pride around her living room. Though the blond brick buildings of Northlawn are nondescript, inside, the Davis home is all gleaming wood floors. On one wall, a glass and pipe bookshelf is lined with family photographs, one picturing a smiling Sabrina Davis in her Urban Day uniform. Voucher advocates and opponents saw the case as the first true test of the concept's constitutionality; for Davis, it was simply about Sabrina.

"Back when the court case was going on, that was for the lawyers to worry about," Davis explains. Her most pressing concern was persuading the public housing authorities to move her family into a better project.

"I was working to get us off Second Street. Some folks wait two years for their name to come up. I couldn't have my kids in a place with no heat and the winter coming—not the way winter is around here. So I used the heat to try to put us in a special situation."

Aware that not everyone prevails over the public housing bureau-cracy, Davis adds: "And I guess my twenty-five phone calls didn't hurt.

"But even Second Street was better than 26th and Brown," she continues, referring to an intersection a few blocks north of Urban Day that most inner-city residents regard as the North Side's most dangerous. "That was a nightmare. I opened my eyes to the police nearly every morning," Davis remembers with the wave of a hand. "One day, I went out the door—the police were taping off the block. No one could go in or out. Someone had thrown a firebomb into one of the houses. There was a drug house across the street. There was a drug house in back of me—another across the alley." At night, prostitutes flagged down traffic at one end of the block.

By nightfall, 26th and Brown was a no man's land. "Every day, when my son walked out the door," Davis recounts, "I told him, 'Don't let dark catch you.'

"This is a better neighborhood. Oh, we still hear gunshots. We still have the drugs—but it's not constant. That's because this de-velopment is veterans and working people only. No AFDC," Davis says, then reconsiders. "Not to be downing them; I was one of them once.

"Like my mother says, 'Never go from bad to worse; always go from bad to better.' "

Like so many of the other actors in the Parental Choice drama, Davis had attended North Division High. School was a struggle. As a senior, four months short of graduation, she dropped out. The de-cision that, when she was a headstrong seventeen-year-old, seemed beyond question has long since become inexplicable. Lonzetta Davis herself has ceased trying to explain why she left high school.

More than a decade after her last day at North Division, married with two children, Davis found her lack of a diploma nagging at her. She had heard of a program downtown at MATC—the Milwaukee Area Technical College—where she could study for her GED. She enrolled; by the spring of 1990, she got her GED, and signed up for a college course at MATC.

That same year, Davis's daughter, Sabrina, entered kindergarten at Urban Day. Sabrina took to school well, her mother noted, and seemed to like Urban Day. Yet tuition was steep, and although both Sabrina's parents worked—she as a secretary at St. Michael's Hospital and her husband driving a Care Cab transporting handicapped people—they had no choice but to send their daughter to MPS for first grade.

Then came a new program called Parental Choice. At a parents' meeting at Urban Day just days before the school year ended, Zakiya Courtney outlined the new program that had just passed the legislature, and then added the bad news: The teachers' unions were suing to stop it. Courtney invited any parents interested in joining a lawsuit to defend the program to come forward at the end of the meeting. Lonzetta Davis didn't hesitate; when the meeting ended and the other parents milled about, she headed for the front of the room.

"I walked up to Zakiya and said, 'Where do I sign?' The school was doing right by my daughter, and I saw what they were talking about was my only way to keep her there." Davis recalls Courtney asking her whether she knew what her involvement would mean. "I said, 'If it means suing the superintendent of the State of Wisconsin, so be it.'"

"YOU'RE GOING TO HEAR, REAL LOUD"

Lonzetta Davis was not the kind of parent teachers like to see heading toward their classroom. When her older child, Vonzell, was having trouble in MPS, Davis would sneak into the school and stand outside his classroom door. "You can learn a lot, just going to that classroom."

Getting there wasn't easy. For grade school, Vonzell went to Victory Elementary, on the Far South Side near the airport. "We had Harambee just up the street at Burleigh, and a Catholic school just down the block from that," neither of which was financially feasible for the Davis family at the time. "And here he was getting bused to the last school on the district line."

Vonzell Davis was on the bus as early as 6:15 for a school day that began at 7:45. He'd spend three hours a day on the bus and five and a half hours a day in school. To be more involved at her son's school, Lonzetta Davis signed on as a room mother, even though that meant an hour on the city bus, followed by a four-block walk to the school.

Her son's teacher was, in Davis's words, "a yeller." The murmur of student voices would build from whispers into shouts, then the teacher would scream back. Walking down the hallway, Davis could hear the class, like the roar of the ocean. Vonzell would come home with headaches. Information on her son's progress was incomplete, and warnings were often delivered too late to be useful; at one point, Davis was told her son was twenty assignments behind—the night before grades closed.

Davis went to the principal to transfer her son to a different teacher's class; he turned her down.

"You're stuck with her," the principal said.

"You mean she's stuck with me."

At school, Davis fought for her son; at home, she fought Vonzell on his homework.

Her son is now a student at Milwaukee Tech High, and Davis is proud of the progress he's made. "My son's grade point has gone from 1.58 to 2.58 in one term. He was upset when he got the low marks, so I sat him down and had him write in what he was going to get next term. He got what he put down—and some classes, he got even higher than what he put down.

"With my son, the way I see it, he's been with MPS and he's got to finish with MPS. I just couldn't see going through that same struggle with Sabrina. Mind you, Urban Day is far from perfect. What I do with my son's teachers in MPS, I do the same thing at Urban Day. If there's a problem, I say, 'Fix it—or you're going to hear, real loud.'"

Although she was never called on to deliver oral testimony in *Davis v. Grover*, Lonzetta Davis had her fifteen minutes of fame. She was interviewed several times by the local papers, which she knew to be opposed to Parental Choice. "They came round, trying to trip you up." Out-of-town reporters, like the one from the *Wall Street Journal*, were sometimes more sympathetic. The Milwaukee reporters wrote down what Davis said, but they never seemed to use it in the paper; yet two days after the case was filed, Davis was quoted in the *Wall Street Journal:* "The public schools are basically just losing interest. . . . I refuse to put up with it. I know a specific place where Sabrina can get the education she deserves."[1]

On the first day of school in September 1990, as Lonzetta Davis delivered her daughter to her classroom, news cameras were gathered around Urban Day's front door. Zakiya Courtney handed Davis a button that read "I am a Choice Parent"; Davis pinned it to her coat a moment before a reporter approached. Later that day, CNN came to the Davis home to interview the woman who had sued the state superintendent.

With no cable TV and no friends with their own VCR, Lonzetta Davis never did get to see herself on television.

"NEVER THE CHILDREN"

With the filing of *Davis v. Grover*, Polly Williams sensed a slight shift in the momentum. They were fighting back, a posture Williams always found comfortable, but more than that, she believed they had turned a corner in correcting the distorted portrayal of Parental Choice: "We got parents back in the picture."

The earliest evidence of the change came in the symbolic battle for the civil rights mantle. For nearly a month, Felmers Chaney's name atop the lawsuit and Grover's constant characterization of vouchers as a route to resegregation had paid off; as late as June 29, the *Milwaukee Journal* could still characterize the suit to stop Choice as "filed by civil rights groups." With the filing of *Davis v. Grover,* however, that began to change.

The first shot was fired June 6, when the *Wall Street Journal* editorialized about the suit Grover had instigated, under the title "Teachers vs. Kids." In it, Polly Williams cast the challenge squarely as the new struggle in civil rights: "We have to be saved from our saviors. . . . Our liberal friends have built their whole lives around taking care of us and they still want to feed us Pablum. At some point, we want real food. We want to make our own decisions whether our liberal friends like it or not."

On June 27, two days after the case was filed, a second *Wall Street Journal* editorial, this one titled "Blocking the Schoolhouse Door," cast Herbert Grover as heir to America's retrograde segregationist legacy:

> Arkansas Governor Orval Faubus called out the National Guard in 1957 to prevent black children from attending all-white Central High School. In 1963, George Wallace stood in the schoolhouse door to block two black students from enrolling in the school of their choice. Now, in 1990, Herbert Grover . . . is openly trying to block a law that will allow 1,000 low-income black children in Milwaukee to use vouchers to attend a private school of their choice.

The editorial, complete with the *Journal*'s signature pointillist portrait of Grover, stung the state superintendent. In a series of interviews, he lashed out against Parental Choice and also Governor Thompson—whom Grover implausibly alleged had a "private, pecuniary" interest in the *Wall Street Journal*.[2] News accounts, which variously described Grover as "frustrated" and "indignant," detailed new Grover allegations that Parental Choice would give rise to a "right-wing radical" Posse Comitatus school[3] and that Parental Choice in schools would soon "spread to other school districts . . . and similar plans could be adopted to give people choice for services such as police and fire departments"[4]—a flare fired off by Grover to enlist other public employee unions in the antichoice cause.

Williams read every word of Grover's rhetorical fusillade, but noticed most what he didn't say. "He talked about the schools, the teachers, the unions, and of course every last one of his enemies," Williams recalls.

"Never the children."

A STUDY IN CONTRASTS

Even as Clint Bolick and his Washington colleagues were racing to file their suit, he was working with Polly Williams to address the administrative straitjacket Grover had sought to shackle prospective Choice schools, and frighten others from the program altogether.

Just after Grover's DPI issued its June 14 release identifying only two schools as participants in the program, Williams came to Washington and, together with Bolick, met with Ted Sanders, Undersecretary of Education. The two briefed Sanders on the strictures Wisconsin's state education authority had imposed on the Parental Choice program—strictures based on what Bolick believed was a punitive if not perverse reading of federal statutes. While most state education authorities enlisted their own legal counsel to defang onerous federal guidelines to whatever extent possible, Wisconsin's DPI seemed intent on construing federal rules as applied to Parental Choice as intrusively as possible.

As allies, Williams's in-your-face style and Bolick's earnest and affable way were a study in contrasts. After initial reservations about Bolick, Williams had warmed to the Washington attorney. At one point, Williams was pressured by a female African-American lawyer to replace Bolick; Milwaukee's parents should be represented, the lawyer argued, by a woman of color. Williams refused. She realized she'd come to trust the acumen of the man she teasingly called "my white Washington lawyer."

Having come to Washington, Williams watched Bolick operate on "his turf." Bolick made his case to Sanders. Grover had sought to conjure an administrative catch-22: The beauty of the scheme was that it rested on the concept of Choice itself—insofar as special-needs students could conceivably choose to pursue a voucher to attend a Choice school. With Choice schools forced to at least acknowledge the possibility that the voucher lottery might bring them a special-needs student, DPI was able to demand that *each* school comply with *every* special-education statute, state and federal. It would not be enough to accommodate a blind student or a deaf child or a student with mental or motor handicaps; because a school could conceivably get not one but all of these special students, it had to be ready to educate all of them.

For private inner-city schools for whom collecting tuition was a constant adventure, the cost of complying with the special-needs provisions was catastrophic: Embedded in Grover's "compliance assurance" document were provisions for special counseling, evaluation, and teaching staff as well as guarantees regarding physical access that would require renovating bathrooms, hallways, doorways, and playgrounds. Because the Parental Choice legislation, in a sensible move to prevent the ratcheting up of tuition costs, forbade schools from charging any costs in addition to the voucher—and there was no likelihood that Grover would authorize vouchers in the amount of full per-pupil funding for special-needs students—Choice schools would be forced to undertake the expense of special-needs students on their own. "And when all that was done," Bolick added, "your school might not even get a handicapped child through the [Choice] lottery."

As a result of Bolick and Williams's entreaty, Undersecretary Sanders authorized a review of the DPI's "compliance assurance" document by Richard Komer, a young lawyer who was Deputy

Assistant Secretary of Education for Civil Rights. Among other offices in the Department of Education, the Office of Special Education and Rehabilitative Services was instructed to cooperate with Komer's review.[5] The date was June 20—just twelve days before the Parental Choice deadline for new schools to declare their intent to join the program.

LEGAL LEGERDEMAIN

No public money for private schools: While voucher opponents often employed this shorthand summary of their argument against Parental Choice, the lawsuit invited by Herbert Grover based its case not on broad principle, but on essentially procedural grounds. The three key charges advanced in *Chaney v. Grover* and carried over into *Davis v. Grover* were:

1. The Parental Choice Program was a "local and private" bill, and therefore unconstitutionally "tacked on to" omnibus, "multi-subject" budget legislation.[6]

2. Parental Choice violated Wisconsin's "public purpose" doctrine. Here, the antivoucher side insisted that public purpose, in the instance of education, cannot be satisfied absent state accountability and hence government control.

3. Parental Choice violated the Wisconsin constitutional provision for "district schools, which shall be as nearly uniform as practicable."[7] To arrive at this conclusion, the antivoucher brief argued essentially that public funding transforms private Choice schools into *public* institutions governed by the state's "uniformity" clause.

In broader terms, Grover's allies sought to paint a portrait of unaccountable schools of uncertain educational quality. Parental Choice schools were branded "standardless private schools": "Teachers [in the

Choice schools]," antivoucher forces alleged, "may be wholly unqual-
ified, curriculum may be empty, advancement may be automatic."[8]
They also charged: "The state has not guaranteed that the character
of instruction in the participating private schools will be comparable
to that in MPS and other public schools throughout Wisconsin."

Learning of this line of argument, Polly Williams marveled at the
legal legerdemain in transforming the difference between the public and private schools into a deficiency in the latter. "They said the
education at our Choice schools isn't comparable with MPS?"
Williams laughed incredulously. "Guilty as charged."

In her affidavit, Williams hammered at the claim that Choice
schools ought to be brought under state regulation—a claim present
not only in the court case but in the rationale for Grover's administrative edicts. Williams reminded the court:

> Efforts to subject the private schools under the program to the
> entire range of regulations applicable to public schools were de-
> feated both in the committee that approved the Milwaukee
> Parental Choice Program and on the floor of the Legislature.
> The entire concept of this law is to allow low-income students
> to patronize schools outside the public system. The intent of
> the law was not to transform these schools into public or quasi-
> public schools.[9]

THE "AT RISK" ARCHIPELAGO

There was a reason antivoucher forces could not allege the legal
impropriety of public funding for private schools: the existence of
the "Children at Risk" program—ironically, the very law MPS had
made the basis for its expanded "choice" bill, triggering Polly
Williams's Parental Choice alternative.

While MPS's "At Risk" expansion had failed in the legislature,
the original "At Risk" program had been operating since 1987.
Given the more than 3,500 problem students outplaced from MPS
to alternative schools, many of which were private, all under the ul-

timate administrative authority of State Superintendent Herbert Grover, antivoucher forces lost the opportunity to play the purist in opposing any and all public funding for private education. Had such a barrier ever existed, MPS and the DPI had breached it with "At Risk."

By 1992, "At Risk," with 3,500 students and a $12 million budget,[10] was, in the words of the program's outside evaluator, Tony Baez, "larger in student enrollments and staff than the average school district" in the state of Wisconsin.[11] It was also a scandal waiting to be discovered. Baez's report documents a system akin to an educational penal colony, an island of internal exile and second-class schools.

The irony was palpable. After all, a key article of faith in the antivoucher catechism was that school choice would allow private schools to skim the cream from public schools, leaving behind a caste of educational "untouchables." In the indelible image of American Federation of Teachers president Albert Shanker, public schools would become the "educational equivalent of charity wards." In fact, in Milwaukee the public education authorities had devised a program that was almost a reverse negative of the allegations made about voucher schemes: a program to exile "problem" students from the public system to private schools.

Baez described a system of once-proud alternative schools that had, with the passage of the "At Risk" statute, begun a "shift from being 'choice' alternatives to schools which operate as MPS 'last chance' programs." As Baez put it: " 'dumping grounds' for 'bad kids.' "[12]

A champion of alternative education in the truest sense of the word and scrupulously thorough in discharging his investigative responsibilities, Baez was shocked at what he found:

> In theory, students choose to attend an MPS alternative. In reality . . . a student is given little choice but to accept an assignment to an MPS, or community-based alternative, once a

traditional school has recommended a transfer out. Similarly, most of the teachers and administrators in these schools have been placed at these sites after they were "bumped" or "excessed" from traditional schools.[13]

In a number of schools, the Baez team discovered, "students did as they pleased. . . . There was very little teaching going on in more than half of the schools visited."[14]

Several were viewed by staff in the main MPS schools "as places where they send youngsters they no longer want." Students shared this assessment. "The school system wants to get rid of us because we are *losers,*" one of them reported to the Baez team. Another student called the "At Risk" schools "dumping grounds for dummies."[15]

Astonishingly, MPS's "At Risk" empire ran with a skeleton staff of four professionals and three office support staff in the Department of Alternative Programs.[16] The small staff was actually a tip-off: far too few bodies to keep tabs on what was going on in the program, but more than enough to provide a steady stream of "problem" students with a one-way ticket out of the public schools.

Baez formed a picture of a program devised to isolate a specific population. "What drives this program is not concerns for the kids. It's to make things easier for the schools."

In some cases, Baez learned that the worst students were told by staff not to come to school on the day the evaluation took place. In one school, Baez's team witnessed a fistfight that ended when one student leaped from a second-story window and sprinted down the street. In that same school—since closed as a result of Baez's report—a man whose job was "school disciplinarian" banged elementary students against metal lockers hard enough to leave dents.

Baez's group was often approached by teachers themselves: "In some schools teachers are terrified by students. . . . Individual teachers said 'We want out NOW.'" In other schools, the atmosphere evoked one researcher's characterization of such schools as "soft jails for court adjudicated kids." In two-thirds of the alternative schools Baez examined, instruction was limited to three hours a day, "and a large portion of their students do not attend more than three days a week."[17]

The "notes on school visits" excerpted at the end of the Baez report capture the conditions all too typical of "At Risk" schools:

> In one elementary partnership, violence among and on students was so pervasive that only closing the place down can correct it. Children did not want to be in this school and many asked [the Baez team examiners] that they be taken out. All the kids observed were Black . . . This was plantation education at its worst. How can MPS allow this . . . ?
>
> MPS Principals, counselors, etc. continue to view alternatives as dumping grounds. As a consequence they may practice a form of "minority youth cleansing" out of traditional schools. . . . 20 of 27 schools evaluated were 75+ [percent] minority.[18]

The dubious distinction of being the worst of the twenty-eight "At Risk" schools went to a private school run by the Milwaukee Urban League. A three-teacher "high school" for about forty students, Urban League's school had, the Baez team discovered, "no curriculum." Students arriving at the school picked up their folder, with worksheets inside. Their day consisted of working in their folders. The teacher was to be approached only if a student had questions. Otherwise, interaction between teacher and student—the mental friction that might be called the essence of education—was nonexistent. Baez's report described the Urban League school as "a holding tank for African-American students."[19]

On any given day, attendance averaged 51 percent, by the school's own accounting. Twenty percent of its students got straight U's, doubtless the ones who missed the most days. Yet lack of attendance was by no means a barrier to promotion. One student accumulated seven credits, although attendance records indicated he had been in school just 30 days out of 180.

The Urban League school was dimly lit, "prison-like," in the words of the Baez report. The dangers of the facility were driven home when one of Baez's evaluators opened an unmarked third-floor door onto a thirty-foot drop to the parking lot pavement.

Urban League's "At Risk" school suspended operations in fall 1992—when it lost its school permit—and reopened in the early spring of 1993. While it was closed, some of its students were reassigned; others simply stayed home or cruised the streets. Funding was never interrupted. Still, in June the Urban League graduated a perfect four for four of its "seniors."

With the publication of the Baez report, the Urban League school closed its doors for good. Yet the MPS teachers who worked there were simply reassigned within the "At Risk" archipelago.

With a few heroic exceptions, "At Risk" constituted a kind of educational netherworld, where students were "slots" or "seats"; where fly-by-night schools sprang up, attracted by the lure of public lucre; where schools closed their doors and continued to collect public funds: In short, "At Risk" was everything antivoucher advocates luridly claimed Parental Choice would be.

One of the questions asked by a Baez team member hangs in the air: "Why doesn't MPS require those agencies interested in setting up alternative programs to register as schools with DPI?"[20]

"The difference is," Polly Williams posited, "MPS wants those kids gone. If a private school takes them, then don't raise a fuss."

A MORE OPEN ADVERSARY

Amid the affidavits and the legal motions, Parental Choice crept forward. By July 11, Urban Day had received 225 applications for the 135 seats it projected for fall 1990. Woodlands School, a multi-racial private K–8 school on Milwaukee's near South Side, with 25 voucher seats open, had not only invited all 25 prospective students and their parents to meet with teachers and administrators, it had already begun working informally with the students on reading, writing, and math. The school had also ordered additional textbooks, renovated its third floor, and hired a new kindergarten teacher and teaching assistant.[21] Woodlands's principal had even been approached by parents of Choice students who were searching for ways to pay tuition to enroll their other children at Woodlands.

As the date for oral argument neared, Herbert Grover took his opposition to Parental Choice to a new level. With the filing of *Davis v. Grover*, the superintendent sought to shift his legal status from nominal defendant of Parental Choice by virtue of being the state's chief education officer to a more open adversary of the voucher program. Grover urged Governor Thompson to allow him counsel, rather than having to rely on the state attorney general, who was duty-bound to defend the legality of Parental Choice. Thompson refused; thus denied, Grover unilaterally filed a brief on July 16, drafted by his DPI attorneys.[22]

At the same time, MPS quietly used its authority to raise Milwaukee's local property tax levy by $2.5 million, an amount sufficient to offset the funds that would be withheld by the State of Wisconsin if every one of the 1,000 vouchers was used in the 1990–91 school year. The effect of the fiscal maneuver was more than merely allowing MPS to be "held harmless" for any exodus to Choice schools that might take place; by using what for it was a worst-case scenario, every unused voucher below the 1,000 maximum—which would therefore involve no diminution of the state contribution—meant a per-pupil windfall from the increased local tax levy.[23]

Yet, in court, weeks after the tax levy adjustment, Grover's allies continued to assert that "irreparable harm" would ensue if funds flowed to Parental Choice, "as $2,500 per MPS student enrolled in the program is diverted from MPS to the participating private schools. In the event that money is illegally expended, there is no likelihood of recoupment."[24]

In fact, MPS had devised a way to insulate itself against any possible loss due to Parental Choice—and, quite possibly, to reap a profit.

MADISON APPEAL

Back in Washington, Deputy Assistant Secretary Richard Komer delivered his opinion to Undersecretary Sanders. Komer's closely argued brief indicated the extent of Grover's regulatory zeal: "In short, it seems fair to say that with respect to handicapped students the DPI equates the obligation of the participating *private* schools to those of a *federally assisted public* school."[25]

According to the Department of Education, Parental Choice enrollments were "private placements"—essentially, parents' decisions—under the Education of the Handicapped Act. "In the language of the regulations, the private schools are not 'recipients' of federal funds and their programs and activities are not federally assisted."[26] Grover's concept of federal reach far outstripped any statutory power recognized in Washington.

Komer's brief arrived just as Sanders was responding to a letter from MPS superintendent Peterkin requesting Department of Education clarification. Sanders responded by appending Komer's advisory brief in full—in effect, publicly releasing the internal Department of Education opinion. The date was July 27. On July 28, Clint Bolick was due in Dane County Trial Court for oral argument.

Bolick armed himself with a motion challenging Grover's regulatory authority to extend and interpret federal statutes. Polly Williams rented a bus and filled it with parents wearing red, white, and blue buttons. "I had planned to try to go over my argument on the way up," Bolick remembers. "Instead, we were stapling those opinion letters all the way up to Madison."

The parents Polly Williams brought to Madison made an impression. A few weeks later, on August 6, Judge Susan Steingass, a jurist whose pronounced liberal leanings had worried Bolick and Williams, upheld the program on all grounds and, in addition, accepting the arguments of the Department of Education advisory, reined in Grover's regulatory gambit.

The uniformity and public-purpose arguments advanced by Grover and his allies were rebuffed by Steingass: "I am not persuaded that this program turns private into public schools." Nor did she find Parental Choice a local and private bill. Steingass did not believe Parental Choice had been smuggled into an omnibus bill; she also viewed the program, though limited to one city, as an education experiment of broad interest, "both by lessons learned and the education improved."[27]

On the question of regulatory power, Steingass found that Grover's "intent forms" imposed on private schools what she termed "an amazing array" of state and federal laws, a burden "more onerous for this program than for others."[28]

In fact, Steingass observed, Parental Choice schools were the subject of ample supervision: "[T]he legislature requires detailed, direct reporting to a degree that I, at least, have not previously seen in its enactments regarding education." Steingass counted an annual report supervised by the superintendent and delivered to the legislature; the superintendent's power to monitor and certify participating schools; an audit by the Legislative Audit Bureau to be submitted to the relevant legislative committees; the creation of a pupil assignment council with representatives from each school; and finally, the superintendent's right to order financial or performance audits as deemed necessary. "The presence," Steingass concluded, "of these reporting requirements must mean that the legislature intends to keep a close eye on this program."[29]

Indeed, a comparison with the abortive MPS "choice" legislation, AB 995—a comparison nowhere evident in the court proceedings— provides an interesting perspective on the "accountability" provisions built into the Parental Choice law. In fact, the performance criteria Grover and his allies attacked as "standardless" in the case of Parental Choice are *drawn almost verbatim from the performance benchmarks written into the MPS law*. Both Parental Choice and the MPS bill based program performance on meeting any one of four measures (language in brackets indicates the only differences between the Choice bill and the MPS bill):

1. At least 70 percent of the pupils in the program advance one grade level each year.
2. The partner [or Choice] school's average attendance rate for the pupils in the program is at least 90 percent.
3. At least 80 percent of the pupils in the program demonstrate significant academic progress.
4. At least 70 percent of the families of pupils in the program meet parent involvement criteria established by the board [in the case of Choice: by the school].[30]

Both bills mandated compliance with but a single federal law: 42 USC 2000d, the federal antidiscrimination statute.[31] The MPS bill stops there, while Parental Choice's statute goes on to mandate that "the private school meets all health and safety laws or codes that apply to public schools" and limits voucher students to no more than 49 percent of the school's student body.[32] This last was a means of preventing the so-called fly-by-night schools predicted by voucher opponents. The 49 percent rule meant every Choice school would have to have a majority of "paying" clientele, which would preclude schools being formed simply to cash vouchers. Even at the time the Choice bill was written, a number of private "At Risk" schools—with no such 49 percent rule—were dependent for almost all their revenue on MPS placements.

As for annual reviews, the MPS bill mandated them to begin after the program had been in operation for two and a half years.[33] Parental Choice's evaluations began immediately, with a first-year report due in December 1991, based on school visits in April and

May of that year—just seven and eight months into the voucher experiment. Parental Choice students were being measured—and found wanting—after less than one school year. At least one education expert believes this was part of Herbert Grover's ongoing crusade to, in effect, study the program to death.[34]

Injunction Denied

Agreeing with the Department of Education's "cautious opinion letter," Judge Steingass observed that Grover's regulatory requirements in the area of special education amounted to ordering every private school to provide full programs to the handicapped. Indeed, Steingass noted, "not even every public school does so." The judge took note that Grover not only sought to appear before the trial court as "the titular defendant charged with facilitation of the Law" but also sought permission to file a brief and make arguments against Parental Choice. "From this I can but conclude that he [Grover] does not wish the Law well,"[35] Steingass observed acerbically.

The judge invalidated Grover's expansive regulatory requirements and ordered DPI to draft a scaled-back intent form within two weeks or face court action.

Grover's rage boiled over. Officially neutral, Grover prided himself on being attuned to partisan politics. He vented his scorn for Steingass to his hometown *Capital Times:* "I absolutely thought she was going to be a liberal stalwart."[36]

Grover turned his wrath on Washington, heaping ad hominem invective on President Bush, deriding him as a "preppy" who "is not the 'education president.'" For Secretary of Education Lauro Cavazos, whose support for school choice was often tepid, Grover coined the title "secretary of private education." Of Wisconsin, Grover said the state would now be spending $2.5 million a year on segregation. Calling the Choice program a "disgrace," Grover reacted as if his faith in democracy had been shaken: "Has the citizenry in Wisconsin lost its common sense?" he thundered.[37]

In Washington, Clint Bolick hailed the victory as the "most important educational breakthrough for low-income youngsters since *Brown v. Board of Education.*" Taking the debate on vouchers to the court of public opinion, Bolick rebutted the allegation that Choice schools were not accountable; in fact, as Bolick put it, Choice schools were required to meet the most exacting standards of all: performance standards. "The achievement of these low-income students will be compared to public school students," Bolick argued. "If performance continues at present rates, far more private school students will graduate and go on to college. The ultimate safeguard is that if these schools don't perform, no one will send their children there."[38]

Yet the antivoucher forces were anything but disarmed. Morris Andrews, the executive director of the Wisconsin Education Association Council, speculated on a new avenue of attack: a new suit, this one arguing that the Choice schools had not been inspected for safety violations.[39] Andrews' harrassment case was never pursued; instead, on August 9, the teachers' unions and their antivoucher allies appealed the trial court ruling. On August 10, they filed for an injunction to stop the Parental Choice program. Once again, Bolick made the trip to Madison; Polly Williams headed for the courtroom with a special weapon of her own, her five-year-old cousin James, kindergartner-to-be with coloring book in hand, who was awaiting word from the court as a Choice applicant at Harambee School. The injunction was denied. It was August 20. Jerry Hill, president of the Landmark Legal Foundation, termed this victory the most important of all.[40] The first day of school was just fifteen days away.

Chilling Effect

But while Grover had lost the first round, his legal assault had cast a significant chilling effect on the Parental Choice program. At

the predominantly Hispanic Bruce-Guadalupe School on Milwaukee's South Side, for example, 130 children had initially applied
for Choice vouchers, but as the summer and the court case wore on,
80 had withdrawn their applications. "Some parents," opined Bruce-
Guadalupe's executive director, Walter Sava, "felt they couldn't wait
any longer, and I think many, since they have not heard from us, felt
they had to make other arrangements." Sava laid the blame for this
turn of events at the doorstep of Superintendent Grover. Sava said:

> If he [Grover] wanted to sabotage this program, he certainly ac-
> complished his goal. . . . School is starting in three weeks, and
> things we should have taken care of months ago—such as find-
> ing space and hiring teachers—were not done because of Mr.
> Grover. He can sit over there and pontificate about constitu-
> tional issues; we still have a 50% dropout rate in the Hispanic
> community.[41]

As the *Milwaukee Journal* reported a week before school opened,
"Schools said space limitations and legal challenges—including a
challenge by the state's top education officials—had limited the
numbers" in the program: 1,037 students had initially applied for
vouchers; on September 4, when doors opened at schools across the
city, 341 Choice students took their seats.[42] Three-quarters were
African-American, 20 percent Hispanic, and the remaining 5 percent white.

The small size of the "freshman class" did nothing to dampen
Polly Williams's spirits. "If Grover still wanted to stop Choice," she
recalls thinking, "he was going to have to go in and pull those kids
out of their chairs."

The passage of Parental Choice created at least a rhetorical need
for MPS to sound the call for reform. Superintendent Peterkin,
describing himself as "impatient" for improvement, introduced
"Milwaukee's promise to our children for our future": five goals
schools would be required to meet through objective, measurable

improvement, including grades, test scores, attendance, and dropout rates. Schools that reached the goals could expect rewards; schools that fell short, punishment.

MPS, Peterkin went on to explain, would have until 1995 to meet the standards.[43]

"LIKE I WAS ON THE EDGE OF A CLIFF"

For nearly two months the school year unfolded without incident. Parental Choice parents, often bewildered by the attention lavished on a program that to many of them seemed straightforward if long overdue, grew used to grapevine gossip about visits from various dignitaries. On October 10, Governor Thompson visited Harambee School with Vice President Dan Quayle in tow; on October 18, Bill Clinton, the governor from Arkansas carving out a national name as an education reformer, sent a letter of congratulations to Polly Williams praising her "visionary" program—a letter that would later cause presidential candidate Clinton embarrassment when the national teachers' unions demanded and won his opposition to vouchers as the price of their support.[44]

Then, just after grades for the first marking period went home to parents, on November 13, 1990, the Wisconsin Court of Appeals struck down the Parental Choice program. Lonzetta Davis remembers the day news of the decision flew through the halls at Urban Day. "It felt like I was on the edge of a cliff. You know the wind's coming—and it only takes a little push to put you over the edge."

This time, the immediate appeal was filed by Clint Bolick, taking the case to the Wisconsin Supreme Court. To Polly Williams's relief, the Choice students were allowed to continue in school while the appeal was pending.

The legal reversal was a jolt to Williams. She fought back with the fury of a back-alley boxer, seizing on a 1987 study by the Urban

Research Center at the University of Wisconsin–Milwaukee that found just 38 percent of MPS teachers willing to allow their own children to attend the school in which they taught.[45] To Williams, the survey was a smoking gun. "Something's rotten with the system," she told parents she met with and the press alike. "Something's wrong when teachers pull their kids out and send them to private schools or hide them out in the suburbs.

"Put their children in their school," Williams urged, "and see what happens. Teachers will report another teacher who's not performing, they'll report the principal if that's what it takes—because they won't tolerate bad teaching if their child is sitting in that classroom.

"The schools will get better—and it won't take five years."

For Williams, it was time to fight fire with fire. The "educrats" had gone to court to kill her program. If her parents couldn't have choice, she'd do what she could to cut out MPS teachers' options. Williams smelled hypocrisy: "These same people are trying to block low-income people from doing what they're doing every day."

The Closing of Juanita Virgil

With the program in legal limbo, these were the dark months for Parental Choice. Struck down on the procedural point that Parental Choice was a "local and private" bill improperly bundled into an omnibus state budget act, Clint Bolick held out hope the Wisconsin Supreme Court would find the program's passage constitutional. The reversal turned on the narrowest of legalisms; even the appeals court all but invited a benign alternative reading of the state constitution that it, as "an error-correcting court," lacked the power to reach.[46] The Supreme Court could.

To Williams, all of the lawyerly talk could not mask the fact that the appeal seemed never to progress; parents occasionally asked, only to be told there was no news on the legal front. Christmas came and went, while worries nagged that Choice children might at any time be forced out of their private schools and onto the buses of MPS.

Halfway through that first year, Parental Choice proponents suffered another setback. One Friday in January 1991, Juanita Virgil Academy announced to its students it was closing its doors for good. One of the original six Choice schools, Juanita Virgil was widely known to be troubled; suddenly it was bankrupt. Sixty-three Choice students—more than one-sixth the total for the entire Choice program—were without a school.

In the years since January 1991, Juanita Virgil Academy has achieved folkloric status among the opponents of school choice. In the national voucher debate, the saga of Juanita Virgil is a staple in American Federation of Teachers and National Education Association literature.

According to the NEA's National Coalition for Public Education, what happened at Juanita Virgil was evidence of the harsh winds that could blow through a market-based voucher system:

> One such school that took in a large number of voucher students had been a religious school until it decided to participate in the program. The non-voucher parents then became unhappy with the switch, feuds broke out and religion classes were reintroduced. In the middle of the year, the 63 voucher students were suddenly expelled, and mostly into the public schools. And only then did the public discover the claims this private school had made to attract customers were mostly bogus, that it had done a terrible job of feeding, transporting and providing books or desks for the kids and that its facilities violated many safety standards and were even more decrepit than those of the public schools. As for education, little, if any, seemed to take place.
>
> The entrepreneurship of the Juanita Virgil School's owner notwithstanding, the school collapsed. The fate of the school's non-voucher students, who lost a year of schooling, is unknown.
>
> The tale of Juanita Virgil School is dramatic, but it is not unique.[47]

Not everyone shares the AFT/NEA interpretation of the closing of Juanita Virgil. Education researcher George Mitchell sees the school's demise as a stern but salutary affirmation of the marketplace working as it ought: In this view, better that schools fail than students fail.[48]

ON THE INSIDE

The case turned on a single vote, 4–3.

In the oral argument in Madison, antivoucher forces had pulled out all the stops, scrabbling for any legal handhold they could find. At one point, Felmers Chaney's lawyer argued that the "uniformity" clause rendered Parental Choice schools *public* schools, and therefore subject to the full range of state regulation; when the argument turned to the "public purpose" doctrine, Chaney's counsel claimed Choice schools were *private* schools incapable of meeting the public-purpose test.[49]

On the procedural point at issue—that the Parental Choice program was a "local or private" bill "smuggled" or "logrolled" through the legislature—evidence mounted that dispelled doubt about the passage of the voucher plan.[50] The state attorney general tallied thirty-one instances in fifteen years in which budget bills had included amendments relating to "first class cities," a category comprising Milwaukee alone; at least a half-dozen of the amendments pertained to education.[51] In no instance had their constitutionality been challenged. The majority opinion also noted that in addition to vouchers being debated in the State Assembly over the course of several years, even the State Senate had amended the Parental Choice program in the brief period preceding the budget vote; this act of "noticing" the bill undercut the procedural claim that Parental Choice had been "smuggled" past an unsuspecting Senate.

Yet in addition to the legalisms at issue, Justice William G. Callow's majority opinion also captured a sense of the concept at the core of

Parental Choice. Against the weight of the arguments on account-ability, Callow noted: "Concerned parents have the greatest incentive to see that their children receive the best education possible."[52]

In addition to the supervisory mechanisms built into the statute, "Control is also fashioned within the [plan] in the form of parental choice. Parents generally know their children better than anyone. . . . If the private school does not meet the parents' expectations, the parents may remove the child from the school and go elsewhere."[53]

Or, in the florid dictum of Judge Louis Ceci's concurring opinion:

> The Wisconsin legislature, attuned and attentive to the ap-palling and seemingly insurmountable problems confronting socio-economically deprived children, has attempted to throw a life preserver to those Milwaukee children caught in the cruel riptide of a school system floundering upon the shoals of poverty, status-quo thinking, and despair. . . .
> Let's give choice a chance.[54]

Superintendent Herbert Grover, once again, saw politics at work. "This Supreme Court has recently become political and has not exercised the traditional independent judicial review that has been the tenor of that body," he stated. He went on, according to the *Milwaukee Sentinel* account, to question the moral courage of the judges.[55]

While Grover raged, a disappointed Robert Friebert, attorney for Felmers Chaney and the teachers' unions, ran up the white flag. Friebert told the *Milwaukee Journal:* "There's no place else to go with these issues. There are no federal issues in this case. We delib-erately avoided all federal issues. So there's no other court to go to with these issues."[56]

When Clint Bolick took the call that told him of the Wisconsin Supreme Court's decision, he thought back to the unseasonably hot Saturday morning, October 4, 1991, when he argued the case before the court. A bus had been chartered to bring a group of parents and children from Milwaukee to Madison; the bus was late. As Bolick arranged his papers, he noticed the courtroom's limited spectator section filling with court personnel and the usual assortment of arm-chair attorneys and lookee-lou's who populate the Supreme Court gallery.

As the proceedings began, Bolick looked back one last time at the glass doors to the chamber. The children had arrived. He could see them peering through the door, their noses pressed against the glass.

"I remember really being struck by that," Bolick recalls. "All those little faces on the outside, always looking in.

"And I thought: Well, they're on the inside now."

PART III

Church, State, and Choice

CHAPTER SEVEN

The Battle of Sister Leonius

Rules for St. Matthew Playground," announces the sign on the playground at St. Matthew grade school, faded paint on a thin metal sheet.

1. Christian Speech and Conduct.

2. Proper Dress.

3. No Bike Riding.

4. No Batting of Balls.

5. Respect for Parish Property.

Farther down the same wall, in slanting strokes of silver paint on the blackened brick, dances an indecipherable hieroglyph, the "tag" of a neighborhood gang.

Sister Leonius Skaar—known simply as Sister to both the children and the adults in St. Matthew's South Side neighborhood—makes a note to remind Bill Zembrowski. The school's unpaid handyman, Zembrowski lives across the back alley from St. Matthew. Lately, he's been experimenting with a special cleaner he claims removes all traces of graffiti with a scrub brush. Long unemployed, and now a stay-at-home father to his children who attend St. Matthew, Zembrowski jokes with Sister Leonius that he's thinking of patenting his "secret formula." "Maybe," he muses, "I could sell it to the poor guys who have to take care of the subways in New York."

A WALK THROUGH THE NEIGHBORHOOD

The South Side streets around St. Matthew are home to a melting pot of Milwaukee's low-income families: majority Hispanic, mostly Mexican, some blacks, and some whites like Zembrowski, holdovers from the days the neighborhood welcomed immigrants from Warsaw and Krakow, and Polish was spoken over corner store counters.

Today, the average household income in the census tract in which St. Matthew sits is just above $11,000. On the streets around St. Matthew, every sixth house stands vacant; four in ten newborns in 1990 were out-of-wedlock births, double the rate a decade earlier.

Before she came to St. Matthew, Sister Leonius worked in the migrant camps north of Milwaukee, educating Mexican children brought by their parents to help with the harvest. Life in the camps was hard; Sister had expected that. Coming to St. Matthew, she thought, would be like returning to civilization. From her new vantage point, the change looks somewhat different. "I'd never say it was better in the camps." She pauses in thought. "But there are things here that make life hard for kids, harder than it should be.

"The other day, we had a fight, a mother and her daughter. It started out front, in the street, but it rolled right into the hallway. We had our kids wondering what was going on, trying to come out into the hall. Then, that night, we had a child disappear. She never went home after school. We didn't find her. It turned out she ran away.

"After that, we had a parent call—late, around eleven. His son was threatening to commit suicide. They call me." Sister sighs. "I'm the principal. I told them, 'Call the police. You've got to get help.'"

Sister manages a wan smile. "I was lucky I made it to school on time the next morning.

"There's always something happening. We're not bored here," she says, smiling at the irony that is very much intentional.

We walk past a row of postage stamp lawns, past neon-lit neighborhood bars that emit the trailing echo of jukebox music in the afternoon air. Sister points out one corner store. "Nasty stuff went on in there," she says opaquely, looking into the middle distance at something no one else can see. *Nasty* is a word Sister Leonius uses often, to draw a curtain across what she knows to be reality but wishes were otherwise.

Pressed to be specific, she relents. "Drugs were sold in there. And there was child prostitution, too." Despite Sister's persistence, the police never managed to uncover any illegal activity on their visits to the store. Yet her repeated calls resulted in repeated visits from the police; in time, the attention caused the landlord to evict the store owners. They went away, somewhere else, Sister doesn't know where. "Away from St. Matthew."

Sister quickens her pace and crosses the street. "When they get hold of children, you know, that's too much. I want to stand 'em up in front of a firing squad and mow 'em down." Sister delivers this death sentence in the flat, laconic Milwaukee accent that has been the South Side's only apparent gift to her. Surprisingly, the sentiment seems neither uncharitable nor un-Christian.

A mile north, across I-94 and the viaduct that separates the South Side from the streets around Urban Day, the gangs are black, the Disciples and the Lords. In St. Matthew's neighborhood, the gangs are Hispanic, the Cobras and the Latin Kings. The Cobras are Mexican, part of the national "family" known as Folks; the Latin Kings are Puerto Rican, a subset of the People family. In a place where family relations are shifting and uncertain, the gang hierarchy branches like a luxuriant tree, offering comfort and certainty in a place where both are in short supply.

"It seems to get worse one week to the next. There are a lot of shootings. It's not racial," Sister opines, a kind of connoisseur of casual violence. "Most are gang-related, intentional. But last week, we did have an eleven-year-old shot, about a block from the school. There had been an argument. Some of our kids say the boys with the gun had been on our playground a few minutes before the shooting."

On we stroll, past the "Polish flat" walk-downs, past the alleys with the "back houses," this one with seven children in a space no more than twenty-five feet across, that one with tarpaper walls.

"We buried a relative of one student last week, shot to death. We had a girl, fifteen, who graduated from St. Matthew and then went to Pulaski," a public high school in the neighborhood. "They found her body in the park. She had been beaten to death."

We walk by one house Sister says is regularly blanketed with graffiti. The people who lived there would paint over it; within days, the graffiti was back again. Finally, the people moved and the graffiti stopped. Today, the house is clean. Could it be a sign the graffiti artists are backing off? Sister shakes her head no, and laughs mordantly.

"All it means is the new people belong to the same gang."

Down 21st Street across from a pleasant park, in a row of houses with flowers and well-kept lawns, several houses stand empty. The street has been the scene of drive-by shootings. Random, Sister thinks, because the victims were so young, as young as nine and ten. There is street logic in the violence of gangbangers and drug dealers, with reprisals arising from vendettas or turf wars, but there is no logic in what happened on 21st Street—just bullets sprayed across a park onto a front porch. And so Sister's families moved, some a few streets away, some away for good.

Halfway down 21st, a "For Sale" sign stands on a lawn. The owners are asking $15,000; there are no offers. In time they will move, renting out the house so that it does not stand empty. The renters will run the property down, the neighborhood around St. Matthew will slip a bit more, and the next house will be more difficult to sell. Sister has seen it happen.

Each September at Sister Leonius's school, about 40 percent of the previous year's students don't come back. Among St. Matthew's most recent class of eighth-grade graduates, only two had attended the school from kindergarten on.

"When we have parents get a regular job and move, it's cause for celebration," she explains. "No, we don't like to lose kids. Sometimes it's our best families." Sister pauses. "But what can you say when they come in and say, 'Sister, we can go where it's safer for our kids'?

"I tell 'em, 'Go.'

"Educationally, it makes it difficult. We have to backtrack each year. We can't assume we can build on what children learned in the previous grade—because we don't know what they learned at their old school."

Yet three-fourths or more of St. Matthew's eighth-grade graduates go on to graduate from high school, in a city where four in ten public school students get diplomas. More than half of St. Matthew's children go on to college.

THE BIRTH OF PAVE

By the spring of 1992, the number of tuition-paying students at St. Matthew, never very large, had dwindled dangerously. Sister Leonius understood the economics well enough to know that re-opening in the fall was in jeopardy; as the weeks wore on, she found herself hoping simply to make it through that school year.

"PAVE saved us," she says flatly. "Without it, we would have been boarding up the windows by July." PAVE (Partners Advancing Values in Education), a privately funded organization, began providing voucher-style grants to Milwaukee children in the fall of 1992.

Patterned after a pioneering program in Indianapolis founded by an insurance company executive, PAVE quickly became the largest of a handful of copycat programs scattered across the country. In its first year of existence—the third year of the Parental Choice program—PAVE provided grants to 2,089 students from low-income families attending eighty-six private schools across the city.[1]

Like most of the privately funded voucher programs patterned after the Indianapolis experiment, PAVE paid only 50 percent of private school tuition; parents—no matter how poor—were expected to pay the other half, in order, literally, to invest themselves in the educational fortunes of their children.

While the funds for PAVE came from Milwaukee's philanthropic and corporate community, the catalyst was John O. Norquist, Milwaukee's energetic young mayor. Norquist, a former Democratic state senator representing Milwaukee's South Side, was not originally a supporter of school choice. He had left the Senate to mount his run for City Hall before Polly Williams engineered the passage of her program, but not before her arguments hit home with him. "I listened to Polly," Norquist recalled during an interview in his mayoral office. "She turned me around."

As mayor, Norquist had no line authority over Milwaukee's public schools, which were run by the city's elected school board. Yet the mayor's interest in education, and his belief in its connection to the city's long-term vitality and economic viability, made it a mainstay of his bully pulpit pitch about Milwaukee's future.

Tall, wavy-haired, and bespectacled, Norquist has a way of carefully choosing his words, which gives him an academic air; yet a few moments of conversation reveal him as a man who enjoys an argument. Norquist, who seems to take a delight in stirring things up, sharpens the points of his opinions like arrows, loosed against his intellectual opposites.

Public education has been a frequent target. Norquist made headlines in early 1992 when he wrote an article declaring that the system of urban education "is in shambles," and went on to propose what sounded like pulling the plug on the system's life support:

> I believe the whole system is the problem. . . . I think it should ultimately be scrapped and replaced with a new system—essentially a voucher or choice system. We should give city parents the purchasing power they need to enroll their children in any public or private, non-sectarian school that complies with essential standards.[2]

Mayor Norquist had taken the same position more than a year earlier, at a private meeting of big-city mayors in New York in November 1990.[3] Yet the publication of his views in his home state, amid the roiling debate occasioned by Parental Choice, created a sense that Polly Williams's experiment had acquired a significant new source of support—as well as an ally in any effort to expand the program.

Norquist's involvement was anything but academic. Each spring seemed to bring rumors of the imminent collapse of one or more of the city's religious schools. Norquist, though not himself Catholic, contributed to two Catholic schools in the South Side neighborhood where he lived. At the time he was writing about "voucherizing" the city's private schools, Norquist was also playing matchmaker between Milwaukee's civic leaders and the city's struggling religious schools. During the winter, he had urged the officers of Milwaukee's Bradley Foundation, the city's largest philanthropic organization, to contribute $1,000 apiece to sponsor twenty-five children in Catholic and Lutheran schools; he later asked a wealthy executive of Northwestern Mutual Life Insurance to give $5,000 to St. Matthew—the church where the executive had been married forty years earlier.

As the end of the school year loomed with a number of religious schools in financial straits, Norquist took his crusade public. At a meeting in the basement of Holy Spirit Catholic Church with neighborhood parents and representatives of the Near South Side Catholic

Schools Association, the mayor speculated that the day would come when public funding for private school vouchers would include the city's religious schools—provided civic-minded Milwaukeeans stepped forward to help those schools live to see the day.[4]

Norquist waved away any objections voucher opponents might have on church–state grounds, pointing to the experience of Canada and the Netherlands in providing public money for religious schools without threatening religious freedom, and, closer to home, citing the United States' experience with "vouchers" under the GI Bill, which could be put toward tuition at any university, public, private, or religious. Norquist also labored to keep the debate focused on the realities of urban education: "Given what we see every day with guns, drugs, and violence in the public schools," Norquist argued, "I think it's kind of hard to claim the real danger is religion."

Norquist's efforts, however persistent, were ultimately piecemeal; there was nothing he could do as mayor to shape MPS policy or legislation in Madison. Yet the mayor's personal crusade triggered something far larger and more systematic: the private-sector push to fund vouchers that gave birth to PAVE.

PAVE's supporters, Norquist included, understood that Parental Choice as it was then configured—constrained by statute to the city's twenty-odd *nonsectarian* private schools, of which a dozen chose to participate in the Choice program—could never accommodate student demand. Choice opponents delighted in pointing out that, although the program had increased from 341 students in its first year to 521 in its second, it had not come close to reaching its 1,000-student cap; yet the program's supporters were well aware that the 49 percent per school rule—as well as the "natural" mismatch between seats in specific schools and grades and students—had conspired to create a substantial waiting list for Parental Choice vouchers. In the first three years of the program, in fact, space limitations would result in more children being turned away than accepted.[5]

Yet even Choice advocates had to admit antivoucher forces were right in one respect: A nonsectarian Parental Choice program—

fated never to outgrow its Lilliputian beginnings—could never pose the kind of significant alternative to the public school system capable of creating a real competitive incentive for the public system to change. Sooner or later, the religious school question Polly Williams and her allies had sidestepped would take center stage.

PAVE supporters were certain the demand was there, and with more than eighty religious schools in the city—Moslem, Christian, and Jewish as well as Catholic—ample supply existed as well. With that in mind, according to PAVE's executive director Dan McKinley, the organization printed up and parceled out 4,500 applications to private schools around Milwaukee. "By the end of the first day," McKinley marveled, "they were gone."

In the fall of 1992, Sister Leonius opened the doors of St. Matthew to 150 students, a full 100 bearing PAVE vouchers.

PAVE was one part philanthropy, one part political crowbar. According to education expert Charles Sykes:

> [Bradley Foundation President Michael] Joyce and others behind PAVE are consciously intensifying the pressure on the state legislature to expand the current choice program by limiting their support to three years. After that point, they argue, the state should provide all parents with the option to choose their children's school.[6]

PAVE set up a parallel system, a constellation of private, religious schools separated by a glass wall from the nonsectarian Parental Choice program. The addition of PAVE to Parental Choice confirmed Milwaukee's place at the very forefront of radical education reform; as yet, however, there was no push from Polly Williams or Governor Thompson to break the religious school barrier.

Crossing the divide from private philanthropy to public policy would fall not to an elected official in Madison or Milwaukee, nor to any member of the city's civic leadership. The first foray into the minefield of church–state questions was made by a high school on Milwaukee's Near North Side. Strangely, the effort was made at the invitation of the DPI.

CHAPTER EIGHT

The Inquisition
v. Brother Bob

It's fair to say that there is a direct line, authoritatively, from
you to the pope. Isn't that true?
—*DPI attorney to Brother Bob Smith, October 14, 1992*

It stands as one of the dark chapters of Catholic history: Tomás de
Torquemada, a Dominican monk, scourging heretics from Seville to
Cordova. From 1483 to 1498, 2,000 souls burned for heresies un-
earthed by Torquemada's Inquisition.

Secular society, of course, forswears such inhuman intolerance in
the name of faith; Torquemada stands as a frightening footnote from
an era long since past. Yet in many instances, secular society means
not so much the absence of religious rites and ways, but their tran-
substantiation to secular ends. So it was that Brother Bob Smith, a
black Capuchin monk who was principal of Messmer High School
on Milwaukee's Near North Side, found himself the object of a
modern-day inquisition.

Brother Bob's ordeal took place in a Ramada Inn conference
room in Madison, Wisconsin, in October 1992; in Torquemada's
chair sat an avuncular state university official named Thomas J.
Grogan. Grogan was examiner "In the Matter of the Eligibility of
Messmer High School for Participation in the Milwaukee Parental

Choice Program . . . ," having been duly deputized by none other than Superintendent Herbert Grover.[1]

There, against a backdrop of wheat wallpaper and blond wood, Brother Bob Smith spent seven and a half hours on the witness stand. At issue: whether Messmer High School, a formerly Catholic school now independent of the Milwaukee Archdiocese, was eligible to enroll students receiving public funds under the Parental Choice program.

More than once on the way to the Ramada Inn inquiry, Brother Bob had sensed a through-the-looking-glass quality in his dealings with the DPI. As written by Polly Williams, the Parental Choice statute barred sectarian schools; in accord with the administrative rules promulgated by the DPI after the program's passage, Grover's office sought a statement from all participating private schools of their nonsectarian status. Many times, Bob Smith had been asked by well-wishers and opponents alike how he had ever conceived the notion that Messmer would be allowed into the program. He had to have known, he heard over and over, that the DPI would fight Messmer's entry with every means at its disposal.

No matter who asked, Smith always gave the same answer.

"I have to be honest. The thought that we were eligible never crossed my mind," Brother Bob recalls.

"Until DPI told us we were."

Brother Bob's nemesis was a veritable Goliath: The DPI-designated examiner, empaneled to review the DPI's decision barring Messmer High from a program DPI had claimed, in three court cases in as many years, was unconstitutional. Given the forces arrayed against him, Brother Bob took the stand that day at the Ramada as a man of great faith, but little hope.

His piety, however, wore an intensely pragmatic aspect. Smith had not sought entry into Parental Choice to lay claim to a new page in the Con Law casebooks by challenging the so-called wall of separation between church and state. The fact that Brother Bob's effort had raised such consequential questions did not diminish for him the practical aim—namely, securing access to $2,700 vouchers for twenty-five Milwaukee children too poor to pay their way into Messmer.

Yet Brother Bob's battle was significant for a larger reason as well: Parental Choice, then beginning its third year, included no traditional high schools. SER–Jobs, the alternative school catering to its "At Risk" student population, had been joined in Choice's third year by another "At Risk" high school; Choice students were for the most part clustered in the early elementary grades, while Choice parents were still savoring the newly won court victory that removed the legal storm clouds over the program. For the first time, parents could stop worrying whether the program would be pulled out from under them. Few had looked far enough ahead to notice the dead end that awaited Choice students after grade 8.

In the spring of 1992, filling that gap became Brother Bob's mission: Messmer would become the first Choice high school.

A CAPUCHIN MONK IN DETROIT

Brother Bob's journey to Messmer, like his journey to the center of church–state controversy, was anything but a straight line. Born in Chicago in 1956, Bob Smith was the third of six children; while the family was intensely religious, Bob would be the only child to enter an order.

Smith's parents were active in their local parish, St. Mel's. Once the largest Catholic parish in the world, St. Mel's and the neighborhood around it were changing during Bob's childhood. The riots that rocked America's cities in the mid-1960s did not spare Chicago. In the aftermath, many of St. Mel's white parishioners fled the city for Cicero and Berwyn and Oak Park.

Standing fast in the face of change, the Smith household became a haven in an increasingly harsh urban landscape. Religion, always critical, assumed even greater importance. The church was not simply the subject of Sunday morning visits, it was knit into the everyday fabric of life; priests from St. Mel's were frequent visitors to the

Smith home, particularly Bob's uncle, Booker Ashe, a Capuchin monk. By eighth grade, Bob had set his sights on attending a Chicago seminary for high school, when his father, a department chief for Western Electric, was transferred to Atlanta. Not wishing to move south and not able to live alone in Chicago, Bob Smith made a choice that shaped his life: He chose to leave Chicago and his family, to enroll at the seminary where his uncle taught, St. Lawrence in Mount Calvary, Wisconsin.

By his own account, seminary life and the pastoral rhythms of Mount Calvary set well with Bob Smith. After graduation, he began the nomadic journey that shook Capuchins loose from their worldly attachments, pledged always to go where their work was needed. Brother Bob served a prenovitiate in Milwaukee, then a novitiate year in Huntington, Indiana. Having taken a vow of obedience, oftentimes he simply lived out of his suitcase until the Capuchins sent word of his next assignment. Yet Brother Bob was anything but uninterested in the sort of worldly vocation he would pursue. More taken with social work than "parish work," Bob Smith sought a ministry that would put him in contact with the real world.

He found it in Detroit, where his order sent him to serve as chaplain and counselor to the Wayne County Youth Division of the Department of Corrections. Brother Bob's "cases" were kids who had committed anything from "status offenses," such as running away, up to "Class I" felonies, such as rape, robbery, and murder.

On his first day at Wayne County, wearing his Roman collar with his cell keys on his belt, Brother Bob pushed open a door to find a guard beating a teenage inmate. As the days passed, and the doors closed behind him as he entered "the facility," the visceral feeling he assumed would dissipate did not. On the inside, Smith realized that he, no less than the institution's adolescent inmates, was locked away from the outside world, with its rules and rhythms.

Brother Bob worked at knowing the adolescents in his charge. Some, even in their early teens, were without remorse and, he feared, beyond rehabilitation. Others were little more than lost children, neglected and often abused. At first uncertain of his role, Brother Bob began to feel how much the power of faith was a part of grim prison life. "These kids had lost everything. They had nothing but God to grab on to."

If the youth at Wayne County gave Brother Bob a flicker of hope, his night work nearly extinguished it. In the few spare hours not spent at the youth facility or in class, Brother Bob was a parole officer for the Michigan Department of Corrections. He forced himself to read through the fat files that contained lifetimes worth of heinous crimes, signaling by sheer weight alone criminals set in their ways. He made unannounced home visits, walking up darkened stairways past a dozen sullen men to check whether his "case" was obeying curfew. He felt fear, but even more frightening, Brother Bob learned what it was to minister to men whom he felt himself powerless to change.

For his parole work, he kept his Roman collar in the closet. In the new night world he had entered, belonging to a religious order marked a person as a soft touch—one person in an otherwise unfeeling system ex-cons could work for sympathy. Brother Bob never hid his religious identity; but then ex-convicts don't make much of an effort to get to know their parole officer. Most of the convicts who were Brother Bob's cases were unaware that their P.O. was a Capuchin monk.

One day, Brother Bob got an emergency call to come to the youth facility. He rushed into a cell to find a teenage boy known to the staff for his histrionic behavior. "I'm going to kill myself," the boy proclaimed. Smith pulled in a deep breath and said evenly, "Okay." Then he turned and walked out of the room. He was emotionally exhausted. That same day, he called his superiors to request a transfer. He had been in Detroit three years.

Soon Brother Bob was back at St. Lawrence, where he taught and coached and put some distance between himself and the scarring experiences in Detroit. His old seminary proved to be a way station to another urban mission. In 1986, Smith was sent to St. Benedict the Moor parish in downtown Milwaukee, across the street from the jail. He ran the meal program for the poor, as well as St. Benedict's Minority Ministry. Nights, Brother Bob studied at the University of Wisconsin–Milwaukee toward a degree in education administration.

Several months after coming to Milwaukee, he was asked to teach a course at Messmer High School, where his uncle, Brother Booker, was a board member. Brother Bob's "World Religions" was an instant success; popular with Messmer's students, Smith was just the kind of strong male role model a Central City school wanted. That summer, the school board asked him to stay on at Messmer—and assume the position of principal. Smith accepted.

A RIBBON OF NAMES

Messmer was an anomaly. Established in 1926 as the first Catholic school in Milwaukee, it was, by the mid-1980s, the only Catholic high school still operating in the Central City, and its existence was increasingly precarious. The flight of white parishioners to the suburbs, a migration repeated in Smith's old Chicago neighborhood and in nearly every northern city in the United States, left the school strapped for cash and short of students. In 1983, the archdiocese had advised Messmer to prepare a five-year plan for privatization. Financial pressures mounted; in the spring of 1984, the school was notified by the archdiocese that financial support would end a bit earlier than planned—with the last day of school in May.

News that Messmer would close rippled through the Central City community. Alumni, board members, and parents joined to form the Save Messmer Committee. Working feverishly over the summer months, Messmer found a savior in the form of the Milwaukee-based DeRance Foundation,[2] established by heirs to the Miller Brewing Co. fortune, which donated funds to Messmer High School Title Holding Corp., which in turn bought the building and leased it to the newly formed Messmer High School Inc. for $1 a year. Abandoned by the archdiocese, the school survived. Messmer reopened on time in the fall of 1984, in its new incarnation: "an independent high school in the Catholic tradition."

The complexion of the school literally changed overnight. "White parents pulled their kids the minute they heard the archdiocese was closing the school," Brother Bob says. "Messmer went from majority white to 'majority minority' almost instantly." Total enrollment plunged from 350 students to 115; 90 percent of the teaching staff left. By the early 1990s, more than half of Messmer's students came from families earning less than $14,000 a year; just one in five could pay the school's full $2,200 tuition.

Yet, in spite of the changes, the school kept its feet. The high school Brother Bob Smith inherited in 1987 was in many ways the diamond in Milwaukee's rough-and-tumble Central City. And Brother Bob, after years of constant change, had found a home.

As the end of his first year as principal approached, excited seniors began to burst into Brother Bob's office, anxious to tell their principal they'd been accepted to college. One day after classes, Brother Bob rummaged for a box of plastic letters in the main office. In the school entryway, fixed high on the wall at the top of the stairwell, was an empty black felt board; in the days when Messmer's chapel was home to the priests' prayer service, the felt board was where the hymnal numbers were posted.

When the students arrived the next morning, the board had a new use: White plastic letters spelled out the names of Messmer's seniors and the colleges they'd attend.

Each year, the list grew longer. When the black felt was filled, Brother Bob taped sheets of paper end to end, a ribbon of names and colleges running the length of the shining tile wall.

DPI'S EVALUATION TEAM

The fortunes of Messmer High and Milwaukee's Parental Choice program did not intersect until the spring of 1992. One day in April, Brother Bob received a phone call from Professor John Witte, the academic whom Herbert Grover had designated to conduct an annual evaluation of the Parental Choice program. Witte wanted permission to tour Messmer; Brother Bob asked why. "You're on the list," Brother Bob remembers the evaluator telling him. Somewhere in the bowels of the DPI's Madison bureaucracy was a list of all private schools eligible for the Milwaukee Parental Choice Program— and Messmer High School was on it.

Two weeks later, the mail brought a DPI application inviting Messmer to register as a Choice school. Brother Bob directed his development staff to fill out the form.

According to administrative rules drawn up by the DPI, a *nonsectarian* school was defined as "a school that does not include a pervasively religious curriculum and is not sponsored, administered, or funded by any religious group or organization."[3]

Brother Bob did not hesitate to certify Messmer High School as nonsectarian. In his assessment, the school met both standards set out in the DPI Administrative Code. First, Messmer did not have a "pervasively religious curriculum": Theology, the one department that could have occasioned concern, accounted for just eight of the school's ninety courses. At any rate, in Brother Bob's view, six of those eight courses might as easily have been classified as sociology, psychology, or philosophy, had Messmer been large enough to sustain those departments.[4] Finally, students and parents who objected to theology study were exempted and given an alternative "independent study" instead. Of the forty-four teachers and administrators on the staff, just three, including Brother Bob, belonged to religious orders, and one of the two nuns taught math. Outside of theology, courses in math, science, English, and history were taught in a manner indistinguishable from public school pedagogy; in fact, although a private school, Messmer followed the DPI recommended course of study in these subjects.

Nor in Brother Bob's view was Messmer "sponsored, administered, or funded by any religious group or organization." Since the archdiocese had abandoned Messmer to its fate eight years earlier, the school had not only been cut off from church funding, it had been removed from the list of parochial schools in the Catholic Directory and disallowed from recruiting prospective students in the archdiocese's grade schools. Messmer was on its own, a fact of life that, in time, had become a point of pride.

Finally, there were the facts of the unsolicited application form from DPI, and Examiner Witte's intended visit. It was well known that Messmer had survived its ejection from the archdiocese system and was making its way as a kind of educational asterisk—a neither/nor school at once independent and yet, almost in spite of the archdiocese's abandonment, tenaciously Catholic in its sense of mission. No other school had survived what Messmer had, and no other school was in the same position. Surely, Brother Bob reasoned, state education authorities recognized Messmer's peculiar status as proof of its eligibility for Parental Choice. Brother Bob mailed Messmer's "Intent to Participate" back to Madison.

In mid-May, the DPI published its first notice of participating Parental Choice schools for the 1992–93 year. Messmer's name appeared on the list. Almost immediately, the phone calls began, not only from parents as the word trickled out, but from the newspapers as well. On June 2, Brother Bob awoke to a front-page *Milwaukee Sentinel* headline, "Catholic School OK'd for Choice: Decision to Get Review." Brother Bob's office was besieged by interested parents.

Two days after the *Sentinel* article, at approximately 9 A.M. on Thursday, June 4, Smith received what he assumed was another of the endless phone calls from excited parents. Instead, Smith found himself talking to a DPI official, who asked whether an "evaluation team" could visit Messmer—at noon that day. Brother Bob assured them they could.

The inquisition was about to begin.

The DPI team that came to Messmer that day brought with them an eighteen-point memorandum, requesting financial and real estate documents, copies of Messmer's course catalogue, required-reading list, tests in religion classes, and a list of faculty, "identifying any presently serving as a nun, priest, brother or holds [*sic*] any office, positions or status within any nationally recognized religious sect, church or religious society in a capacity other than as a member of the faithful or member of the congregation."[5]

For four hours, the DPI team set up shop in Brother Bob's office, scoured the school's books, and wandered Messmer's halls unattended.

The team departed, only to return the following Tuesday, this time armed with a detailed eight-page checklist.[6] Compared to the memorandum from the previous visit, the new document left no doubt as to the intent of the DPI inquisitors: "#1: Are religious symbols such as crucifixes displayed in the school building? . . . #7: Review trophy case(s) for references to conferences like Catholic Conference."

Brother Bob looked on as members of the group clustered around the trophy case in the school's entryway—a few feet from the list of college-bound seniors. Smith marveled at the importance the DPI team apparently attached to the dusty WCIAA Champion trophy Messmer's basketball team had won back in 1966, and wondered whether the DPI officials would realize the "C" in WCIAA stood for "Catholic."

All told, the DPI team combed Messmer for seven hours. Classroom sweeps revealed crucifixes, but—as the DPI team would ultimately report—"not in every classroom."[7] The team did notice the inexpensive print of the Last Supper in Messmer's basement cafeteria—a painting some people at Messmer thought lent an unintended comic effect, as a kind of commentary on the quality of the cafeteria food.

Brother Bob thought the interests and approach of the DPI investigators curious. Although the school year had ended, Messmer was by no means empty. Never once on either visit did the DPI squad talk to Messmer's teachers or the small but steady trickle of students who came and went freely. "They went through our books and curriculum looking for what we did in theology," Brother Bob recalls, "but they never once tried to talk to the theology teacher— or talk to a student about what he or she did in theology class."

June 10, 1992, just two days after the second visit, a fax clattered across the machine in Brother Bob's office from Superintendent Herbert Grover. The DPI had reversed itself; Brother Bob's school was denied entry into the Parental Choice program.

The Media's Message

The question had always played at Brother Bob's mind: Who had requested that the DPI investigate Messmer?

The mystery begins with the fact that the administrative rules for Parental Choice drawn up by the DPI made no provision for investigating prospective schools.[8]

In all the public testimony that would follow, no DPI official was ever able to point to a complaint by a parent or interested member of the public that led to the investigation of Messmer. To be sure, there were references in the hearings to phone calls between various unidentified offices within the DPI, as Wisconsin education authorities woke to the fact that, somehow, a Catholic school had infiltrated Parental Choice.

In the end, however, the DPI seemed to lay the whole episode at the doorstep of the *Milwaukee Sentinel*, which had published the Messmer story June 2.[9] Indeed, Examiner Grogan's "Final Factual Stipulation of the Parties" is clear on this point:

> The DPI's school administration consultant with responsibilities for overseeing the implementation of the Milwaukee Parental Choice Program, Earl G. Knitt, Jr., testified that DPI's practice was *not* to consider schools' Notice of Intent to Participate forms as an application which called for Department approval or denial. . . . [N]o Department investigation to verify the assurances was or had been undertaken absent a complaint

or other outside question being raised. Prior to the question raised about Messmer, no previous investigation of the Choice schools' assurances had been undertaken. In this instance, the interest by the news media . . . was the basis for the agency's decision to conduct the subsequent investigation that followed.[10]

The DPI's ad-libbed investigation met with Examiner Grogan's complete approval. Even the role of the media as catalyst of the investigation was, in the examiner's view, cause for celebration rather than concern.

[W]hatever "spin" is placed on the facts, we are left with a condition where the interest by the news media provided help or encouragement for the Department of Public Instruction to conduct the review that followed. To the extent that the media has a role to oversee the affairs of government, this case can be described as a classic example of the media helping government make a correct decision.[11]

With such a sunny view of the public-spiritedness of the press, Grogan did not pause to speculate that a state agency, absent even a single complaint from a public citizen, might engineer a leak to a friendly member of the press—and then use the resulting "publicity" to trigger an inquiry, sparking a chain of events that would allow a public authority to initiate, investigate, and ultimately exonerate itself.

Having showered kudos on the media, Grogan tipped his hat in wonderment at the DPI:

The nature of the review that was conducted by the Department . . . constitutes a very impressive record of a responsive and thorough state agency. . . . Given the complexity of the issues involved, this review must represent a "high water" mark that is not likely to be equalled soon by any other state agency.[12]

And all of it was done between June 2 and June 10—quickly enough to strike Messmer from the list before eligible schools could formally receive applications from interested students.

For the DPI, it was a case study in crisis management.

A Last Chance

The inquisition at the Ramada Inn represented Brother Bob's last chance to reverse Messmer's precipitate ejection from Parental Choice. The fact that the DPI was judge and jury did nothing to sway Brother Bob's determination to right what he perceived as a grievous wrong. Back in his office, he still kept the list of families who had applied to Messmer during the brief time it had been approved for Parental Choice. The list contained ninety children's names.

Brother Bob made it plain he was in no way renouncing Messmer's Catholic patrimony. "Messmer," he told the examiner at the Ramada Inn hearing, "has never denied being a Catholic school. Being a Catholic school is something that we don't—and won't—apologize for."

Yet to Brother Bob, Messmer's mission was not to proselytize:

> We hope that any student we touch leaves our building being a good Christian, if they're Christian; if they're a non-Christian, being a good non-Christian; if they're an atheist, being a good atheist.
>
> We simply want to support whatever choice they make in regard to religion, but more, we want to help students choose to be good human beings. We are in no way out trying to get more members for the Catholic faith—and the evidence simply is that since the school's reopened in 1984, we haven't had a single Catholic converted. We haven't talked about conversion; we haven't had a baptism; we haven't even mentioned it.
>
> What we're more interested in is that students be given a solid education, and walk out of there with some values—values that any human being should have.

To Brother Bob, the traits and teachings he freely described as "religious" might just as easily and interchangeably be described as "values-based"—and often were. The fact was, the majority of Messmer's students were non-Catholic: Most were Baptists, just one in four was Catholic—and a full 11 percent were without religious belief of any kind. At the hearing, Brother Bob affirmed that an avowed atheist could be admitted to Messmer, though the student would have to volunteer the information, since religious affiliation was not requested in the application process.[13] Scholarships—in effect, tuition discounts—were awarded in proportions roughly equal to the school population at large; in other words, about 75 percent of scholarship aid went to non-Catholic students. Brother Bob and his staff had crafted a very careful approach to maintain a values-based curriculum without offending the beliefs of non-Catholic students. Yet DPI and the examiner seemed uninterested in the exquisite balancing act that was taken so seriously by Messmer's principal.

Instead, the DPI counsel piled up fact after fact that proved the alleged pervasiveness of religion at Messmer:

Daily prayer.   The DPI cited a fifteen-second daily prayer over the PA system, "a one or two sentence statement that begins by invoking the name 'God' or 'Lord' and that ends with 'Amen.'"[14] Brother Bob took pains to point out that prayers endorsing any one religion were prohibited, and often consisted simply in invoking God's help at school and through the day, followed by a quote from a "famous individual."

Theology.   The DPI cited the fact that texts used in the theology courses contained the "imprimatur" of the Catholic church, were published by Catholic or religious presses, or included editors or authors of articles who belonged to church orders.[15] Brother Bob pointed out that no theology teacher was required to use approved texts; that any student objecting to an individual class, an assignment, or even to an entire course was excused—in the latter case, required to enroll in independent study; and finally, that for transfers to Messmer, theology requirements were routinely waived in order to allow a student to graduate or stay "in grade."[16]

Prayer services.   DPI cited "prayer services" held in Messmer's gym or auditorium. Brother Bob explained the nature of these services, which proved remarkably secular in subject matter and substance:

> The service usually has a values-based theme, [e.g.], respect, and other topics have been discussed, such as the Smithsonian . . . in Washington, D.C. Also a rapper named Big Daddy Kane spoke with the students. An outside person generally presents the theme and spends time talking with students. The school choir may sing a song during the service. Certain main speakers are priests or ministers. One was a priest who talked about experiences he had as a senior at Messmer and what to expect upon graduation. Others were: The Rev. Gerald Saffold, a Baptist minister who spoke on self-esteem of the students; the Rev. Jim Leafry, a Calvary Baptist minister who discussed feeding the poor; and Steven Reitman, a person of Jewish descent who spoke about a foundation he created for Messmer. Messmer also had subjects discussed such as recycling and other forms of waste conservation, summer jobs for teenagers, teenage pregnancy, and drug use.[17]

As the particulars attest, just how these assemblies met the description of "prayer services" is not easily discerned.

Messmer's faculty and student handbooks. The DPI cited quotations containing references to Messmer's mission as advancing Christianity and Catholicism;[18] Brother Bob cited passages testifying to the explicit injunction that Messmer recognize and honor the diverse beliefs of its students.[19] Smith labored in vain to explain that an organization could be religious in its motive—whether helping the poor, for instance, or educating children—and yet not proselytize in its means.

Brother Bob's view of the matter had the clarity of a logical syllogism. If Messmer's mission was to create Catholics, then it was failing miserably.[20] If, however, Messmer's mission was to educate students, it was by all accounts performing miracles. To hold—as the examiner ultimately would—that Messmer was in essence a *church* rather than a *school* was to assert an inversion of the facts.[21] Messmer would, under such a definition, be an utter failure at its primary mission—raising Catholics—and an accidental success at its secondary goal, educating students.

GETTING HIS MAN

In the end, the Catholic Conference trophies, the Capuchin monk principal, the nondenominational prayer over the PA, the funds from a philanthropic organization that was not itself tied to the church but targeted much of its giving to religious organizations all conspired to stamp Messmer as "pervasively religious."

The question is how this finding relates to the precise wording of the statute, which requires a finding of a "pervasively religious *curriculum*." If we begin by adopting the "plain reading" rule Examiner Grogan claims as his guide to the convoluted language of the DPI regulation, it is patently impossible to convict Messmer on the charge of having a "pervasively religious *curriculum*." Wishing the DPI definition had been more broadly written is no mandate for making it so. Nevertheless, that is what Examiner Grogan did, at the behest of the DPI and the amicus brief entered by the Wisconsin Education Association Council.[22]

The DPI opened the assault that would drive the word *curriculum* out of its own regulatory rule:

> Arguably, the rule phrase "pervasively religious *curriculum*" is narrower than the classical one used in the courts' establishment cases, "pervasively sectarian *institution or organization*." This and the next subsection suggest that the examiner must construe the rule phrase "pervasively sectarian [*sic*] curriculum" broadly.[23]

It was a suggestion seconded by the WEAC and eagerly adopted by Grogan:

In conducting such an examination, the Department must view "curriculum" as not only coursework, but rather, as the overall package of knowledge, tenets and beliefs that the school seeks to impart to students during the regular schoolday, or during school-sanctioned extracurricular activities.[24]

Thus having expanded the word *curriculum* in a way that emptied it of all meaning, the examiner read the word out of the DPI definition altogether. *Curriculum*, once a word with a precise meaning, became elastic enough to serve as a legal duffel bag for whatever evidence the DPI had collected.

A similar fate befell the word *pervasive*. Under the plain-reading rule, "pervasively religious" would have some meaning distinct from simply "religious." Indeed, the implication is that "religiousness" alone is not sufficient to transgress the nonsectarian rule: Religion must not be incidental or intermittent, but pervasive.

Yet the DPI and Examiner Grogan consistently conflated the mere *presence* of religion with *pervasiveness*. The effect was to render *pervasive* superfluous, a violation of the plain-reading rule that passes without comment. Indeed, the entire line of U.S. Supreme Court establishment-clause case law under which "Congress shall make no law respecting an establishment of religion . . ."—decisions sanctioning everything from textbook loans to transportation reimbursements and the like to private religious schools—is opaque apart from an understanding of the difference between "religious" and "pervasively religious."

The DPI's reading abandoned any pretense to neutrality in matters involving religion, rendering religion a virus, the presence of which in the smallest form infects the whole. As Grogan put it: *"Messmer High School has a religious purpose that permeates all aspects of the school's organization, operation, and administration."*[25] Viewed from this vantage point, Messmer, closed down and cut loose by the archdiocese eight years earlier, separated from potential donors by its exclusion from the Catholic Directory, simply could not eliminate the taint of religion that remained.

The viral nature of religion is evident in microcosm in the way Messmer's class retreats were characterized in the hearing. What the DPI insisted, contrary to Messmer's own practice, on calling *"religious* retreats"[26] in fact possessed only a small tincture of religion. A careful review of the retreats, differentiated by subject matter for freshmen, sophomores, juniors, and seniors, revealed that

> The freshman retreat usually deals with getting to know one another, awareness of each other, realizing similarities and differences. The sophomore and junior retreats deal with sexuality, sexual activity as it relates to teenagers, responsible sex, HIV/AIDS, and lifestyles focusing on single life, married life, raising children and the economics of these choices. The fall senior retreat dealt with communications across cultures. . . . A part of that retreat, about 1 and $^1/_2$ hours, deals with a Bible activity where students look up stories as they relate to our present society, i.e., how the Bible could be made relevant to today, and then discuss with the group, such as the Good Samaritan Law that is debated today or the prodigal son as it may apply to their families. In general, students are given time for private reflection, but they do not have to pray. The spring retreat dealt with gangs and their influence on the community, Len Bias's mother showed the danger of drugs. Another topic dealt with teenage pregnancy. *A review of the retreat programs for the 1991–92 year did not indicate religious content except for the senior retreat which had a prayer service (Bible reading and discussion) scheduled for part of one evening.*[27]

The presence of religion in a part was considered sufficient to taint the whole. By treating the *presence* of any religious trappings as *pervasive*, the DPI, WEAC, and Examiner Grogan were able to knit together all manner of extracurricular strands into a hanging rope for Messmer High School.

The DPI counsel also seemed, incredibly, to imply that *private* religious belief alone might taint an institution.[28] At times, the hearing took on a serio-comic aspect, as when the DPI's attorney asked the chief financial officer of the DeRance Foundation in all earnestness whether his organization funded any *anti*-Catholic activities.

Laughing, the DeRance officer admitted they did not. The DPI attorney stopped there; it was never made clear just how much antireligious activity might be required to cleanse DeRance of its alleged religious taint.

As to the second sectarian "test"—whether a school was sponsored, administered, or funded by a religious organization—Brother Bob recounted the ways Messmer was divorced from the Catholic hierarchy: the fact that Messmer was prohibited from recruiting in the Catholic grade schools; that its employees were not eligible to participate in the diocesan insurance program; that Messmer had been dropped from the Catholic Directory in 1985—and was therefore not eligible for the IRS group tax exemption granted the U.S. Catholic Conference. Nor, Smith testified, did the school appear in the Official Wisconsin Pastoral Handbook under the listing of the Archdiocese of Milwaukee—by tradition, regarded as a kind of imprimatur by private donors seeking to contribute to Catholic organizations.[29]

The DPI counsel's response to the school's absence from the Catholic Directory typified the kind of conspiracy theories he found so easy to entertain when the subject was Catholicism. Seizing on a standard disclaimer in the preface to the Catholic Directory that "neither the publishers nor the ecclesiastical authorities assume responsibility for any errors or omissions,"[30] attorney Robert J. Paul insisted more than once that the disclaimer be made part of the record—as if to imply that Messmer, like some educational equivalent of a Cold War "sleeper" spy smuggled into place with instructions to await word of its mission, had somehow engineered its removal from the Directory in 1985, in preparation for the day seven years hence when it would burrow into a Parental Choice program that, at the moment of Messmer's expulsion from the archdiocese, did not exist.

For the DPI and ultimately Examiner Grogan, the question of Messmer's funding, sponsorship, and administration was never a difficult one. The DPI totted up the substantial funding Messmer received from the DeRance Foundation—$1.5 million pledged or paid out between 1988 and the time of the hearing in 1992—took note of the fact that DeRance grants, made to PAVE with the proviso that they be used only at Catholic schools, included Messmer on the list, and reached the conclusion that Messmer was indeed sponsored, administered, and funded by religious organizations or groups. Examiner Grogan, devoting to this test less than one page of his fifty-seven-page Order, "accept[ed] the DPI's theory at face value," throwing in, for good measure, an endorsement of the amicus briefs of the ACLU, Americans United for the Separation of Church and State, and WEAC. In the end, however, Grogan went a step further, ruling that Messmer High School Inc. was "itself a religious group or organization"—again citing Messmer's own definition of itself as an "integrated Catholic High School."[31]

One of the keys for Grogan was Messmer's self-characterization as a Catholic entity while seeking the religious exemption from unemployment tax in a 1990 case before the State Department of Industry, Labor and Human Relations (DILHR) in 1990. Brother Bob argued that Messmer's theology courses and curricular objectives had undergone a systematic reappraisal and revision between the DILHR proceeding in 1990 and Messmer's 1992 application for Parental Choice.[32] The examiner, however, remained unconvinced; in finding Brother Bob's school to have a pervasively religious curriculum, he claimed only to be taking Messmer at its word.[33]

At times, the DPI attorney's knowledge of Catholic doctrine itself helped clinch the case. Time and again, the DPI counsel circled back to the small school chapel across the hall from Brother Bob's office. For Messmer's first half-century the chapel was a place for the religious among its teachers and staff to celebrate daily Mass; its four pews, however, could seat just a fraction of Messmer's student body. Yet attorney Paul questioned whether and when the chapel was still used to celebrate the Mass (several times a year, Brother

Bob reported), and whether consecrated hosts were stored there (Brother Bob testified they weren't).[34] Almost in the manner of a gumshoe, the DPI attorney went about "getting his man"—in this case, according to Brother Bob's faith, the son of God.

PAUL: Let me get a clarification regarding the consecrated hosts . . . not being resident on the premises in the chapel. But . . . it's true that at any of the Masses that occur throughout the year, hosts *are* consecrated at those Masses—
BROTHER BOB: Yes.
PAUL: —and in the Catholic faith, that's the conversion of the bread and wine into the body and blood of Christ Jesus.
BROTHER BOB: That's correct.
PAUL: And that takes place at the Mass, and then those articles of bread and wine are consumed—
BROTHER BOB: Yes.
PAUL: —then they are no longer on the premises.
BROTHER BOB: That's correct.
PAUL: Then—*in the time between consecration and consumption*—then the conse-crated host of the blessed sacrament *is* present.
BROTHER BOB: That's correct.
PAUL: With that clarification, that ends my cross.

Paul's persistence paid off. Brother Bob may have testified that Messmer's chapel was not a church; yet, however fleetingly, Jesus had been placed at the scene. Months later, in a passage near the end of the DPI brief, Messmer would be identified not as a *school* at all, but a *church*.

There were times when Brother Bob suspected that had he offered at any point in the proceeding to abolish the theology requirement, Messmer might have won DPI approval. "At one point during preparations [for the appeal], an attorney advising me said, 'Brother Bob, why not just discontinue Theology I and II? Why not move the elective courses into a philosophy department or psychol-ogy—get rid of theology altogether?' "

Brother Bob batted it down. "I had said all along we would not apologize for what we were. To compromise by changing the nature of our school, for the sake of twenty-five Choice students—I couldn't imagine it. I knew our board would be as adamant as I was.

"I was confident there was no way DPI could ever find us 'pervasively religious.' And I was wrong."

Smith thought the theology courses well tailored to respect the full range of religious and even antireligious belief. He took seriously Messmer's policy giving students the right to opt out of any course, class, or activity incompatible with their religious or areligious beliefs. Offering to abolish the theology courses would have been an admission of sorts, and who could tell whether it might suffice in satisfying the DPI? After all, the Department could simply find other reasons to rule against Messmer. To secularize his school was to criminalize belief. Messmer was what it was, Smith decided. Stand or fall, it would stay the same.

TWO MASTERS

Brother Bob saw his inquisition as a comment on the culture. At a time when students in the public high schools walked through metal detectors every morning—when four in ten students who entered high school left with a diploma—Messmer High, in a North Side neighborhood afflicted with the same gangs, graffiti, and guns, managed a graduation rate of 98 percent and a college-bound rate of 79 percent. And yet, Brother Bob ruminated, Messmer High School was on trial.

At times, the proceeding seemed a flashback to an earlier era of unapologetic anti-Catholicism. DPI counsel Paul methodically evoked the dangers of dual allegiance—and the primacy of Catholics' allegiance to Church over Country.

PAUL: We left off with the Minister General in Rome—is he the top person in the province of St. Joseph?
BROTHER BOB: The top Capuchin.
PAUL: There is a general for that Congregation—

BROTHER BOB: Correct.

PAUL: —who is in turn answerable to the pope.

BROTHER BOB: That is correct.

PAUL: So it is true in a disciplinary chain, for doctrinal purposes, if you will
. . . for religious purposes, it's fair to say that there is a direct line, authoritatively, from you to the pope. Isn't that true?

BROTHER BOB: No. You could stretch it out there was a connection, but the
reality—

PAUL: —No; I just went through the chain step by step for who answers to
whom, and in fact if we were to diagram the structure of the Franciscan order,
and you in it as a Capuchin, I can make that line.

Moments later, the DPI counsel sums up for the examiner.

PAUL: In the Department [of Public Instruction]'s view, it is significant that
there is a line between the pope and Brother Bob.

EXAMINER: It's the Department's view that there is a direct line of authority?

PAUL: And it's significant, yes.

Seldom has the hostility between sacred and secular been more
sharply drawn. Backed into a corner by the DPI attorney, Brother
Bob could renounce the authority of his highest superior—or stand
revealed as an agent of the pope of Rome.

The moment marked an epiphany. In the eyes of the secular state,
Brother Bob could not serve two masters, the pope and the DPI.

CHAPTER 9

Constitutional Daylight

As a question of constitutional law, should Messmer High School have been allowed into the Parental Choice program?

Any attempt to answer must begin by noting that the DPI tribunal was not a court of law. The Messmer affair was an administrative, not legal, hearing, turning on the definition of an administrative, not statutory, guideline.

That said, however, the DPI attorney went to significant lengths to base his argument on U.S. Supreme Court case law. At one point, challenged by the examiner to provide a citation for his definition of "pervasively religious," the DPI counsel cited *Tilton v. Richardson,* a 1973 case in the line of establishment-clause cases descending from *Lemon v. Kurtzman.*[1] According to the DPI brief: "Lemon and the cases since then reflect a consistent application of the three Lemon prongs that when applied to K–12 cases, hold that the RISK or PO-TENTIAL for indoctrination, is sufficient to run afoul of the effects and entanglement prongs of Lemon."[2]

The three-prong *Lemon* test requires that legislation (1) reflect a clearly secular legislative purpose; (2) have a primary effect that neither advances nor inhibits religion; and (3) avoid excessive government entanglement with religion. While the *Lemon* test was advanced by the DPI as well as the ACLU amicus, the examiner did not rely on either to reach his decision. The Messmer hearing merely set the stage for the church–state questions destined to dominate the extension of vouchers to religious schools.

BREAKING THE BARRIER

Several months before Messmer's appeal would be denied, the first legislative effort was made to open Parental Choice to religious schools. The vehicle was a bill introduced in March 1993 by State Senator John Plewa, a Milwaukee Democrat whose South Side district included St. Matthew School. Plewa's bill called for $1,000 tax credits to families sending their children to private schools, religious as well as nonsectarian. In the spring of 1993, neither Polly Williams nor Governor Thompson seemed inclined to invest political capital in breaking the religious school barrier.[3] Plewa's bill languished, and the legislative session ended.

A more sustained effort to break the religious school barrier would come in the fall of 1993.[4] The push came not in the legislature, but in U.S. District Court, in the form of a suit pitting four low-income Milwaukee parents against new State Superintendent John Benson—another vigorous opponent of Parental Choice, if less voluble than Grover.[5] Each of the parents in *Miller v. Benson* had applied to nonsectarian Choice schools; having lost in the lottery, they were placed on the waiting list while their children attended or prepared to enter MPS. Cynthia Miller, Zachery Gray, George Richardson, and Faye Henry looked to the court for permission to use vouchers to enroll their children in private *religious* schools, an option expressly forbidden by the Choice statute. Counsel to the *Miller* parents was once again provided by Landmark Legal Foundation; with Clint Bolick having left Landmark to establish his own organization, the Institute for Justice, the position of lead litigator went to Bolick's colleague from the *Davis* case, Mark Bredemeier.

Bredemeier's argument was breathtakingly activist. His intent was to frame the question of religious school choice around the First

Amendment's free-exercise clause, in distinction to the long line of establishment-clause cases reaching back in varying degrees to *Lemon*. In doing so, Bredemeier was breathing new life into what had become the forgotten half of the First Amendment's religious clause: "Congress shall make no law respecting an establishment of religion, or prohibiting the free exercise thereof. . . ." The plaintiffs' claim hinged on a careful distinction from the *Pierce* precedent, the 1925 case that ratified the right to private schooling in the United States.[6]

> A state decision to fund only its public schools is valid. However, an entitlement program that benefits all similarly situated public and private entities, but purposefully excludes only religious families who choose religiously affiliated organizations, is *prima facie* violative of the Free Exercise Clause.[7]

Wisconsin provided public funds for public school choice, and with the passage of Parental Choice, it provided *publicly* funded *private* school choice as well—although limited to nonsectarian schools.[8] For Bredemeier, the limitation was critical, and ultimately unconstitutional: As a result of the state's actions, only parents seeking to choose religious schools for their children had been singled out and deprived of a government benefit.

> Plaintiffs are not asking this Court to create a right that does not exist. They are asking the Court to order the State of Wisconsin to provide the government benefit of an existing public-funded private school choice program on a fair, equal and nondiscriminatory basis. . . .
>
> The State of Wisconsin may have been under no constitutional or legal obligation to create a government benefit that provides public funding for low-income families who choose private schools. *But once it did, the State was obligated to confer such benefits in a nondiscriminatory manner.*[9]

Bredemeier found support for this line of argument in *The Culture of Disbelief*, Yale law professor Stephen Carter's penetrating examination of American law's assault on religion:

> Parents who choose to send their children to religious schools
> should be eligible alongside parents who send their children
> elsewhere. . . . For the government to subsidize some private
> schools but refuse to subsidize the religious ones would make
> religious schools more costly and would thus constitute a
> government-created disincentive to use them.

Carter was categorical in the constitutional implications: "In
other areas of constitutional law, we do not call such disincentives
'neutrality'; we call them 'discrimination.' "[10]

Miller's proposed remedy? Simply by striking the word *nonsectarian*
from the Parental Choice statute, the court would render the Choice
program neutral as regards religion, and therefore constitutional.[11]

At that point, the *Miller* claim would take its place not in the line
of establishment-clause case law descended from *Lemon*, but in the
line of free-exercise cases beginning with the GI Bill, and followed
by *Mueller* in 1983, *Witters* in 1986, and *Zobrest* in 1993. Each had
recognized a free-exercise right in cases where the law was neutral
in conferring a government benefit, and whatever aid might incidentally flow to religious institutions was "driven by the private
choices of individual parents."[12]

Indeed, the two lines—*Lemon* and *Mueller–Witters–Zobrest*—
touched at one point in *Witters*. In that 1986 case, the court justified
its approval of a neutral government benefit to individuals with an
incidental benefit to religious institutions by citing a distinction
drawn in the *Nyquist* case, a 1973 ruling that applied the *Lemon* tests'
three prongs to strike down a New York state statute providing tuition reimbursement to parents with children in religious schools.
Witters went so far as to quote *Nyquist's* proviso that the court

> need not decide whether the significantly religious character of
> the statute's beneficiaries might differentiate the present case
> from a case involving some form of public assistance (e.g.,
> scholarships) made available generally without regard to the
> sectarian–nonsectarian, or public–nonpublic nature of the insti-
> tution benefited. [13]

Nyquist, in this reading, had left the door open for a certain species of voucher program. Bredemeier buttressed his case with support from an unlikely source, liberal legal icon Laurence Tribe:

> These decisions [*Mueller* and *Witters*] suggest that the [Supreme] Court would uphold an educational voucher scheme that would permit parents to decide which schools, public or private, their children should attend. The Establishment Clause probably would not stand as an obstacle to a purely neutral program, at least one with a broad enough class of beneficiary schools and one that channeled aid through parents and children rather than directly to schools.[14]

Not all advocates of school choice proved supportive of the *Miller* suit. Some feared the attempt might backfire and bring down the original Choice program in the process;[15] others simply exhibited the nervousness natural in the face of an aggressive attempt to encourage the very sort of "judge-made" law conservatives had long decried. For conservative jurists instinctively distrustful of Warren Court activism, *Miller*'s brand of right-wing Warrenism would prove an acquired taste.[16]

A FINAL IRONY

As in *Davis v. Grover*, the state superintendent erected the foundations of his defense against the *Miller* parents on procedural rather than substantive grounds. The *Miller* children, Superintendent Benson argued, lacked standing; having suffered no direct harm, there was no "case or controversy," the sine qua non of any court proceeding. Benson claimed there to be "no evidence . . . from which the court can conclude that any sectarian institutions would participate" in an expanded Parental Choice program; granting a right to *Miller* parents would give them no place to go. Since the statute pertains to *schools*—none of which were party to the suit—Benson's brief concluded the children's suit represented an impermissible attempt to assert third-party rights.[17]

Bredemeier battled back with affidavits indicating a readiness of religious schools to participate, which—in addition to the plain language of the statute telling them religious schools were barred from Parental Choice—raised the experience of Messmer High School as proof of the futility of any effort to apply.[18] Bredemeier scored Benson's attempt to undercut his plaintiff's standing through such procedural "sleight-of-hand": "We have no doubt had religious *schools* filed a complaint instead of parents, defendants would claim they were attempting impermissibly to assert parents' third-party rights."[19] Benson's benchmark for standing—that religious schools ought to have applied to Parental Choice, only to be turned away— was to condition legal rights on an exercise in futility.

Benson added a second procedural defense, attacking the sincerity of the religious beliefs espoused by the *Miller* parents. According to Benson, the schools sought by the *Miller* parents might be religious, but their impetus in choosing them was actually secular—like Thoreau at Walden Pond, Cynthia Miller and her fellow plaintiffs had come to their views through "philosophical and personal" cogitation, rather than religious belief.[20]

On this point, the ACLU—not in the habit of parsing private beliefs and very much in the habit of entering court to defend the peculiar, if not perverse, against the inroads of state authority—parted company with Benson: "Amici do *not* challenge the plaintiffs' sincere religious beliefs."[21]

Yet if the ACLU's refusal to follow Benson was an admirable exercise in adhering to principle, the rest of the ACLU brief offers arguments that ought to have made a card-carrying member of the organization shudder. Rather than claiming itself the defender of establishment-clause strictures, the ACLU announced itself the true defender of the free-exercise clause: *Miller* parents might see themselves as wronged, but in fact, the ACLU was focused on a day when religious schools, welcomed into Parental Choice like a fly into a spider's web, would find themselves subject to intrusive state regulations.[22] Like "virtual reality," a kind of lifelike projection of what might be, the ACLU found in the *Miller* case a kind of "virtual" lawsuit, far more important than the immediate case at hand.

> Indeed, if religious schools were included in [Parental Choice], it is not difficult to imagine that the first enforcement of the statutory requirements and regulations would result in a challenge by a religious school that the [Choice plan], as applied, poses a burden on religion.[23]

Miller parents might not understand, but religious schools would learn to thank the ACLU later.

Ironically, the ACLU's case was built on the rigor of Parental Choice's many supervisory strictures—the very provisions presumed so weak and ineffectual in *Grover v. Davis*. In the ACLU's view, those requirements and regulations were so onerous, extensive, and intrusive that they constituted prima facie evidence of "excessive entanglement" on the part of the state.[24]

The Lewis Carroll quality of the ACLU brief did not stop with its imaginary suit. The ACLU proceeded to argue the impermissibility of expanding Choice to religious schools on behalf of an imagined "outsider" religious school whose views caused it to be denied entry into the Parental Choice program by the state.[25] In addition to stretching to include the hypothetical rights of a hypothetical school against a hypothetical infringement on the part of the state (the only entity in the ACLU scheme that did in fact exist), the ACLU did not acknowledge the non sequitur at the heart of its scenario: The outsider school was being denied its right to enter a program bound—by the ACLU's previously imagined case—to excessively entangle itself in the affairs of the "outsider" school. By the ACLU's logic, or lack of it, the state should have welcomed the "outsider" school into the program—in order to regulate it to death.

As a final irony, the ACLU brief cast the civil liberties defender in the role of strict constructionist and defender of the state legislature. The remedy sought by the *Miller* parents—striking the word *nonsectarian* from the Parental Choice statute—was, the ACLU argued,

> an impermissible encroachment on the Wisconsin legislature and thus invites this Court to violate the separation of powers between the judicial and legislative branches. The court should decline this invitation. . . . This Court should not now be asked to redraft the statute in the very manner rejected by the legislature.[26]

It was one instance where the ACLU—imaginative in the extreme in the rest of its brief—would prove to be shortsighted. Such exaggerated deference to the legislature's actions was fine in the immediate case, but it raised a question: What if the legislature itself decided to expand Choice to include religious schools?

Lemonade

Like the ACLU, Superintendent Benson advanced an excessive-entanglement argument, based on the oversight and audit functions built into the Parental Choice statute.[27] It was testament to how far things had come since the Wisconsin Supreme Court issued its ruling in *Davis v. Grover:* Benson was now resting his case on the *strength* of the regulations his predecessor had claimed were tissue-thin.

Yet the core of the superintendent's defense was to drive the *Miller* claim into the well-worn establishment-clause line tracing back to *Lemon* and its rigorous three-prong test. Here again, however, Benson sought to rest his defense on a point of process: In *Miller*, the method of payment, "directly from the state to the private school," ran afoul of *Lemon*'s second prong.[28]

The difficulty for Benson's argument was *Witters*. The 1986 case "did not violate the second prong of *Lemon* because the aid to religion resulted from private decisions of the beneficiaries." Benson's answer served the immediate case: "That case [*Witters*] is not apposite here.

The Milwaukee Choice program is *not* a voucher system. The money is not given to the parents. It goes directly to the institution."[29]

For Bredemeier, this fixation on the mechanics of payment was something the Supreme Court had already considered—and dismissed. "There is no 'kinship' whatsoever between the MPCP's individual choice-driven tuition benefit and the broad government-controlled assistance-to-institutions packages struck down in years past."[30]

To support this claim, *Miller*'s parents cited the *Committee for Public Education and Liberty v. Regan* (1980):[31]

> We decline to embrace a formalistic dichotomy that bears so little relationship either to common sense or to the realities of school finance. None of our cases requires us to invalidate these reimbursements simply because they involve [direct] payments in cash.[32]

Such was the power of *Lemon* that even Bredemeier could not run the risk of ignoring it. With the secular intent of Parental Choice beyond question, Bredemeier asserted that—true "neutrality" having been achieved by striking the word *nonsectarian* from the statute—Parental Choice would neither advance nor inhibit religion; nor would the continuation of Parental Choice's regulatory regime create excessive government entanglement in religion.[33] When given lemons, make lemonade.

FINE LINES

"Ruling Bars Religious School Choice," trumpeted the *Milwaukee Journal* on March 15, 1995; "Expansion of Choice Ruled Unconstitutional," headlined the *Sentinel*. "We are disappointed. It was a close call," both papers quoted Landmark's Bredemeier as saying of Judge John W. Reynolds's decision to rule for the state and against the *Miller* parents.

Whatever the legal grounds of the ruling, there was no denying the negative political impact on the fortunes of religious school choice. Less than a month before Reynolds handed down his ruling, Governor Thompson had put in his budget a bill to amend and expand the Parental Choice program to include religious schools.

After several years and several ineffectual efforts to expand Parental Choice, Wisconsin's correlation of forces had shifted. In November 1994, just a week before *Miller v. Benson* was scheduled for oral argument, the state elections had swept Republicans into power in the Assembly, even as they maintained their majority in the Senate. One early sign pointed to potential movement on Parental Choice: The Assembly's new Republican leadership, parceling out the spoils of victory, nonetheless reached across the aisle to name Polly Williams chair of the Urban Education Committee—giving the Milwaukee maverick a political plum she'd never dreamed of while her own Democrats were in power.[34]

Thompson's budget and Williams's ascension fed the fears of antivoucher forces. Several new groups, composed of many of the teachers' unions and other alumni of the *Davis v. Grover* suit, sprang into existence to oppose religious school choice. One, the Wisconsin Coalition for Public Education (WCPE), dusted off the old antichoice rallying cry as its new motto: "Public funds for public schools only."[35] WCPE, described in news accounts as a "citizens' organization," in fact included not only the Wisconsin Education Association Council, the Wisconsin Federation of Teachers, various other public education unions, and the NAACP, but also public agencies such as the DPI and even MPS. Just how public agencies could enroll themselves in a "citizens' group"—or how they might participate in *any* private organization, for that matter—was something WCPE's spokesman could not explain. WCPE's grassroots might be astroturf; in the media, however, that didn't matter.

Nevertheless, while opposition to Thompson's proposed Choice expansion was vigorous and full of the predictable vitriol, it was to all appearances not very effectual. Now, with the *Miller* ruling, Choice's opponents had a new weapon in their arsenal: Governor Thompson's plan was unconstitutional.

The argument, though incorrect, was easily made. Unlike in the *Davis* case, in which Clint Bolick and Polly Williams enlisted parents and prospective Choice children at every turn to make their case in the court of public opinion, Landmark's Bredemeier made no attempt to pack the courtroom with parents for the oral argument in *Miller*. The tactical decision, while it had no bearing on the legal proceedings, had the effect of rendering the *Miller* case essentially invisible to the public. Thus the ruling, when it came, looked as though it was a legal ruling on the Thompson plan.

Bredemeier struggled to put a positive spin on the ruling. He treated the defeat as strike one, nothing more. In fact, Reynolds's ruling did answer several concerns in ways quite favorable to Parental Choice: First, against the arguments of the state superintendent, a federal court had acknowledged that the children and their parents had standing to file suit. Second, Reynolds had ruled the existing Parental Choice program constitutional—a verdict in federal court that affirmed the judgment of the Wisconsin Supreme Court.[36]

Yet on the central element of the *Miller* parents' argument, Reynolds remained unpersuaded:

> The plaintiffs have argued that the present state of Establishment Clause jurisprudence is in flux, and that the current Supreme Court might be more likely to allow a tuition reimbursement program flowing to religious private schools. The plaintiffs have even suggested that the current Supreme Court would overrule *Nyquist*. However, this court may not speculate on future decisions of the current Supreme Court and decide a case on such speculation when a directly relevant Supreme Court case decides the issue. The present state of First Amendment law compels this court to hold that the plaintiffs' request to expand the current Choice Program to make tuition reimbursements directly payable to religious private schools who admit eligible Choice Program schoolchildren would violate the Establishment Clause.[37]

For Reynolds, the case turned on the mechanics of the payment.[38] Having failed to meet the *Mueller* method, in which the benefit flowed *to the parents* in the form of a tax credit, Reynolds held that the *Miller* complaint would be governed by *Nyquist*: "[I]t is clear from our cases that direct aid [to religious schools] in whatever form is invalid."[39]

"As the Supreme Court has repeatedly stated," Reynolds noted,

> tension between the Free Exercise Clause and the Establishment Clause is inevitable, and "it may not be possible to promote the former without offending the latter." The Supreme Court's cases interpreting the First Amendment religion clauses in the area of economic benefits to religious schools draw fine lines between what a state may or must do, and what a state may not do. These lines may not be logical or rational, but they represent the best efforts of the Court to resolve these most difficult problems.[40]

Yet what began for Reynolds as an observation of the unsettled and uncertain course of establishment-clause case law became a license of sorts to choose among the menu of cases that might plausibly govern *Miller*. In Reynolds's hands, the inarguable tension between the religious clauses turned into a trump card favoring establishment concerns over free-exercise claims.

On what possible constitutional basis could one elevate one religious clause over the other—and assuming one could take precedence, why would it be the establishment clause?[41] *Nyquist*, Reynolds's template for the *Miller* decision, holds no answer; indeed, *Nyquist* acknowledges that neither clause naturally outranks the other: "[T]he Court has struggled to find a neutral course between the two Religion Clauses, both of which are cast in absolute terms, and either of which, if expanded to a logical extreme, would tend to clash with the other."[42]

In what Bredemeier termed a fatal flaw,[43] on the critical commentary the Supreme Court had offered in *Witters* and *Regan* on *Nyquist* Reynolds was altogether silent. Bredemeier's scorn was evident.

Recalling Reynolds's refusal to speculate about what the current Supreme Court might decide, Bredemeier pressed forward with his planned appeal: "Landmark will now proceed to give the Court of Appeals and the Supreme Court the chance to end this speculation."[44]

NEW LIFE

As the immediate impact of the *Miller* defeat gave way to a closer reading of the decision, one passage in particular seemed to take on new meaning. It was an argument advanced in Superintendent Benson's brief:

> Thus it is clear that the direct payment to the religious schools violates the Establishment Clause *even though such might not be the case under a voucher system. Plaintiffs must take the program the Legislature adopted not the one they would have preferred.*[45]

Like the ACLU's newfound appreciation for judicial restraint and deference to the wisdom of the legislature, Benson's argument had an unintended effect: In defeating the *Miller* claim, it illuminated precisely what kind of religious school voucher plan *would* withstand First Amendment scrutiny.

It bore an uncanny resemblance to the expanded Choice plan contained in Governor Thompson's budget bill. Thompson seized the implication immediately: "Judge Reynolds' decision will not deter our efforts. If anything, it helps reaffirm that we are going in the right direction with a voucher system that gives tuition money *directly to the parents, not the schools.*"[46]

On June 29, 1995, the Wisconsin legislature passed Governor Thompson's budget. In it was funding sufficient to provide 7,250 vouchers for the 1995–96 school year to enable low-income Milwaukee children to attend the school of their choice—nonsectarian or religious. For 1996–97, the budget allotted funds for the program to double again, to 15,700 students. The bill also amended the payment mechanism, providing for payments from the state treasury directly to parents, who would then deliver them to their Choice school.

The next twenty-four hours were busy ones in the private schools around the city. On June 30, 1995—the very date Herbert Grover had declared would be Parental Choice's last day—seventy-two religious schools across Milwaukee sent the DPI notices of intent to join the Parental Choice program.

PART IV

Report
Card

CHAPTER TEN

Accentuate the Negative

But does it work? The question is asked as frequently and impatiently by Parental Choice's advocates as by its enemies. Indeed, with all that hinges on the Milwaukee experiment, a visitor to Choice schools might expect to encounter halls thronged with teams of researchers in hot pursuit of empirical proof. The reality is far different. Most of the opinions on Parental Choice—and the vast majority of the criticism—amount to "received wisdom," borrowed from the studies of one man: John F. Witte, Herbert Grover's hand-picked outside evaluator of the Parental Choice program.[1] From the publication of Witte's First Year Report in November 1991 to his fourth report in December 1994, the public education establishment has drawn ammunition for its campaign against school choice.[2]

ECHO EFFECT

The result is a sort of echo effect: What appears on the national scene to be a chorus of voucher critics amounts, upon examination, to a kind of scholarly ventriloquism—commentators who share a common antipathy toward vouchers parroting the partial findings of one examiner.

The oft-quoted 1992 Special Report on School Choice by the Carnegie Foundation for the Advancement of Teaching provides a case in point: Released one week before the 1992 presidential election,

Carnegie's findings—harshly critical of vouchers in general and Milwaukee in particular—made Page 1 of the *New York Times*. On Milwaukee, Carnegie was categorical: "Milwaukee's plan has failed to demonstrate that vouchers can, in and of themselves, spark school improvement. . . . Inflated promises have outdistanced reality in Milwaukee." Carnegie's chapter on the Milwaukee voucher program leans heavily on Witte, citing him in six of thirteen footnotes.[3]

The echo effect becomes evident elsewhere. Scratch the surface of almost any criticism of the Milwaukee program, and Witte is often lurking in the footnotes. In a 1994 pamphlet prepared by the Texas State Teachers Association (TSTA) and the National Education Association, titled "Our Public Schools: The Best Choice for Texas," Witte—identified as an independent evaluator—is invoked in a chapter called "The Hollow Promise of Vouchers: The Failed Milwaukee Experiment." A few pages later, to add ballast to TSTA/NEA's antivoucher argument, Witte's criticism is backed up by the influential Carnegie school choice study; no mention is made of Carnegie's reliance on Witte. Having achieved a certain hall-of-mirrors effect, the Texas report concludes: "There is only one publicly funded voucher program in operation. It is confined to the Milwaukee, Wisconsin, school system and by all accounts, after four years, it is a dismal failure."[4]

Witte's work has also found favor with the American Federation of Teachers. Bella Rosenberg, aide to AFT president Al Shanker and the AFT's point person on school choice, refers interlocutors to Witte's reports, which prove, in her words, that "Milwaukee has not made one bit of difference."[5]

Because so much of the criticism of the country's sole voucher experiment can be traced to the work of one researcher—particularly a researcher appointed by Herbert Grover, implacable enemy of Parental Choice—the remainder of this chapter takes a closer look at Witte's findings, as well as the use made of those findings by high-profile critics of school choice.[6]

One month before Grover selected Witte to evaluate the program, the Dane County Circuit Court had upheld Parental Choice, dashing Grover's hopes of strangling it before the first students reported to their new private schools in September 1990. In Witte, Grover turned to an academic with a pronounced and public antipathy toward school choice. In contrast to Grover's bombast, Witte's position was more measured, yet unmistakable. In a 1990 book on choice that he coedited, Witte prophesied that "singular adherence to choice will have us in ten years looking backward on . . . choice as simply another set of failed reforms."[7] Witte's negative views on choice were known outside Wisconsin circles; his antivoucher stance was noted approvingly by the AFT's Al Shanker, in the fall of 1990.[8]

In selecting Witte, Grover did not open the examiner's position to a competitive process; according to George Mitchell, who dissected Witte's First Year Report for the Wisconsin Policy Research Institute, neither Grover nor Witte responded to written requests for a copy of their grant agreement or documents related to the selection process.[9] One can imagine Grover, still smarting from his setback at the hands of Judge Susan Steingass, making his selection with the same objectivity of the sheriff in Old West lore confronting an alleged horse thief: "First we'll have a trial, then we'll hang you."

WITTE'S CHARGES

Surprisingly, Witte's reports have not been so critical as alleged. While his findings remain remarkably constant, his inferences in many respects grow more favorable to Milwaukee's Parental Choice program. Witte's findings fall into three groups, each handled in a different way by voucher critics. In a nutshell, Witte's negative findings have been headlined and hyped; his cautions and caveats unheeded; his positive findings all but ignored.

Consider the following key criticisms that prove upon closer examination to be questionable—many of which Witte modifies or qualifies in subsequent reports but which, a full four years after the fact, form the basis of choice critics' ongoing assault on the Milwaukee program.

Witte Charge: Attrition from Parental Choice Is High

Witte's First Year Report cites it as "perhaps the most troubling aspect" of his research: "Attrition appears to be high." This criticism, while at first glance seemingly peripheral, is potentially damning: How good can the program be if parents pull their kids out of it? Like canaries in a coal mine, parents can be counted on to serve as an early warning system for programs in distress. In a speculation unsupported by any evidence, Witte takes the additional step of linking attrition to achievement, or rather the lack of it: "[I]t is possible that problems in the schools, especially modest achievement gains, could have been a factor."[10]

This proved to be a key line of attack in the 1992 Carnegie report, which ostensibly demonstrated that parents do not really want school choice and seldom use it when it is available. So what of Witte's attrition assertion: Has there been a large exodus out of the Milwaukee program?

The short answer is no. To the extent the allegation of high attrition is valid at all, it is as true or truer for public schools as for Choice schools; to the extent it implies parents voting with their feet against Choice, the data prove nothing of the sort. Indeed, a case can be made that Parental Choice has significantly *lower* attrition than the "background" Central City rate.

The numbers are these: The bulk of the first-year attrition from the Parental Choice program can be traced to the sudden closing of Juanita Virgil Academy five months into Choice's first year in February 1991. Discounting the 63 Juanita Virgil students, 29 children left the Choice schools in the program's first year. That amounts to 10 percent attrition (29/278)—even when the lone alternative, "At Risk" high school in the Parental Choice program, SER–Jobs, is included.[11]

Elsewhere in Witte's First Year Report, a footnote reveals that the SER–Jobs "non-completion" rate for Choice students was 14 of 27.[12] That is, *half* the in-year attrition from the Choice program came from students designated "at risk" for dropping out—the category that Wisconsin law defines as including pregnant teens or teen parents, adjudicated youths, children with drug or disciplinary problems—*before* they began the program. Without SER–Jobs, the Choice attrition rate shrinks to under 6 percent.

The question remains: Can we justify factoring out Juanita Virgil? Again, according to a DPI official charged with overseeing the Choice program, the children from Juanita Virgil were not allowed to transfer to another Choice school; when Juanita Virgil closed, they were simply reassigned to the Milwaukee Public Schools.[13] To count them in any attrition figure is to sanction a strange species of "forced attrition." To his credit, Witte—while he says nothing about the state's administrative diktat to deny reenrollment into Choice schools—separates out the Juanita Virgil experience as a special case.

Not everyone does. The 1992 Carnegie report, for one, saddles Parental Choice with a 40 percent attrition rate. Herbert Grover preferred the same inflated attrition statistic, as does the TSTA/NEA report.[14]

There are other reasons to doubt that attrition is unusually high in the Parental Choice program. Witte does not separate out for economic ineligibility—that is, students who leave Parental Choice because their parents' improved economic circumstances push them past the program's income cutoff of 175 percent of the poverty line. Pressed to account for the number of students scored as "attritions" because their mother or father finds a good job, Witte admits he has not measured this species of attrition, but assures this author it is "minimal." Nor does Witte separate out remarriage, a factor Harvard's Paul Peterson identifies as pivotal in explaining the fluctuating economic circumstances of families. Witte's own reports confirm that three-fourths of Parental Choice families are single-parent homes. A parent's marriage to an employed spouse may well result in students becoming ineligible for vouchers. For these reasons, Peterson states flatly in his comments on Witte's First Year Report: "The attrition rate in the Choice schools is impossible to evaluate."[15]

Finally, how high is high? How does the attrition rate of Parental Choice compare with that of the public schools? According to Witte, the average "mobility rate" in the Milwaukee Public Schools is 33 percent—which, because this does not differentiate between students entering or leaving a school, Witte treats as 16.5 percent movement in and 16.5 percent out. Hence at 10 percent, the Choice program has slightly more than half the attrition rate of MPS; excluding SER–Jobs—just as the MPS rate excludes its own "At Risk" students—the Choice attrition rate drops to *about one-third* the level in the Milwaukee Public Schools. It is difficult, even on the basis of Witte's own evidence, to see how he can sustain the claim that Choice's attrition rate is high.[16]

As for attrition in the public schools, Witte claims no exact figures are available for MPS, hence the necessity of using the 33 percent mobility rate for an estimate. Strangely enough, however, a figure on public school attrition *was* available in the most comprehensive study done to date on metropolitan Milwaukee schools. "Better Public Schools" reported that "attrition rates of 40–50 percent . . . are common across many cities."[17] In this light, Parental Choice's attrition rate is remarkably low. The author of the study? John F. Witte.

Another reviewer might even consider Choice's attrition rate remarkably low for an inner-city program—particularly given the legal cloud hanging over it through two of its first three years.

Peterson, for his part, calculates the in-year attrition rate—excluding "At Risk" students—as being "as low as 3 percent during the third school year and 2 percent during the fourth." Indeed, Peterson concludes,

> [T]here was by the third year no "attrition rate problem" in choice schools during the school year at all. On the contrary, it appears instead as if *choice schools were ten times as effective* as public schools at retaining their students during the school year, when change in school can be most disruptive to a child's education. . . .
>
> If public elementary school year to year turnover rates for low income students are 35 percent, as Witte suggested in his second report, and if choice elementary school turnover rates are now 23 percent, then *public school year to year turnover rates are 52 percent higher than choice turnover rates.*[18]

Even so, as late as his Third Year Report, Witte concludes in his Executive Summary: "By any measure, the private schools are having difficulty retaining students."[19]

Witte goes on to identify what he calls a high "non-return rate"—over-the-summer attrition from the Choice program. Yet again, on closer examination, the Choice nonreturn rate differs little from that in MPS: In the body of his Third Year Report, in language far different from that of his Executive Summary, Witte reports that "Mobility out of Choice schools *may be very close to the norm for MPS;* and . . . for both systems, the data suggests considerable problems."[20]

Indeed, each subsequent year, without withdrawing his charge, Witte moves away from his first-year finding of high attrition; what he has discovered is the high transiency in *all* Central City schools, public *or* private. Calling in his Third Year Report for a separate study of attrition in *public and private* schools in Milwaukee's Central City, Witte grudgingly reports: "Attrition appears to be high *although it is declining.*"[21] In fact, the situation is considerably less dire: As Witte notes in the body of his report, "not counting Juanita Virgil, attrition during the year was *less than MPS in all three years* and is reasonable given the residential mobility of inner-city families."[22]

Yet the damage is done. The initial charge is repeated uncritically as fact, Witte's caveats notwithstanding. For example, the Carnegie report states: "Another disappointing aspect of the Milwaukee program has been the high attrition rate."[23]

Witte Charge: Choice Parents Have Fewer Children and Thus More Time to Invest in Their Education

This finding surfaces for the first time in Witte's Second Year Report: Choice families are smaller, "thus providing an opportunity for parents to focus more on any single child"; or, as Witte puts it in his Third Year Report, permitting a "higher education 'investment' per child."[24] Witte's readers are free to picture a kind of "yuppie effect" at work among the Choice subset of the urban poor—doting parents nurturing their only child.

The import for evaluating the Choice program is clear: If Choice families are indeed a privileged population, then any academic progress on the part of Choice students may be attributable to factors having nothing to do with their Choice school—and everything to do with their favored family circumstances.

In fact, Choice families *are* on average smaller when compared to low-income public school families. Yet 55 percent of the Choice families, according to Witte's statistics, have two or three children; a full 44 percent have *three or more children.*[25] Overall, the average is 2.6 children per Choice family, compared to 2.95 children for all MPS families and 3.24 children for low-income MPS families.[26]

Choice families may be slightly smaller; they are also overwhelmingly single-parent families. Once we notice Witte's finding that Choice families were "much more likely" to be headed by a nonmarried parent, this putative advantage in parental involvement vanishes.[27] It is more than offset by the multiple demands made on a single parent raising two or three children. Despite the smaller average number of children, the ratio of parents to children in Choice families—the only relevant ratio for making inferences about parents concentrating time and resources on their children— is worse than for the average Milwaukee Public Schools family.[28] Witte tells us Choice parents have little money to lavish on their children; his data reveal they also have precious little time.

Again, as in the case of the attrition allegations, critics pick up on Witte's strained suggestion that Choice parents are a specially privileged population.

Carnegie's spin is particularly ingenious. Learning from Witte that Choice mothers have a higher average high school completion rate and college attendance compared to public school mothers, Carnegie leans on this finding to conjure up visions of relatively affluent, well-educated families benefiting from Parental Choice. Yet nowhere does Carnegie report Witte's finding that Choice families have an average annual income of $10,700.[29] It is, to say the least, odd to see such families trotted out to uphold Carnegie's sweeping claim that "School choice works better for some parents than for others. Those with *education, sophistication, and especially the right location* may be able to participate in such programs."[30] Milwaukee's impoverished inner-city Choice parents would be bewildered by the enviable advantages the Carnegie authors attribute to them.

Witte Charge: Achievement Scores Are Inconclusive

For many observers, the success or failure of school choice hinges on hard statistical data: Are Choice students' test scores higher than those of their public school peers?

Measurements of Milwaukee's Parental Choice program began almost immediately; Carnegie's negative judgments, for instance, were based on tests taken when the students had spent just seven to eight months in the program.

In contrast to Choice critics' rush to judgment, Witte's reports on these test data reveal him at his most cautious. After four years, he states, "outcomes . . . remain mixed," and "results are less clear-cut." Choice critics, however, easily twist Witte's neutral assessment into a negative; Albert Shanker asserts: "Private schools are not out-performing public schools."[31]

What can we learn from Witte's score data? Here, the challenge is sifting what data Witte chooses to reveal in his reports.

FRUIT SALAD: CHANGE VERSUS COHORT SCORES

The key in any comparison is to set like against like. Witte's First Year Report falls short of this standard, comparing apples to oranges in what becomes a statistical fruit salad of questionable conclusions. The problem revolves around Witte's use of *change* scores—scores on successive tests taken by the same student; and *cohort* scores—a year-to-year group average, when the group itself consists of a shifting mix of new and old students.

Witte himself makes a strong case for preferring change scores over cohort scores *"for individual students* . . . [as] the most reliable measure of achievement based on test score results."[32] In his Second and Third Year Reports, Witte's endorsement of change scores becomes more insistent: "Because the cohort scores do not report on the same students from year to year, the *only accurate measure of achievement gains and losses* are [*sic*] *change scores.*" In the Third Year, again: "[T]he only accurate measure of achievement gains and losses are [*sic*] change scores."[33]

So why does Witte report cohort scores at all? Stranger still, why does Witte's First Year Report base its findings—findings that reflect negatively on Choice students—on *cohort* scores?

Consider Witte's First Year finding that "Preliminary outcomes . . . were mixed."[34] Close reading shows that Witte bases his finding *not* on whether Choice students have improved their change scores or gained ground on a test group of similarly situated low-income public school students, but on whether Choice students, who began measurably behind their public school counterparts, have caught up to *the average MPS student of all income levels.* Not surprisingly, after just seven to eight months in their new schools, Choice students come up short: "Choice students clearly are not yet on par with the average MPS student in math and reading skills."[35]

The relevant comparison would have been to Choice students' own previous public school scores, their change scores.

Does Witte make such a comparison? He does; characteristically, however, Choice students' change score statistics—for a small group of seventy-six students—appear in a footnote in the First Year Report. Those scores show that measured against public school students in both reading and math, *Choice students narrowed the gap.* In a parenthetical aside within the footnote, Witte drily observes that this finding is "counter to the results" of the *Cohort* Score Table published at the back of the report—the scores that form the basis for his mixed judgment on Choice students' performance.[36]

Still, Witte's assessment is cautious compared with the rush to judgment others made to damn the Choice program. Witte wrote:

> If there is any firm conclusion from these results, and we are not sure if there is much of one, it is that when students begin as far behind as the students apparently did in the first year of this program, *seven or eight months will not produce dramatic changes in test scores.*[37]

Yet Witte's footnotes and fine print did not make it into headlines; witness the *Milwaukee Journal*'s story after the release of Witte's initial review: "Scores Aren't Up Under School Choice."[38]

Years 2 and 3

Again, Witte reports that after two years, "preliminary outcomes . . . were mixed." And again, caveats abound:

There is simply a great deal we do not know about these patterns at this point in time. Although it is not possible to use these data to support a picture of miraculous outcomes occurring in the private schools, the relative comparison to the public schools is not yet clear. . . . We continue to interpret these short-term changes in very small numbers of students with great caution.[39]

Cohort scores in particular are of questionable utility in the second and third years, as Witte makes clear, because of the changing nature of the Choice student cohort: The Choice program drew significantly lower-scoring public school children in the second and third years, and, in the second year especially, when Choice was still under a legal cloud, lost better-than-average students. In other words, the composite Choice student profile was losing ground against the first year group.[40] Witte wisely avoids conclusions based on such a shifting test population.[41]

For *change scores*, Witte reports "the results differ somewhat."[42] On reading scores, the Choice gain from the first year—which Witte assessed as statistically insignificant—is followed by significant declines in years two and three. For MPS low-income students, slight increases in the first and second year give way to a decline in the third—none of which Witte assesses as statistically significant. While MPS students are flatlining, the trend is troubling for Choice.

Math scores, in contrast, yield a slightly more positive picture for Choice students. Both the all-MPS and low-income snapshots show first-year gains in math, second-year scores flat—and third-year a significant decline. For Choice students, according to Witte: "In Math, choice students were essentially the same in the first two years, but recorded a significant *increase* in the third year."[43]

For public schoolers the trend is ominous; for Choice students, optimistic. Yet Witte's regression analysis allows him to scamper back even from a mildly positive finding for Choice students and end his report with the far fuzzier statement: "When we controlled for other relevant variables, however, the effect of being in a Choice school was insignificant."[44] Not surprisingly, in his 1994 column, it is this sentence AFT's Al Shanker stripped out to characterize the Milwaukee program.

Year 4

Once again, "outcomes remain mixed"; once again, the snapshot permitted by change scores compared to cohort scores "differ[s] somewhat."[45]

Yet even around Witte's carefully phrased conclusions, the concrete is beginning to harden. "For all groups [Choice and both MPS samples] reading scores effectively did not change." For Choice students, however, "after a large math increase in 1993, there was a decline of 2 NCE [normal curve equivalent] points in 1994."[46]

In fact, Choice students' two-point decline comes off of an average math score of 44.0 NCE—a score eclipsed only once in the four years surveyed, and then only by the all-MPS sample.[47]

Without claiming that this is in itself a sign of superior achievement, it is interesting to note that Witte's method of reporting plus-or-minus NCE change rather than NCEs alone obscures Choice students' comparatively high math achievement scores. No one consulting Witte's graphs at the front of the statistical tables in the Fourth Year Report, with their plunging bar for Choice math achievement, would know that Choice students' math "decline" left them *above* the low-income MPS math score, and 0.7 points behind the all-MPS score.[48]

This performance was all the more remarkable given the academic achievement profile of the average Choice student. Choice students began the race well behind the starting line:

> In all four years, ITBS [Iowa Test of Basic Skills] scores taken in prior public schools by students applying to the Choice Program were significantly below [that of] the average MPS student taking the same test. The scores were also below [those

of] the low-income MPS cohort in each year. . . . The latest
year prior scores for 1993–94 [in other words, the fourth-year
group] were lower than the previous year for both tests. Based
on median scores, they were very low on math and similar to
prior years on reading. . . .
   In short, the choice students in this program enter very near the
bottom in terms of academic achievement.[49]

   In any case, Witte acknowledges the "key test" is the "longitudinal effect of being in the Choice Program . . . 1, 2, 3, or 4 years," a
factor obscured by tables that aggregate data for constantly shifting
groups of students entering the program in different years with different degrees of prior achievement. Here,

   [t]he fourth year is *inconclusive* because of small changes in test
   scores for all groups, *but it appears that the advanced choice stu-*
   dents did better than the first-year students. Thus there is some
   mixed and relatively weak evidence that students who remain in
   these schools do better than students who do not.[50]

   "When the impact of factors which in part control for those
changes [is] taken into account, there are no significant differences
in the achievement gains between choice and MPS students in
1994." Witte's regression analysis once again smoothes away any
ripples in the data: "Thus as with last year's conclusion, it appears
that choice and MPS students do not differ in any predictable way
on achievement tests over the first four years of the Choice program." And, finally, in the words of Witte's conclusion: "[A]chieve-
ment [for Choice students], as measured by standardized tests, was
no different than the achievement of MPS students."[51]

SECOND OPINIONS

   While outside researchers, including even the Wisconsin Legislative Audit Bureau (LAB), are limited to reviewing the data Witte
reveals to them, not all reach Witte's conclusions.

Paul Peterson, in particular, deems Witte's reports "methodologically flawed," "based on procedures that fail to comply with basic principles of evaluation research," and "biased against finding choice schools effective." Witte's regression controls—the screen so useful in rubbing away the occasional hint that Choice might be benefiting its students—come in for a scathing critique: Peterson cites seven specific student characteristics omitted from Witte's regressions.[52]

Failure to control for native language, for instance—given the fact that the second-largest Choice school, Bruce-Guadalupe, is heavily Hispanic and officially bilingual—skews results against Choice students. The Choice student population, Witte's data indicate, is twice as likely to be Hispanic as the average or low-income MPS sample;[53] at Bruce-Guadalupe, nearly two-thirds of the school's Hispanic students speak English as a second language.[54] MPS test data do not include tests of ESL students. Indeed, Peterson relies on Witte himself to underscore the importance of language proficiency in test results, quoting Witte's First Year Report: "Students with poor English reading skills may also do worse on math and on other tests."[55]

In fact, even change scores—the scores Witte himself, in accord with research conventions, identifies as the most accurate measure of achievement—are suspect. Witte's Choice change score sample disguises the fact that the group lumps together students with just one change score (prior–post years) and those with several (Choice "veterans"); that attrition and new arrivals alter the sample each year in a manner similar to—and just as damaging to their reliability as—what happens to cohort scores;[56] and finally, that the MPS and low-income MPS samples, because the students in them move up one grade each year, measure an increasingly test-savvy group of students against a Choice group the bulk of which is enrolled in kindergarten to third grade.[57]

In fact, as the LAB audit reveals, of the 733 students in Choice's fourth year, just 145 had been in the program three or more years, only 57 since the program began and, of those, only 29 had been tested in all four years. Moreover, the LAB audit reports that 61.1 percent of the Choice students entering the fifth year of the program were in grades K to 3. For the LAB auditors, this fact is significant: "[T]he young age of a majority of participants and the limited time most participants have been in the program make it difficult for the program to have demonstrated significant gains in student achievement thus far."[58]

Witte, too, was well aware that many if not a majority of Choice students are concentrated in the early grades, having entered the Choice program as kindergartners.[59] What Witte therefore calls the "last test" in a student's file may be for many of the predominantly young Choice students their "first and only" test, most likely taken in second grade. Measuring changes in such early grades, with children engaged in their first encounter with "pencil and paper" testing, may make results less reliable. Witte's own words put it best: "It is extremely difficult to measure outcomes or achievement for children at those ages."[60] Yet this is precisely what Witte's reports go on to do.

While Witte's data do not permit such a calculation to be made, the LAB's chart of "Choice Students, By Grade, All Schools" makes it possible to assay an estimate of the number of Choice students in Year 5 for whom their last change score is in reality their *only* change score, based on measuring their first two achievement tests, in second and third grade.[61] Following Witte's observation that the testing years are typically grades 2, 5, 7, and 10—and also following his practice of throwing out tenth-grade scores[62]—as many as 152 of the 335 Choice students between third and eighth grade would be judged by their first and only change score. In other words, 45 percent of all Choice student change scores would be based on a student's first and second experience taking achievement tests, in the second and third grades.

In the end, the LAB audit found that

> Professor Witte's conclusion that there is no difference between
> the academic performance of students in choice schools and

> [the academic performance of students] in MPS schools . . . is stronger than can be supported by the limited data available. In fact, no conclusion can be drawn because too few students have provided test results over too short a period of time.[63]

Even so, the Legislative Audit Bureau offered an alternative interpretation of Choice achievement sharply at odds with Witte's:

> [I]f students experiencing problems make up a significant portion of all other [post-kindergarten] students, then achievement test scores . . . showing choice students holding even with MPS students' scores could be considered to show program success.[64]

REFUSENIKS

However inconclusive or incomplete these early assessments may be, the final question regarding test data is *whether Witte is studying the right group at all*. Clearly, comparisons of Choice students to MPS students of all income levels are suspect—which is why Witte shifts in his Second, Third, and Fourth Year Reports to a comparison between Choice students and a subset of low-income public school students.

Yet suppose Witte were to compare Choice students with a group of public school students identical in all important respects—even including their desire to transfer to a Choice school—and differing only in that there was insufficient room in the Choice program to allow these students in. These refused students, continuing on in public school, would be a near-perfect control group against which to gauge Choice students' progress.

In his 1990 letter to Superintendent Grover acknowledging his appointment, Witte himself promised to study precisely this group.[65] As late as his Third Year Report, he had not done so—in spite of the fact that, as several telltale footnotes and appendices in his Second and Third Year Reports attest, he apparently had access to the refused students and their scores.[66] That changed in the

Fourth Year Report.[67] Suddenly, the Choice refuseniks emerge as a group, with Witte accounting for their earlier absence with a kind of researcher's reticence, claiming that deficiencies in the sample size were not overcome until the fourth year.[68]

Yet, the claim that the refusenik cohort was too small is undercut by the fact that Witte had been teasing conclusions from data on Choice students from samples as small as 84 and 88 students as early as Year 2.[69] At that time, there were already 314 refuseniks.[70] Witte's reason for suppressing the refusenik data until Year 4 does not square with his willingness to publish and interpret far smaller subsets throughout the Choice study.

Stranger still is Witte's evident haste to usher these students into and out of the spotlight after their long-awaited appearance in Year 4. Recalling the phrase he had used in the Grover appointment letter about the "unique research opportunity," we might expect Witte to publish detailed year-by-year NCEs and change scores alongside—or indeed in place of—those of the low-income MPS group that served as Witte's stand-in for the prodigal refuseniks.[71] Instead, Witte offers a single, composite chart, with score differentials that cannot be derived from the data at hand. Witte's convenient conclusion: "There was no difference in terms of achievement between those who got into the program and those who did not. . . . These findings exactly parallel the differences noted between choice and our MPS random sample control group."[72]

Whether there is more to the story of the refuseniks remains a mystery. As with all of the data gathered under the exclusive arrangement between the DPI and its chosen examiner, we know only what Witte tells us.

As the Choice program matures and Choice students move through the pipeline, examiners will doubtless shift their attention from achievement tests to graduation rates. As originally designed—and as the vain attempt of Messmer High School served to illustrate—the Parental Choice program carried within itself a structural obstacle to success: Like a bridge that ends midway across the river, Parental Choice could not carry its students to their goal so long as it lacked a high school. For this reason, Choice's expansion to include religious schools looms as pivotal to the program's success.

Access to private Choice high schools would make moot the current wrangle over change scores and conventions of statistical significance. A program from which 90 percent of inner-city students graduate—compared to a public school population where only 40 percent do—would remove any remaining doubt as to whether school choice "works."

Yet, here again, the fate of Parental Choice may rest with the courts. Should voucher opponents succeed in litigating away the legislature's expansion, few if any of the children in Parental Choice would be able to afford private high school tuition. Milwaukee's Choice program would then be judged on its "graduates'" success rate in surviving reentry into a Milwaukee public high school from which—to cite one sobering statistic—African-American students have just a one in four chance of graduating.[73]

CHAPTER ELEVEN

Eliminate the Positive

If many of Witte's negative conclusions that critics find so quotable are in fact questionable, another group of Witte's findings are solid—and surprisingly friendly to school choice. Not so surprisingly, voucher critics who eagerly invoke Witte's reviews to blast Milwaukee's experiment remain silent on the positive findings in his reports.

What makes this omission all the more interesting is the fact that Witte's positive findings explode some of the most serious charges leveled against school choice.

Myth #1: Choice Will Hurt Minorities

It is a constant refrain of voucher critics: Choice will help those who need help least and further harm the disadvantaged—especially minorities. Witte's findings, interestingly, point to precisely the opposite conclusion: Milwaukee's program has been disproportionately popular with minority families.

Through the first four years of Parental Choice, an average of 92 percent of all children receiving Choice vouchers were African-American or Hispanic—a percentage well above their presence in the Milwaukee public schools.[1]

Witte's evidence provides ample proof that Choice families are in fact not only below the program's cutoff of 175 percent of the poverty line, but are among the poorest of the poor:

- Of Choice families, 57 percent were on AFDC or general assistance.

- Seventy-six percent were single-parent households.

- For 1990 through 1993, the average income of Choice families was $11,630—*half* that of the average Milwaukee Public Schools family, itself hovering near the low-income line. In a city where poverty is widespread, Choice families are among the most impoverished.[2]

The positive impact for minorities is reflected in the Milwaukee media. The daily newspapers, the *Journal* and the *Sentinel*, consistently editorialized against Parental Choice; only the tiny African-American *Milwaukee Community Journal* came out in support of it.

Myth #2: Choice Will Lead to Resegregated Schools

Once again, the AFT's Albert Shanker takes a typical approach when he writes of Milwaukee: "With few exceptions, students ended up in segregated schools with an ethnocentric educational program." Shanker's studied vagueness is anything but unintentional; his words evoke images of the Old South's Freedom of Choice plans, which used vouchers to help white families dodge court-ordered desegregation.[3]

Closer to home, the Milwaukee-based *Rethinking Schools*, a self-styled "independent education journal" whose masthead nonetheless includes a number of past and present officers of the Milwaukee Teachers Education Association, echoes Shanker's image of segregated schools employing vouchers. In the lead essay of *False Choices: Why School Vouchers Threaten Our Children's Future*, a thirty-two-page pamphlet published by *Rethinking Schools* and distributed by the National Education Association in its packages of antivoucher material, *Rethinking School*'s editor, Robert Lowe, writes: "The first choice program provided white students in Virginia public funds in order to attend private academies in order to avoid attending public schools with blacks."[4]

Lowe's reference is to the infamous example of Prince Edward County in the insurrectionary years after the Supreme Court's *Brown v. Board of Education* decision. Rather than comply with court-ordered desegregation, the county closed its public schools for five years and issued students vouchers for private schools.

The objective of Lowe and Shanker, apparently, is to taint the very idea of vouchers by portraying it as inherently racist. On closer examination, however, their history lessons prove nothing. In Georgia, for instance, an old statute enacted to circumvent desegregation through the use of vouchers slumbered unnoticed and unused on the state law books for thirty years. Rediscovered in 1993 by a black state senator and a white legal activist, the Jim Crow–era statute was invoked by Georgia parents—this time African-Americans—to obtain vouchers so that their children could escape the public schools. Even Lowe admits in a footnote that Prince Edward County's vouchers were available to black students as well as to whites.

But what about the claim that vouchers lead to resegregation? Again, in contrast to Choice critics like Shanker who twist the truth, Witte emphatically exonerates Parental Choice. While Choice schools such as Harambee and Urban Day stress African-American culture, and Bruce-Guadalupe puts a special emphasis on bilingualism, Witte finds no evidence of "teaching cultural superiority or separatism."[5] In contrast to the "intense debate" created by this type of cultural emphasis around the country, Witte finds that "in these schools the approach seemed positive."

In all, Witte finds the Choice program fosters *diversity*—an ideal otherwise dear to the public education establishment, but inconvenient when it comes as a consequence of school vouchers. Witte writes: "The student bodies of participating [Choice] schools vary from schools that are almost all one minority race, to racially integrated schools, to schools that have used the program to diversify their almost all White student bodies."[6] This finding, like others encountered by Choice critics, is inconvenient—and thus ignored.

Myth #3: Choice Schools Will Skim the Cream

Again, the AFT's Shanker serves to state the charge: "If private schools can pick and choose the most promising students . . . what are the prospects for providing equal education opportunity to the children left behind?" Shanker is quick to answer his own rhetorical question: Allow school choice, and public schools will be filled with the children of "the indigent . . . cared for in the educational equivalent of charity wards."[7] Again, seconding Shanker, the editors of Milwaukee's *Rethinking Schools* conjure an image of Choice schools siphoning off the public system's best and brightest: Voucher schools would become "islands of excellence for the already privileged."[8]

For the editors of *Rethinking Schools*, well aware that Milwaukee's Parental Choice program was limited to families at or below 175 percent of the poverty line, the notion that the North and South Side Milwaukee families receiving vouchers were members of a socioeconomic elite marks that publication's determination never to let reality stand in the way of rhetoric.

Even so, *Rethinking Schools'* rush to condemn Choice begets a certain schizophrenia. In the very same issue, Lowe, for instance, recounts the saga of Juanita Virgil and observes: "Like nineteenth-century charity schools, such [voucher] schools would compose the bottom tier of an educational hierarchy based on privilege."[9]

The result is typical of the grab-bag of anti-Choice arguments appearing in *False Choices:* Some critics say vouchers will create a sink pool of substandard charity schools; others claim vouchers will constitute a special preserve for the privileged. For *Rethinking Schools,* the inconsistency hardly matters: Either way, vouchers are bad.

So is there truth to the charge? Has Parental Choice drawn the cream of the crop into private schools, leaving public schools the dregs? Again, Witte's data shatter this cherished myth: "[Choice] students were not succeeding in the MPS and probably had higher than average behavioral problems. . . . In short, the choice students in this program enter very near the bottom in terms of academic achievement." As Witte puts it in his Fourth Year Report: "The students in the Choice Program were not the best, or even average students from the Milwaukee system."[10]

On average, at the time of entry into the program Choice children were more likely to underperform their counterparts in the public schools—and were more likely than their peers to have had a history of behavior-related problems in their old public schools. As early as his First Year Report, Witte's own words could hardly be more categorical: "Rather than skimming off the best students, this program seems to provide an alternative educational environment for students who are not doing particularly well in the public school system." His Second Year Report stated:

> One of the most striking and consistent conclusions from the first two years is that the program is offering opportunities for a private-school alternative to poor families *whose children were not succeeding in school.* This is a positive outcome of the program.[11]

In the end, even *Rethinking Schools'* Lowe feels compelled to admit a positive outcome for Parental Choice:

> In the face of [public schools'] miserable average grades and appalling suspension and dropout rates, [Polly] Williams has enabled a small number of students to seek an education elsewhere—partly in community-based schools that have long served African-Americans and Hispanics. Under the circumstances it makes little sense to berate the program for violating the ideal of the common school or the goal of an integrated

society. Such unrealized visions are inadequate justifications for denying a few children a potential opportunity to pursue an education of value. As advocates of choice are quick to point out, the Milwaukee program gives some options to low-income families that the well-to-do have long exercised, and virtually no one challenges the right of the privileged to either move to their schools of choice in the suburbs or to attend public schools.[12]

Is it possible Parental Choice is having a positive impact? Consider these findings on parental involvement—a factor often associated with superior student achievement:

> [T]he findings ... are consistent across three years: They [Parental Choice parents] have high parental involvement coming into the schools and even higher involvement once there. ...
>
> The bottom line of this report is a recommendation to continue the program for at least several more years. ...
>
> Despite some problems and difficulties, engendered both by the uncertainty of the program's future (because of court challenges) and by limited demonstrated educational success to date, it is clear this program continues to offer opportunities otherwise unavailable to some Milwaukee parents. ...
>
> [Parents] were seeking a better learning environment, with a better disciplinary climate. They turned to the private schools in the hope of finding that environment. ...
>
> [Parents] who responded to our surveys believe they found in the Choice schools what they professed they were looking for when they entered the program—increased learning and discipline. ...
>
> The Choice program was targeted to provide an opportunity for relatively poor families to attend private schools. In the first three years the program has clearly accomplished this goal. ...
>
> To the extent that this purpose of the program was to create these opportunities, the program is succeeding.[13]

Who is the researcher whose reports paint such a positive portrait of Milwaukee Parental Choice?

John F. Witte.

WHAT PARENTS KNOW

The portrait that emerges from the Witte reports is one of a still skeptical reviewer, gradually warming to a program—a reviewer far more cautious than the critics who champion his work. The fact remains, however, that Witte's own data often war with the bumper sticker conclusions Choice critics find so easy to manipulate and magnify.

All of this is good reason for Wisconsin to end Witte's effective evaluation monopoly and open Parental Choice to a truly competitive review process—a wall-to-wall comparison of change scores, with careful methodological controls for nonschool factors and a consistent approach to control groups. Until such an independent examination occurs, we will continue to witness what has become business as usual: The anti-Choice public education establishment using Witte's work as convenient scholarly cover, dipping into his data in selective ways to condemn school choice in ways even Witte's reports do not.

Among the findings in Witte's reports is a survey on parental satisfaction: "Respondents almost unanimously agreed the [Choice] program should continue (99% in 1991; and 97% in the respective [second and third] years)." In Parental Choice's fourth year, the figure reached 98.7 percent.[14] Even more impressive, this enthusiasm reached to parents who, for whatever reason, withdrew their children from the program.

Witte's response? He drops the parental satisfaction chart after his First Year Report.

In the end, even Choice's critics ought to be unsettled by the fascinating paradox they claim to have found in Witte's studies of Parental Choice: Why is a program so inconclusive in terms of test scores so beloved by parents?

One obvious hypothesis would be that Milwaukee's Choice parents are dolts or dupes—an explanation the AFT's Shanker hints at when he writes of parents "pushed or seduced" into accepting a voucher program;[15] Witte, to his credit, resists such a slanderous explanation—perhaps because his own data demonstrate that Choice mothers in particular have more than the average levels of education.

Then again, another hypothesis suggests itself as to why Choice parents think so highly of the program: Perhaps Parental Choice parents aren't simply more educated; maybe they are smarter, too.

Epilogue:
Class Notes

If the government's not going to do it, you have to take charge
and do it yourself.
—*parent from Cleveland's Hough neighborhood*
at a school choice rally in Columbus, Ohio

On July 26, 1995, Wisconsin governor Tommy Thompson con-
vened a signing celebration for the bill expanding Parental Choice
to religious schools. The ceremony took place in the basement gym-
nasium of Messmer High School; Brother Bob Smith received a
souvenir signing pen.

Eric Ransom found the transition from North Division to college
more difficult than he'd imagined; after less than a year, he dropped
out of Marquette, giving up his scholarship. Sensing that he needed
some distance from Milwaukee, Ransom transferred to Jackson
State in Mississippi, not far from his grandmother's home, where he
is working toward his degree.

In June, Messmer High School graduated forty-six students out
of the forty-eight seniors in its Class of 1995; the remaining two enrolled in summer school in order to earn the credits necessary to
graduate by August. Forty-one of the forty-six graduates are going

directly to college, a ribbon of names running down Messmer's entryway wall.

On June 30, 1995, school choice won its second victory, this time in Cleveland, Ohio. Backed by a Republican–urban Democratic coalition reminiscent of Wisconsin's Thompson–Williams alliance, the Cleveland pilot program promised vouchers worth $2,225 each to 1,500 low-income children, for use at any private school, religious or nonsectarian.[1]

Cleveland's voucher program was a victory for City Councilwoman Fannie Lewis, a Democrat representing the Hough district that still bears the scars of the 1968 riots. In January, Lewis had invited Polly Williams to come to Hough to share her strategy and light a fire under Lewis's constituents. In a page torn from the Milwaukee playbook, Lewis organized busloads of 300 Cleveland parents to descend on the statehouse in Columbus.[2]

"You didn't come down here to beg, you came down here to tell people what you want," Lewis told the rally. "This is serious business." Said one Hough parent who had brought his five-year-old daughter on the bus to the Columbus rally: "If the government's not going to do it, you have to take charge and do it yourself."

Voucher opponents vowed a lawsuit.

"If you let it happen here, it can happen anywhere," Congressman Louis Stokes, an opponent of vouchers, warned. "The whole nation is watching us to see whether we allow it."[3]

With summer ending, Sabrina Davis prepared for sixth grade at Urban Day. Lonzetta Davis had a baby girl. She'd left work on maternity leave; with money tight, she hoped in several years to take advantage of the expanded Choice program to enroll Sabrina in one of Milwaukee's Lutheran high schools.

Tragedy has also touched the Davises. Sabrina's older brother, Vonzell, collapsed and died while playing basketball on a church outing. He was sixteen. The coroner discovered a heart condition; his mother, still numbed at the suddenness of it, says, "It was the first we heard of it." Vonzell, his mother says, had finally hit his stride in high school, staying eligible for football and basketball, excelling in his carpentry classes at Milwaukee Tech.

Lonzetta Davis had been following the news accounts of the battle to expand Parental Choice. She knew the schools were looking for parents to step forward for the inevitable lawsuit; she wished them well, but allowed she was not inclined to volunteer: "I've done my bit."[4]

During the 1995 legislative session in Texas, a voucher bill fell short. In Connecticut, that state's Republican governor inexplicably pulled back a bill that would have allowed local districts to opt for vouchers. In Illinois, a pilot choice program for 2,000 Chicago children passed the State Senate but stalled on the House floor. In Pennsylvania, the political allies of the public teachers' unions rallied to defeat Republican Governor Tom Ridge's broad-based $42 million voucher bill for poverty-line families; in the fall legislative session, Ridge came back with a targeted choice plan, aimed at low-income families in Pennsylvania's larger counties and cities.[5]

Antivoucher forces celebrated the string of defeats with an underlying sense of unease. Over the years, they had grown accustomed to picking off the odd voucher initiative with a massive concentration of political force and funding; now, the battle seemed to be breaking out on many fronts at once. "Predictable as crabgrass," groused the National Education Association's house organ, *NEA Today*, "school voucher initiatives just keep sprouting up across the country."

Accompanying the warning: an NEA battle map, listing twelve states plus the District of Columbia where voucher bills would be introduced in 1996.[6]

Regis Chesir is now nearly 6 feet 4, with a size 14 shoe. During the summer, he enrolled in the Science and Math Program at

Marquette, studying robotics, biology, chemistry, and statistics. His mother, Regina, read in the paper that more than three-fourths of MPS seniors failed a math proficiency test, meaning they will have to settle for GEDs instead of diplomas.[7] Now she's worried that Regis's 3.5 GPA may mean less than she'd assumed.

Pleased with Regis's progress at Rufus King High School, she nevertheless planned to start the year with a visit to her son's counselor. She remembers when she was in school how smart the kids from the Lutheran high schools used to be: "Always got the best grades. Always wrote the best papers." She knows some Lutheran high schools are planning to get into Parental Choice. "We're happy with Rufus King, but if I have to take him out, I will," Mrs. Chesir says.

"All options are open."

On August 1, six days after Governor Thompson signed the bill at Messmer, the Milwaukee Teachers Education Association and People for the American Way filed suit against the expanded Parental Choice program.[8] Less than a week later, the American Civil Liberties Union launched a companion suit, joining the MTEA in seeking an immediate injunction to halt the awarding of any vouchers for the coming school year.[9] Within twenty-four hours, a group called Parents for School Choice, represented by Clint Bolick, petitioned to intervene in the case.

The start of the new school year was less than four weeks away.

Enrollment had declined at St. Matthew, from 150 students two years earlier to 115. In July, several weeks after the Wisconsin legislature voted to allow St. Matthew and Milwaukee's other religious schools into the Choice program, Sister Leonius Skaar hadn't yet calculated how many seats she'd have open in the higher grades. Space, she observed, shouldn't be a problem: "These days, we always have room."

Sister planned to phone each St. Matthew family to let them know about the expanded Choice program, and to help them register if they were eligible. She also worried about the lawsuit looming over the new program.

"People here are excited," Sister admitted. Yet excitement is an emotion that doesn't quite sit right with Sister Leonius. "To tell you the truth, you know, I didn't think it would happen."[10]

Passage of the expansion so close to the start of the school year set in motion a hurried, administratively ad hoc transition. Public education authorities, focused on the start of their own school year the day after Labor Day, seemed not to notice that some of the city's private schools would open their doors as early as the third week of August. At the private religious schools that had opted in to the Choice program, a kind of naive optimism prevailed; word went out that even if the voucher payments would not arrive until late September, voucher students would be welcome for the start of classes.

So it was that Monday, August 21, marked a milestone in the maelstrom history of church–state and school relations. At fourteen religious schools across Milwaukee, voucher students reported for the first day of class, with nothing more than a figurative IOU from the Wisconsin state treasury to pay their tuition. By Wednesday, with more schools opening, 375 voucher students were in attendance. By week's end, the number reached 1,000.

The news came Friday afternoon, August 25. The Wisconsin Supreme Court handed down a one-sentence order: The planned expansion of Parental Choice to religious schools was enjoined, pending the outcome of the lawsuit. The fact that the state's highest court had agreed to hear the trial expeditiously, cutting at least a year off the inevitable appeals process, was small consolation to Choice supporters. The vouchers on which so many schoolchildren had pinned their hopes had vanished.

Voucher opponents exulted. MPS board president Mary Bills "smiled when she turned on the news and learned of the preliminary injunction"; Mordecai Lee, head of the Wisconsin Coalition for Public Education—the self-styled "grassroots" citizens' organization that included MPS, the state Department of Public Instruction, both of Wisconsin's statewide public teachers' unions (WEAC and WFT), and the ACLU—hailed the ruling as "the first piece of good news" since the expansion of Parental Choice was included in the governor's budget.[11]

Word spread quickly through the private school community. Administrators at a score of private religious schools grappled with the realization that the children they'd admitted would not be able to pay tuition; thousands more families preparing to send their children to Choice schools the next week learned their children were stranded.

Brother Bob Smith recalls the chaos at Messmer. "It was panic. The phone was ringing off the hook, parents calling to see if it was true—and what it meant." One call in particular stood out for Smith: "It was a grandmother. She promised to come in every morning, answer phones, help around the office, do anything, just as long as we promised not to put her grandchild out of school."

Pilar Gonzales, mother of three school-age children with a fourth still at home, remembers the Friday the injunction was handed down. "I was in tears. We all knew the court could do it. You try to prepare, but you can't prepare."

As a member of Parents for School Choice and a petitioner in the court case, Gonzales had given many parents her phone number with instructions to call with questions or concerns. As news of the injunction spread Friday night, the calls to Pilar Gonzales came one after the other. "That's when I realized how many parents were hurt."

News reached Dan McKinley, executive director of Partners Advancing Values in Education, Milwaukee's privately funded school choice program, at PAVE's offices on Milwaukee's North Side. McKinley talked with a friend at a school that had voted in the wake of the enlarged voucher program to expand its kindergarten-only program to serve grades K–3. "After the injunction," the PAVE director recalls, "the new teachers were discussing how long they could work with no pay."

PAVE, which used its private funds to pay a half-share of tuition for students who met the same income eligibility guidelines as those for Parental Choice, had secured funding of $1.6 million for the school year just started. Judging from the number of students dislocated by the court injunction, McKinley estimated it would take another $1.6 million to pay even PAVE's half-share of their collective tuition. If the funds couldn't be raised by Labor Day, the families displaced by the court's ruling—by definition families with incomes no higher than 175 percent of the poverty line—would have little choice but to send their children back to MPS.

As an accomplished fundraiser, McKinley, PAVE's one and only paid staff member, knew the kind of work it took to raise $1.6 million dollar by dollar over fifty-two weeks.

This time, he had a week and a half.

"Injunction Forces Some Parents to Change Plans Quickly": Above the Saturday *Milwaukee Journal Sentinel*'s[12] front-page story appeared a photo of a mother, her daughter, and the niece under her care who would be out of school; the faces of the stoical mother and sorrowful girls offered mute testimony to the tragedy that had befallen them.

PAVE's McKinley got a phone call from Sister Monica, principal of St. Joan Antida, a Catholic high school for girls. "Sister Monica told me, 'I just got a call from a man who said he'd pay the tuition for the two girls in the picture.'"

Someone else called PAVE offering to pay five children's tuition. In an envelope, McKinley found a check from an elderly couple—

$52 sent to commemorate their fifty-second wedding anniversary. Something was happening. McKinley started to work the phones.

Sunday morning's news seemed to echo the previous day's pessimism: "Choice Schools in Disarray," announced the *Journal Sentinel*. Yet beneath the headline, the piece went on to report something in marked contrast to Friday's panic: The schools were turning away no one.

Once again, PAVE proved to be a more accurate barometer of community sentiment. As Dan McKinley planned a Tuesday morning news conference, to be held at Holy Redeemer Christian Academy with Mayor Norquist and a number of religious leaders, he took a call from an official with the Milwaukee Chamber of Commerce, donating $120,000. Monday morning, McKinley hurried into his office at 8 o'clock to find the phone ringing; it was local businessman Richard Burke. "He said, 'Dan, I'm at O'Hare,'" McKinley recalls. Burke, en route to Southeast Asia on business, told the PAVE director: "I'm boarding in a minute, but I'm calling right now just to tell you a check's on the way to your office for $100,000." Several hours later, a caller promised McKinley a $100,000 anonymous donation. Dick Abdoo of Wisconsin Electric, coping with power line damage caused by a late summer electrical storm, took a minute to call and pledge $100,000. Businessman Mike Cudahy followed with another $100,000.

With the news conference scheduled for the next day, McKinley had pledges of more than $500,000. Wednesday night, once more back at the Holy Redeemer Church with hundreds of mostly African-American parents and children in attendance, McKinley learned the Bradley Foundation would add $800,000 outright, and $200,000 more in matching funds. Pastor Sedgwick Daniels captured the shift in momentum and offered a message to the ACLU and MTEA: "You're picking on a giant that's bigger than you are. . . . My advice to them is to quit while they're behind."[13]

It was August 30, five days since the injunction.

McKinley pulled together his phone lists. With two days until Labor Day weekend, he had to get the word out to more than 2,000 students across the city. Their place in private school was safe, at least for the coming school year.

The expansion of school choice coincided with the increased estrangement of Polly Williams from the movement she had mobilized. Rumblings of Williams's discontent came during the spring legislative offensive; warning signs came in July. At the bill-signing ceremony at Messmer, Williams was a no-show; her office gave out that Williams was tending an ailing family member in Madison. After the injunction was granted in late August, Williams missed the rally at Holy Redeemer. When former Education Secretaries William J. Bennett and Lamar Alexander appeared in Milwaukee for a September 4 Choice rally, again Polly Williams was absent. "It appears," she told a reporter, "they're trying to diminish my role in this choice initiative."[14]

For Polly Williams, the distance between politics and pique has always been narrow. More than once since her masterly performance pushing Parental Choice through the legislature in 1990 had she distanced herself from her allies, only to resume the fight. Said Bennett at the Milwaukee rally, "I hope she'll get back in the fray. She's a great voice, a great witness."

In the District of Columbia, Wisconsin Republican Congressman Steve Gunderson, charged by Speaker of the House Newt Gingrich, fashioned a voucher program for low-income District residents. Provision for a Milwaukee-style program—3,000 vouchers for poverty-line families—was built into the House version of federal budget legislation. As wrangling between the White House and the Congress led to a budget standoff in the fall of 1995, the provision remained in the House legislation. Speaker Gingrich has vowed that whatever compromises may come, vouchers for District students must be part of the final bill.

"MPS May Let Parents Choose," read the headline of a *Milwaukee Journal Sentinel* story in late October 1995. "Parents have told us this is what they want, and now we are in a position to make a positive change," said school board president and voucher opponent Mary Bills. Was it a tactical move to position the public schools for the upcoming court arguments—or the first glimmer of evidence that private school vouchers can in fact leverage change in the *public* schools?

Seven hundred miles away from Milwaukee, Clint Bolick prepares for a return to the courtroom. "We're starting in the [Wisconsin] Supreme Court, which probably shaves a year off the timetable." Since the 1992 ruling in favor of the original Parental Choice program, two judges who ruled for it have since left the bench; one who ruled against is gone. "So of the original 4–3 court," says Bolick, "it's 2–2—with three new judges."

Bolick views the case as a chance to put Parental Choice squarely in the line of *Mueller*, *Witters*, and *Zobrest*. "This is what we've been working towards for a very long time," Bolick says. "There has never been a clearer constitutional test of a voucher plan."

Win or lose, "if the ruling turns on the First Amendment issues," Bolick predicts, "we'll be in the Supreme Court for oral argument in the fall of 1996, with a decision by 1997."[15]

The fallout from a defeat in the U.S. high court, Bolick concedes, is impossible to predict. An adverse ruling could devastate Choice, or merely point the way for a retooled program that would pass constitutional muster.

For voucher opponents seeking to litigate away what the legislature had passed, challenging Milwaukee's Parental Choice program could prove a strategic error of staggering proportions. Seeking to destroy vouchers in one state, they risk a U.S. Supreme Court decision validating vouchers for the nation.

Pilar Gonzales has filed an affidavit; she's ready to make the trip from her South Side neighborhood to Madison to testify before the Wisconsin Supreme Court. "No matter what, I'm going to be there for the case. There ought to be a place for the parents to get their say."

Gonzales has a friend who belongs to the ACLU. "We argue about the case all the time. I always ask, 'Do you really think the biggest thing we've got to worry about in school is our kids coming in contact with religion?'" Gonzales recounts.

"Because if that's what you think," she says with a snort of laughter, "you don't spend much time in MPS."

Gonzales and her husband have just made the first of the monthly payments that will keep their youngest two children in private school. For the year, tuition will total almost $1,800. With winter approaching, the cost is coming home to her; "that's about the same amount as our heating bill." She and her husband have worked out a way to survive this school year. If they win the court case, vouchers will be there for next fall.

"I have so much hope that it will go through. My feeling is so strong: There's just so many kids depending on this."

Notes

Introduction: Milwaukee As Microscosm

1. *Milwaukee Journal*, February 17, 1994.

2. *Milwaukee Sentinel*, January 13, 1994.

3. Department of School Safety, Milwaukee Public Schools (MPS), 1992–93, as quoted in Susan Mitchell, "Why MPS Doesn't Work," Wisconsin Policy Research Institute Report, January 1994, p. 44, n. 109.

4. MPS Division of School Safety, letter of December 2, 1993.

5. National Center for Education Statistics, *Digest of Education Statistics* (NCES 93-292), U.S. Department of Education, 1993, Table 92, p. 103. The rankings include countywide school districts as well as city systems.

6. The Council of the Great City Schools, "National Urban Education Goals: Baseline Indicators, 1990–91" (1992), pp. 166, 219.

7. Ibid., p. 166.

8. 1990–91, GCS's most recent year for membershipwide measurement. Milwaukee led with a 16.1 percent dropout rate. Council of Great City Schools, p. 166; Fig. 28, p. 28.

9. MPS Report Card, 1993–94. Also see "Better Public Schools," Study Commission on the Quality of Education in the Metropolitan Milwaukee Public Schools, October 1985.

Chapter 1: Room 207

1. Census Tract 84, U.S. Census Bureau, 1990 Census. According to Pastor Ivy, principal of North Division, unemployment in the neighborhood is 54 percent (interview during author's visit, February 26, 1994).

2. Census tract data.

3. Interview with Milwaukee historian John Gurda, January 12, 1994; City of Milwaukee Public Safety Report, 1993, p. 14.

4. Interviews with Eric Ransom, August 18, 19, and 21, 1994. Ransom's videotape appeared on NBC's *Exposé* news program, September 1, 1991.

5. Arbitration Summary, Milwaukee Public Schools Department of Labor Relations, September 22, 1992.

6. Arbitration Summary, Milwaukee Public Schools, Department of Labor Relations, January 8, 1993.

Chapter 2: Autopsy Report

1. Geiger is quick to claim the educational implosion of urban schools is no argument for school choice: "But I don't think the solution is to let some kids escape so there are fewer people to be concerned with what's going on." Quoted in Dennis Kelly, "Choosing a School: More States Move to Join Voucher Plan," *USA Today*, October 20, 1993.

2. Albert Shanker, quoted in Jonathan Kozol, *Savage Inequalities*, p. i.

3. *Savage Inequalities'* 233 pages contain twenty-three separate assertions regarding the lack of funding, in addition to tables in its appendix. This author counts only two references to possible waste or inefficient spending in public schools—both of which are no sooner reported by Kozol than dismissed (pp. 38 and 124). In fact, Kozol suggests that the "administrative chaos" he calls "endemic in some urban systems" could be alleviated with greater funding, "by making possible . . . the employment of some very gifted, high-paid fiscal managers who could assure that money is well used" (p. 124). Thus does even the misuse of funds turn in Kozol's hands into an argument for more money.

4. NCES 93-292, Fig. 2, p. 8; Fig. 8, p. 48; Table 41, p. 51; Table 63, p. 74.

5. Council of the Great City Schools, p. 48.

6. NCES 93-292, Table 34, p. 37; Table 41, p. 51; Fig. 2, p. 8.

7. Figure calculated using the same 3.85 CPI inflator used in NCES 93-292 Table 80 to derive constant-dollar public school instructional staff salaries.

8. NCES 93-292, Table 76, p. 84.

9. Council of the Great City Schools, Fig. 63, p. 52 (figures drawn, incidentally, from the National Education Association).

10. NCES 93-292, Fig. 11, p. 50; Table 41, p. 52.

11. Kozol, p. 4.

12. James MacGuire, *Beyond Partisan Politics: A Response to the Carnegie Report on Choice* (1993), p. 9.

13. Richard A. Rossmiller, "Federal Funds: A Shifting Balance?" in *The Impacts of Litigation and Legislation on Public School Finance*, ed. Julie K. Underwood and Deborah A. Verstegen (1990), pp. 16–17, 21. And see p. 20, Rossmiller's tempered and temperate conclusion as compared to those of Kozol and his compatriots: "Thus the Reagan Administration succeeded in holding the line on federal expenditures for education, but it was unsuccessful in reducing overall federal spending for education."

14. Ibid., p. 22.

15. NCES 93-292, Table 125, p. 126. Verbal scores declined from 466 in 1966–67 to 422 in 1990–91; math from 492 to 474.

16. Robert J. Samuelson reports an 84-point decline from 1963 scores (math 502, verbal 478), in "Merchants of Mediocrity," *Washington Post*, July 27, 1994.

17. National Center for Education Statistics, *The Condition of Education* (92-096) (1992), Table 49-1, p. 338; NCES 93-292, Table 389, p. 414; Table 393, p. 417.

18. See NCES 93-292, Table 394, p. 418. See also Douglas P. Munro, "How to Find Out Where the Money Goes in the Public Schools," Heritage Foundation, 955/S, August 10, 1993.

19. Munro, p. 4.

20. Eric A. Hanushek, "The Economics of Schooling: Production and Efficiency in Public Schools," *Journal of Economic Literature*, September 1986, pp. 1141–77, and "Impact of Differential Expenditures on School Performance," *Education Researcher*, May 1989. See also John Chubb and Terry Moe, *Politics, Markets and America's Schools* (Washington, D.C., Brookings Institution 1990), p. 145: "A shade more than half of the effective schools

have *below*-average levels of economic resources. Although our more complex analysis may yet show otherwise, effective schools do not seem to be things that money can easily buy" (italics in original).

21. S. Mitchell, p. 44, n. 105.

22. Munro (calculated from NEA statistics), p. 7.

23. Council of the Great City Schools, p. 85.

24. Cited in Martin Morse Wooster, *Angry Classrooms, Vacant Minds* (1994), pp. 110–11.

25. Chicago's average revenues per student ($5,249), from Council of the Great City Schools, p. 130.

26. NCES 93-292, p. 89.

27. Munro, Table 2, p. 22; p. 9.

28. Ibid., p. 11.

29. Michael Fischer, "Fiscal Accountability in Milwaukee's Public Elementary Schools: 'Where Does the Money Go?'" Wisconsin Policy Research Institute Report, September 1990.

30. Munro, p. 14.

31. Charles Sykes, "Fuller's Choice," *Wisconsin Interest*, Winter/Spring 1992, p. 14; p. 12.

32. See S. Mitchell, p. 46, n. 183.

33. "Better Public Schools," 1985, p. 12.

34. Ibid., p. 20. And see John F. Witte, Metropolitan Milwaukee Dropout Report, #3, October 25, 1985, p. 12.

35. George Mitchell, "The Milwaukee Parental Choice Program," Wisconsin Policy Research Institute Report, November 1992, p. 25.

36. "Race and Metropolitan Educational Inequalities in Milwaukee: Evidence and Implications," delivered at the University of Chicago, September 5, 1986, quoted in G. Mitchell, p. 25.

37. S. Mitchell, p. 44, n. 106; "Bad Apples: Firing Teachers Is Tough," *Milwaukee Journal*, May 2, 1990.

38. S. Mitchell, p. 18. And the dance goes on: See Joe Williams, "Bad MPS Teachers Rotated, Audit Says," *Milwaukee Sentinel*, March 10, 1995.

According to MPS's chief auditor, Ronald J. Vavril, "it is much easier for already-overworked principals to simply recommend a transfer because any suggestion that a teacher be terminated opens up myriad legal concerns because of the teachers union contract."

39. S. Mitchell, pp. 19–23.

40. See "Better Public Schools," p. 20, and MPS Report Card, 1992–93, p. 12.

41. S. Mitchell, p. 19.

42. "Better Public Schools," p. 13; p. 11.

43. Ibid., pp. 14 and 24, emphasis in original.

44. Ibid., p. 24.

45. Ibid., p. 25.

46. Ibid., p. 26.

47. MTEA incorporation documents for 1993, listing officers and their home addresses; telephone interview with Linda Gaston-Mounger of the MTEA, May 3, 1995.

48. P. 4, in Denis P. Doyle's authoritative 100-city study based on U.S. census data: *Where Connoisseurs Send Their Children to School: An Analysis of 1990 Census Data to Determine Where School Teachers Send Their Children to School* (May 1995).

49. In a May 1995 study conducted by the University of Wisconsin–Madison Applied Population Laboratory, commissioned by this author to review and replicate findings reported in 1993. See Richard P. Jones, "Teachers Choose Private Schools," *Milwaukee Journal*, November 14, 1993.

50. While the methodology in any such study can be contested, the Wisconsin Applied Population Lab study tends, if anything, to *overestimate* the percentage of MPS teachers who enroll their own children in MPS schools. Because census data do not permit a differentiation between public suburban schools and the Milwaukee Public Schools, it thereby counts as "MPS" students some small percentage of children who leave Milwaukee to attend suburban public schools as part of the metropolitan area's "220" voluntary desegregation program. Systemwide, the 220 program accounts for 5,000 transfers out of MPS to the suburbs, or about 5 percent of all MPS students. Even if public school teachers were only as successful as the average Milwaukee parent in gaining entry to suburban school transfers through 220, it would push the percentage of MPS teachers enrolling their own

children in "non-MPS" schools into the high 30s. According to Doyle, in terms of the percentage of public school teachers enrolling their own children in private schools, Milwaukee ranks 15th among the 100 largest cities in the United States (Table 23, p. 29).

51. Sykes, p. 11.

52. Ibid.

53. *Milwaukee Sentinel,* April 23, 1991.

54. "MPS Dropout Rate Hits 17.4%," *Milwaukee Sentinel,* January 13, 1994; Witte, p. 12.

Chapter 3: The Lessons of Urban Day

1. In 1995 Cleveland passed a "Milwaukee-style" pilot voucher program, to begin in the 1996–97 school year. See the Epilogue.

2. 1995–96 Parent Guide. For a family of four, the limit is $26,513; the eligibility limit rises $4,480 for each additional family member.

3. Interview with Susan Freeze, Wisconsin DPI, September 1, 1994. The 1993–94 amount was $2,984.

4. In 1993, the legislature raised the school choice–nonchoice ratio from 49 percent to 65 percent, effective in the 1994–95 school year.

5. One school, Bruce-Guadalupe, a predominantly Hispanic school on Milwaukee's South Side, provides the exception that proves the rule: In the fourth year of the program, Bruce-Guadalupe opened a new facility that allowed it to double its enrollment from pre-Choice levels. Even so, as a result of the 49 percent rule, it was faced with the need to add new tuition-paying students in order to take in more children from its Parental Choice waiting list. For 1994–95, Bruce-Guadalupe enrolled 192 Choice students, 56 percent of its 345 total.

6. G. Mitchell, p. 1; interview with S. Freeze.

7. Interview with Milwaukee historian John Gurda.

8. That same year, the first for the Parental Choice program, income eligibility for a family of three was $18,225—more than twice the average household income in the Urban Day area.

9. 1994–95 enrollment figure from Susan Freeze, Wisconsin DPI, August 1994.

10. Courtney has since left Urban Day to become executive director of Parents for School Choice, a local pro-voucher group.

11. See the Witte Reports, analyzed in Chapters 10 and 11.

12. Interview, January 10, 1995.

Chapter 4: White Lies

1. "Bertelle" and "Ellis" are pseudonyms, in keeping with Bertelle E.'s wish to remain anonymous.

2. Ron Grossman, "Polly's Political Paradox," *Chicago Tribune*, August 20, 1993. In 1990, McGee promised violence if the power structure failed to ameliorate conditions among Milwaukee's blacks by 1995 ("Milwaukee School Choice Proposal Ignites Bitter Racial, Political Battles," *Los Angeles Times*, August 3, 1990); in the summer of 1995, McGee went to jail for his part in upending a police car in October 1993 to protest the shooting of a black man by a police officer ("After a Send-Off Rally, McGee Begins Jail Term," *Milwaukee Journal Sentinel*, June 9, 1995).

3. Mikel Holt, "Few Benefit from School Desegregation: Report Calls for Evaluation of Programs," *Milwaukee Community Journal*, September 16, 1992.

4. Paul Haubrich, "Student Life in Milwaukee High Schools," in *Seeds of Crisis: Public Schooling in Milwaukee Since 1920*, ed. John L. Rury and Frank A. Cassell (University of Wisconsin Press, 1993), p. 203.

5. The program takes its name from the chapter in the state legal code in which it is found.

6. Michael Stolee, "The Milwaukee Desegregation Case," in *Seeds of Crisis*, p. 230.

7. Ibid., p. 249.

8. MPS Sending and Receiving Attendance Reports, September 1988.

9. According to Susan Mitchell, former consultant to MPS and author of *Why MPS Doesn't Work: Barriers to Reform in the Milwaukee Public Schools* (January 1994, Wisconsin Policy Research Institute Report, Vol 7. No. 1), three reasons all but guarantee most children being bused will be black: (1) displacement due to the creation of specialty schools in black neighborhoods, (2) the construction of new schools in white residential areas, and (3) the closing of schools without replacing them in the predominantly black Central City.

10. Department of Business Support Services, MPS, as quoted in S. Mitchell, n. 159.

11. According to Williams's aide Larry Harwell; this includes "220" costs.

12. Stolee, p. 257.

13. Ibid., pp. 258–59. Interview with Larry Harwell, December 10, 1993.

14. MPS 1994 Report Card: Enrollment as of September 16, 1994.

15. Stolee, p. 262.

16. " 'Voucher' No Longer Dirty Word," *New York Times,* June 10, 1990.

17. "Williams Offers MPS Alternative Plan," *Milwaukee Times,* January 18, 1989.

18. AB 995, 119.23 Enrollment Options Program, 1989–90 Legislature. Telephone interview with MPS official Douglas Haselow, September 12, 1994.

19. AB 995: Analysis.

20. "Williams Pushes Parental Choice School Bill," *Wisconsin Light,* February 22, 1990.

21. "Milwaukee Parents Get More Choice on Schools," *New York Times,* March 28, 1990.

22. *Milwaukee Community Journal,* February 21, 1990.

23. "Up from Mediocrity," *Wall Street Journal* editorial, March 29, 1990.

24. "Lawmakers Bombarded with Support for Choice Proposal," *Milwaukee Community Journal,* February 28, 1990.

25. Interview with State Representative Kim Plache, June 22, 1995.

26. "Committee Backs Plan to Help Needy Pay for Private School," *Milwaukee Journal,* March 8, 1990.

27. March 14, 1990.

28. "Williams Puts Liberals on Trial: When Push Comes to Shove," *Milwaukee Community Journal,* March 21, 1990.

Chapter 5: The Empire Strikes Back

1. *Milwaukee Community Journal,* May 16, 1990.

2. Joan Kent, "State School Chief Hoping for Lawsuit over 'Choice' Issue," *La Crosse Tribune,* May 8, 1990.

3. Priscilla Ahlgren, "High Court Asked to Kill State's School Choice Plan," *Milwaukee Journal*, May 31, 1990.

4. *Felmers O. Chaney et al. v. Herbert J. Grover et al.*, 90-1200-OA, filed in the Supreme Court of the State of Wisconsin, May 26, 1990.

5. Exhibits to the complaint, p. 2.

6. Steven Walters and Felicia Wilson, "Suit Aims to Stop 'Parents' Choice' Plan," *Milwaukee Sentinel*, May 30, 1990.

7. Steven Walters, "Top Educator Calls Choice Plan 'Flawed,'" ibid., June 2, 1990.

8. "Chaney Gives Reasons for Opposing Parental Choice," *Milwaukee Community Journal*, June 6, 1990.

9. "Questionable Choice," *Milwaukee Sentinel*, "'Choice' Plan Far Too Flawed," *Milwaukee Journal*," May 31, 1990.

10. "Law Firm to Defend Choice Plan in Court," City Briefs, *Milwaukee Journal*, June 1, 1990.

11. *Milwaukee Sentinel*, June 11, 1990.

12. Milwaukee Parental Choice Program Notice of School's Intent to Participate (DPI document), p. 5.

13. As summarized by Trial Court Judge Susan Steingass in her August 6, 1990, ruling, p. 4.

14. "School Choice Plan Is Upheld in Wisconsin," *New York Times*, August 8, 1990.

15. "6 Schools Interested in 'Choice' Plan," *Milwaukee Journal*, May 30, 1990. The DPI official identifying the schools was Assistant Superintendent Steven Dold. The article lists Woodlands School, Bruce-Guadalupe, Urban Day, Harambee, Highland Community, and SER–Jobs for Progress—of which all but Highland ultimately participated in Parental Choice's first year. The fact that six schools were interested in the program was mentioned again the following day, "High Court Asked to Kill State's School Choice Plan," *Milwaukee Journal*, May 31, 1990.

16. DPI press release, 90069-B, June 15, 1990.

17. "Applications Available for Milwaukee School Choice Program," Governor Tommy G. Thompson, June 15, 1990.

18. DPI information: "Grover Clarifies Parental Choice Program," 90072, June 19, 1990.

19. Chief Justice Heffernan, concurring.

Chapter 6: Davis v. Grover

1. *Wall Street Journal*, June 27, 1990.

2. Pamela Cotant, "Grover Defends Opposition to School Choice," (Madison) *Capital Times*, June 28, 1990.

3. "Grover Says Paper's Editorial Made an Unfair Comparison," *Milwaukee Journal*, June 29, 1990.

4. *Capital Times*, June 28, 1990. Only the pro-Grover *Capital Times* editorial page defended the superintendent, declaring the *Wall Street Journal* editorial "one of its more insipid," and advancing the patently indefensible claim that "Everyone's willing to give the [Choice] experiment a try, including Grover."

5. U.S. Department of Education memorandum, June 20, 1990, Milwaukee Choice Program.

6. Petition for Leave to Commence Original Action, *Chaney v. Grover*, May 30, 1990, pp. 6–7.

7. Ibid., p. 10.

8. Motion to intervene in *Lonzetta Davis et al. v. Herbert Grover et al.*, June 27, 1990, p. 15, para. 29; p. 11.

9. Affidavit of Annette Polly Williams, p. 3.

10. "Final Report: An Independent Evaluation of MPS Alternative and Partnership Schools, Spring 1993," Tony Baez, principal researcher, University of Wisconsin/Milwaukee, Center for Urban Community Development, June 1993, p. 10; p. 184.

11. Ibid., p. 61.

12. Ibid., p. 10.

13. Ibid., p. 12. In an interview January 3, 1994, Baez said of the authorities who appointed him to survey the state of "At Risk" education: "They weren't expecting my report—just a cut-and-dried survey, how many seats, attendance figures, etc. But I tried to treat At Risk with respect. What I found, I thought, could kill the program. For the sake of the good schools—and there are a few good schools like Shalom or Grand or Milwaukee Spectrum and Next Door/Cornerstone succeeding in spite of the system—I wanted people to know what was going on."

14. Ibid., p. 53; p. 183.

15. Ibid., p. 42.

16. Ibid., p. 11. The small staff is particularly interesting since the "At Risk" statute mandates a 10 percent premium in state funding to be paid to the sending system to perform its placement and operating functions (Wisconsin Statute 118.153 [4b] and [5]). In a $12 million program, that amounts to a not-insubstantial $1.2 million per year administrative premium.

17. Ibid., p. 182; p. 36; p. 40.

18. Ibid., p. 187; p. 188.

19. Ibid., p. 85.

20. Ibid., p. 190.

21. Affidavit of Susan Wing, principal of Woodlands School, August 17, 1990.

22. Neil Shively and Amy Rinard, "Grover Seeks to Halt Choice Program," *Milwaukee Sentinel*, July 17, 1990. Grover's brief was drafted by Robert J. Paul, DPI counsel, and Julie K. Underwood, "education law teacher at the University of Wisconsin–Madison who was working for Grover as a limited-term employee" at the time. Both Paul and Underwood would figure in the Messmer hearings in 1992; see Chapter 8.

23. Affidavit of John Peterburs, secretary/business manager of MPS, July 13, 1990: "In preparing its 1990–91 budget, MPS was required to anticipate that a maximum of 1,000 MPS students would participate in the Choice program, and that MPS would lose $2,500 per student in direct state aid. Since these students would not come from the same MPS school or program, but from throughout the school district, MPS cannot anticipate any reduction in expenditures based on the loss of these students. *MPS was therefore required to increase its property tax levy by $2.5 million*" (pp. 5–6, emphasis added).

24. "Emergency Motion of Appellants/Petitioners for Advancement of Case," August 9, 1990, pp. 6–7.

25. Komer brief, p. 4, emphasis added.

26. Ibid., p. 2.

27. *Davis v. Grover*, Decision and Order 90CV2576, Dane County Circuit Court Branch 8, August 6, 1990, p. 15; p. 9.

28. Ibid., p. 20.

29. Ibid., p. 10.

30. MPS bill, AB 995, Section 5, and Parental Choice bill, Section 7 (a).

31. MPS bill, Section 2 (a), and Parental Choice bill, Section 2 (a) 4. 42 USC 2000d reads: "No person in the United States shall, on the ground of race, color, or national origin, be excluded from participation in, be denied the benefits of, or be subjected to discrimination under any program or activity receiving Federal financial assistance."

32. Parental Choice bill, Sections 5 (b) 1 and 2.

33. MPS bill, Section 8 (b). When considering their own education experiments, MPS officials understood first-year evaluations to be inappropriate; see, for instance, the Malcolm X black immersion school experiment, in which test scores were inconclusive and turnover high: "Observers, including MPS Superintendent Howard L. Fuller, say it's too early to draw conclusions about the black immersion experiment, now in its second year." "Malcolm X School Hopes Pride Helps Test Scores," *Milwaukee Sentinel*, February 16, 1994.

34. Peterson, in *Seeds of Crisis*, p. 292: "The legislature authorized a comprehensive evaluation of the program to begin simultaneously with its establishment, making it likely that the initial missteps that accompany most innovations would be well-documented, exposing the plan to immediate public scrutiny and undermining its long-term political support." To see how the plaintiffs in *Chaney v. Grover* built their allegations of Parental Choice's "standardless" schools on the supposedly scant requirements, see p. 4 of their "Petition to Commence Original Action." The four requirements quoted from the Parental Choice statute are the same—in some cases verbatim—as the requirements built into the abortive MPS "choice" bill (see p. 108).

35. *Davis v. Grover* (August 6, 1990), p. 23; p. 26; p. 20.

36. *Capital Times*, August 8, 1990.

37. *Milwaukee Sentinel*, August 7, 1990.

38. *Capital Times*, August 14, 1990.

39. "Grover Raps Bush for Backing Choice," *Milwaukee Sentinel*, August 8, 1990.

40. Interview, December 9, 1993.

41. "Teacher Union to Appeal Choice Decision," *Milwaukee Journal*, August 8, 1990.

42. Ibid.; 217 Choice applicants had to be put on a waiting list because their schools did not have openings in their particular grade.

43. "Choice Plan About to Be Reality," *Milwaukee Journal*, September 2, 1990.

44. Clinton's letter to Polly Williams, October 18, 1990:

    "Dear Polly: I read Don Lambro's recent column about your version of the school choice bill in Milwaukee. I am fascinated by that proposal and am having my staff analyze it. I'm concerned that the traditional Democratic Party establishment has not given you more encouragement. The visionary is rarely embraced by [the] status quo.
    "Keep up the good work."

    By June 1993, NEA literature included the following quote from President Clinton: "I am unalterably opposed to a voucher system to give people public money to take to private schools." NEA Center for the Preservation of Public Education, June 1993.

45. Gretchen Schuldt, "Williams Wants Mandatory MPS Enrollment," *Milwaukee Sentinel*, November 26, 1990.

46. *Davis v. Grover*, No. 90-1807-LV, Court of Appeals, District IV, p. 17.

47. NEA, "The Case Against Private School Vouchers," July 1991. The NEA article goes on to say, "Another school has folded. . . ."

    Oddly, the AFT, in the Fall 1991 issue of its *American Educator*, carried a sidebar article, "The Milwaukee Story," which tells of Juanita Virgil in nearly identical words:

    "One financially strapped school that took in a large number of voucher kids had been a religious school until it decided to participate in the program. Then the non-voucher parents became unhappy with the switch, feuds broke out, and religion classes were reintroduced. In the middle of the year, the 63 voucher students were suddenly expelled, and mostly into the public schools. And only then did the public hear that this school had been doing a lousy job of feeding, transporting, and providing books to the kids, that its facilities were even more decrepit than the public schools, and that little, if any, education took place.

    "The owner's entrepreneurship got her the voucher monies, but the school collapsed anyway. The fate of the school's other students is unclear.

    "The tale of the Juanita Virgil School may seem dramatic, but it is not unique. Another school has folded. . . ."

    Most interesting, perhaps, is the erroneous assertion identical to both accounts: "Another school has folded." Besides Juanita Virgil, no other Choice school closed in the first year of the program, or indeed in any following year. The error suggests an uncritical and unexamined reliance on a single source for the Juanita Virgil story.

48. G. Mitchell pp. 35–36.

49. *Davis v. Grover*, 480 N.W.2d 460 (Wis. 1992), p. 474; p. 475.

50. Ibid., p. 467.

51. State Petitioners' Brief, p. 15. Ironically, to those who recall the MPS "choice" plan, the "first class city" argument used to impugn Parental Choice as a local and private bill—pertaining only to Milwaukee—would have also disqualified the MPS bill, which used the same language.

52. *Davis v. Grover*, Wisconsin State Supreme Court, 480 North Western Reporter, 2nd Series, March 3, 1992, p. 47.

53. Ibid., p. 476.

54. Ibid., pp. 477–78.

55. March 4, 1992.

56. "Thompson Jubilant over Choice Victory," *Milwaukee Journal*, March 4, 1992.

Chapter 7: The Battle of Sister Leonius

1. PAVE's largest grant came from the Bradley Foundation, in the amount of $1.5 million over three years.

2. "The Future of Our Cities," *Wisconsin Interest*, Winter 1992.

3. "Mayor Reaffirms Support for School Choice Plans," *Milwaukee Journal*, January 2, 1992.

4. "Norquist Says Parochial Schools Will Soon Get Public Money," *Milwaukee Journal*, April 28, 1992.

5. See statistics compiled in G. Mitchell, p. 14. Mitchell's policy recommendation was a repeal of the 49 percent rule as well as the 1 percent cap.

6. "The Future That Works," *Crisis*, January 1993, p. 32.

Chapter 8: The Inquisition v. Brother Bob

1. Grover's antipathy to Parental Choice never cooled. Having announced his retirement when his term expired in 1993, Grover's final DPI budget

deleted funds for Parental Choice effective June 30, 1995. Grover claimed this move, coupled with a new emphasis on *public* school choice statewide, was in reality an attempt to improve Parental Choice. Called on to explain how termination could be called an improvement, Grover's DPI deputy admitted: " 'Improve' probably isn't the best choice of words" ("School Chief Wants Choice Ended by '95," *Milwaukee Sentinel,* November 14, 1992).

2. The DeRance Foundation ceased operations in December 1992.

3. Chapter PI 35.02 (8), September 20, 1991. The wording of the DPI definition was to be the subject of significant controversy in the hearings. According to the DPI and its attorneys, the definition was meant to provide two separate "tests"—curriculum and sponsorship–administration–funding; failing either would disqualify a school from participation. Yet the language and punctuation—or lack of it—in the DPI definition made it appear that a school had to trigger *both* tests to disqualify itself: "pervasively religious curriculum and is not sponsored, administered, or funded by."

In an amicus brief submitted by the ACLU in support of the DPI position, the ACLU attorney goes so far as hand-editing into the text of the code numerals and emphases to bring the language around to the DPI meaning: " 'Nonsectarian' school means a school that 1) does not include a pervasively religious curriculum *and* 2) is not sponsored, administered or funded by any religious group or organization" (p. 4). The ACLU's slender fourteen-page brief devotes a full eight pages to what it calls "the clear and unambiguous terms" of the DPI rule, arguing the propriety of subjecting the language in question to the "same principles of construction that apply to the construction of statutes" (p. 5). Apparently unsure whether its attempt at deconstruction had succeeded, the ACLU proceeds to a fall back: "Even if PI 35.02 (8) was ambiguous (which it is not) the hearing Examiner should give deference to the DPI's interpretation of the regulation" (pp. 6–7).

Thoughtfully, the DPI provided an affidavit on just this point, from Professor Julie Underwood, author of the administrative code on Parental Choice and, in 1990–92, counsel to Superintendent Grover in *Davis v. Grover.* Underwood explained her intent, in spite of the convoluted language of the code, to set up a distinct two-part test.

Messmer's counsel countered with his own "plain language" claim: "By the use of the word 'and' instead of 'or' if it [a school] does not meet one Choice and of the criteria it will still qualify" (see ACLU brief, p. 4). If the DPI had meant to create a distinct two-part test, it could have circumvented all the uncertainty by changing "and" to "or."

Had the DPI simply been sloppy in crafting the language of its administrative rules—or was it trying to raise the bar on Messmer? In any event, Examiner Grogan was in no mood to take DPI to task for its lax language. He dismissed Messmer's straightforward interpretation and granted the strict construction the DPI claimed it had intended. "The reason for this decision," Grogan wrote without apparent irony, "is the plain reading of the rule." (Grogan, p. 39. Here and at several other junctures, however, Grogan observed that Messmer's counsel had waived Grogan's oft-extended invitation to supply a "reply brief" supplementing its argument; Messmer's counsel never did; pp. 4, 39, 40, 41.)

Attempts to brush up the language of PI 35.02 (8) continued even after the examiner released his ruling; DPI's chief legal counsel sent an erratum to Examiner Grogan proposing edits to the examiner's gloss on "page 39 as follows: . . . means that a school must *avoid both* (strike: not have neither) (1) the characteristic of having a 'pervasively religious curriculum' *and* (Strike: nor) (2) the characteristic . . ." (emphasis in original, letter from Robert J. Paul to Thomas R. Grogan, May 19, 1993). Grogan accepted the "corrigendum" into his final order, essentially adopting as his own DPI's preferred wording. (See Grogan, p. 39, and title page note, bottom.)

4. I observed two theology classes as part of an unannounced visit to Messmer in 1993. I found the first class analyzing rap and rock "love songs" for their message. Each student had brought a tape with a favorite song, which was played in turn, and then discussed; each had been asked to transcribe the lyrics and make a copy for each member of the class to assist in the discussion. The discussions were lively and spirited; no prayer or reading from the Bible took place, nor were students advancing opinions or evaluating others' with reference to scripture. There was a Bible on a lectern in the corner of the classroom. The second theology class was reviewing a worksheet on drug use, which led to a discussion of peer pressure and also the negative effects of drug use, in which the students displayed a great deal of interest as well as expertise. The gist of the discussion concerned whether one had an affirmative responsibility to help a drug user, or whether the limit of responsibility was individual, adhering in each person's decision to use or avoid drugs. There was no Bible on display in the second classroom.

I employed the same unannounced-arrival tactic at Harambee, Urban Day, and Bruce-Guadalupe schools; in every case, I was allowed by administrators to walk the school and offered the opportunity to attend classes at will. I attempted the same at North Division High School and was limited to a "hallway" tour with the principal; while courteous in interrupting his schedule to deal with a surprise visitor, he maintained that an unscheduled classroom visit might prove a disruptive intrusion into the educational process. On my arrival, the principal's first instinct was to check with MPS headquarters about my request; told that the official he had called was unavailable, the principal made a decision on his own authority to escort me around the school's main hallway.

5. "Information Needed," DPI document, June 4, 1992.

6. DPI document, June 8, 1992.

7. Letter from Herbert Grover to Brother Bob Smith, June 10, 1992, p. 2.

8. "[T]he examiner was struck by the fact that the Department of Public Instruction did not include in the rules a mechanism for the review and investigation of issues of this nature" (Grogan, p. 51).

9. Examiner Grogan, based on the testimony of the DPI official in charge of overseeing the Parental Choice program, accepts the fact that the *Sentinel* article " 'triggered' an agency review of Messmer's eligibility" (Grogan, p. 2).

10. Ibid., p. 23.

11. Ibid., p. 52.

12. Ibid., pp. 51 and 52.

13. Ibid., p 33.

14. Ibid., p. 10.

15. Ibid., pp. 10–11.

16. The example given of a typical independent study was a paper on the "Life and Times of Dr. Martin Luther King, Jr." (Grogan, p. 22).

17. Grogan, p. 14.

18. Examples read into the record include:
    From the MHS Student Handbook: "We the community of Messmer High School, affirm that Messmer is a private, Catholic High School seeking to fulfill its mission of faith by educating a diverse urban population." (p. 8)
    From the Faculty and Staff Handbook: "As faculty and staff working at Messmer High, we think that it is beneficial for us to keep in mind that our job/ministry here is to model: . . . a Christian atmosphere where the entire person is developed to his/her potential; a community fostering Catholic faith." (p. 9)

19. The following passages illustrate Smith's claim:

From the MHS Student Handbook: "Messmer's purpose is to educate, challenge and to instill a sense of Christian values in every student. Our students come from a variety of backgrounds and we at Messmer welcome you as you are" (p. 11).

"We are committed . . . to inspire Christian leadership and service with others; and to appreciate the multiplicity of social, cultural, and religious heritages" (p. 8).

From the objectives for the Messmer retreats: "8. To value spirituality regardless of religious background" (p. 16).

20. In stipulated fact 4.27: "No students have been converted to Catholicism or the religious life" (Grogan, p. 22).

21. The DPI press release announcing the reversal on Messmer listed as evidence of the school's "pervasively religious curriculum" four factors: "Each school day . . . begins with a prayer, students are rquired to attend six prayer services a year, all students are required to take a religion or theology course each year, and the faculty and staff handbook talks about the school's Christian mission" ("DPI Rules Messmer High School Is Ineligible for Choice Program," DPI 92084, June 10, 1992).

22. The very acceptance of amicus briefs in an administrative procedure was acknowledged by Grogan to be unusual; allowing his inability to locate "a source of specific authority under Wisconsin law on this subject" (p. 4), Grogan allowed WEAC, the ACLU, and Americans United for the Separation of Church and State to enter the "case" against Messmer.

23. DPI brief, p. 16.

24. WEAC brief, as adopted by Grogan, p. 41.

25. Grogan, p. 47, emphasis in original.

26. See also Herbert Grover's letter to Brother Bob Smith, June 10, 1992, p. 2.

27. Grogan, p. 15, emphasis added.

28. Quite often in the hearing, DPI counsel asked after the private beliefs—as distinct from any organizational or official affiliation with a religious group—of various people involved with Messmer. That DPI would condition *public* benefits on the status of *private* individuals' religious beliefs is implied, but never stated outright.

29. Grogan, p. 9; p. 10.

30. Ibid., p. 10.

31. Ibid., p. 48.

32. Smith offered as the motive for the "self-study" review Messmer's recognition that the student body had shifted between 1990 and 1992 from majority Catholic to minority Catholic, and offered as proof such changes in the theology curriculum as the discontinuation of a course called "Christian Morality." Examiner Grogan did invite Brother Bob to provide a systematic record of the postreview changes; neither Smith nor his counsel responded.

33. Grogan, p. 47.

34. My first visit to Messmer included a visit to the chapel as well. The chapel, which is kept locked, seemed more a storeroom than a place of worship. At one corner of the altar leaned a miniature Christmas tree; in a back pew next to a stack of Xerox paper boxes were strewn a dozen basketball practice jerseys. The door off the altar opened onto a room overflowing with more trophies (perhaps more evidence of illicit Catholic Conference glory). All told, the room measures five strides from front to back, with capacity to seat approximately two dozen.

Chapter 9: Constitutional Daylight

1. *Lemon v. Kurtzman*, 403 US 602. This is strange for several reasons: First, *Tilton* does not mention the phrase "pervasively religious"; second, in *Tilton* the Court *upholds* a statute allowing state aid to a religious institution, in this instance, a university. Was the DPI attorney guilty of sloppy lawyering? There is some support for this: In response to the examiner's query, Paul states with misplaced pride that " 'inextricably intertwined' is the exact phrase." This well-worn colloquialism, however, appears nowhere in *Tilton;* the DPI attorney is, one assumes, reaching for the phrase "excessive entanglement," the standard that grew from the third prong of the *Lemon* test. At any rate, no one at the Ramada Inn hearing was conversant with the seminal church–state cases; neither the examiner nor Messmer's attorney nor Brother Bob questioned attorney Paul's wobbly discourse on establishment-clause case law.

2. DPI Brief, p. 12, emphasis in original.

3. Surprisingly, Polly Williams's name could not be found among the cosponsors of the Assembly version of the Plewa bill. "I was never consulted. I was never even called," she said.

4. See Daniel McGroarty, "A Prayer for a Better Education," *Wall Street Journal*, October 1, 1993.

5. *Miller v. Benson* would later add a fifth plaintiff, Valerie Barrett.

6. *Pierce v. Society of Sisters*, 268 U.S. 510 (1925), struck down a state law banning private schools and mandating public education.

7. *Miller*, p. 10. Throughout the case, Superintendent Benson persisted in demonstrating a certain legal astigmatism—an inability to see without distortion the plaintiffs' basis for claiming a right to public funds for the private school of their choice. Thus Benson refuted a claim *Miller* parents never made: the ability "as a matter of federal constitutional right, to choose a sectarian school and have the state pay for their children's education in this religious setting" (Defendant's brief, p. 11; Plaintiff's reply, p. 8). Bredemeier labored to bring to the court's attention his more nuanced view: "Plaintiffs do contend that when the government creates a benefit such as this private school choice program, it cannot confer that benefit in a discriminatory manner—at least not without a compelling state interest" (*Miller*, p. 9).

8. Against the claim that government aid to religious institutions was impermissible, *Miller* parents advanced evidence that such aid was in fact extensive. One of the few clear lines in the tangle of establishment-clause case law was a distinction between aid to college-age students and their younger elementary and secondary school counterparts; among the cases where aid to religious schools had survived post-*Lemon* scrutiny were a number of laws extending benefits to religious colleges and universities, on the grounds that students at that age were less impressionable and indoctrination less intense. In Wisconsin, however—and also nationally as a result of federal assistance to private and even church-run day care centers—that "firewall" had been breached. *Miller* adduced the various ways Wisconsin religious school students of all ages benefited from public funds: from college students at religious colleges and universities (the Wisconsin Tuition Grant program), to preschool children in religiously run day care, and even "At Risk" students in grades 3–12, who were, in some instances, placed by MPS in private schools with religious affiliations. (See *Miller*, Plaintiffs' Proposed Supplemental Findings of Fact, pp. 2–3, and also D. McGroarty, "Private Choice, Public Dumping," p. 26.)

    There was apparently only one place government aid could not follow children to religious institutions: the Parental Choice program.

9. *Miller*, pp. 5–6, emphasis added.

10. Stephen Carter, *The Culture of Disbelief: How American Law and Politics Trivialize Religious Devotion* (1993), p. 200.

11. *Miller*, p. 16.

12. Ibid., p. 7. "In *Mueller*, the Court upheld a state law allowing educational expense income tax deductions for parents whose children attended private schools. Despite the fact most of these families selected sectarian schools, the income tax benefit was found to apply broadly to the educational expenses of all parents. 463 US at 398. Moreover, public funds became available to sectarian schools 'only as a result of numerous private choices of individual parents of school-age children'" (*Miller*, pp. 22–24). *Witters*, in which the Supreme Court upheld a scheme providing vocational assistance to a blind student studying at a private Christian college to become a pastor, and *Zobrest*, which allowed public aid to a deaf child enrolled in a religious school, both recognized that the "primary" beneficiaries of these government programs were children and parents, with participating schools, whether sectarian or nonsectarian, "only incidental beneficiaries," aided only "as a result of the private decision of individual parents" (*Zobrest*, 113 S. Ct at 2467).

13. *Committee for Public Education v. Nyquist* (1973), 413 US at 783 n. 38.

14. Laurence Tribe, *American Constitutional Law*, 2nd ed. (1988), p. 1223. Tribe repeated his view to the *Congressional Quarterly*'s Jill Zuckman ("School 'Choice' a Tough Choice for Members of Congress," April 27, 1991): "I don't think there is any chance at all that the [Supreme] Court as currently composed would find a reasonably designed school choice plan as a violation of church and state. . . . If there are objections, they should be debated on policy grounds and not recast as constitutional arguments."

    Bredemeier's use of the Tribe quotation was just one of a number of indications a new activism was afoot: The *Miller* brief closes by citing *Swann v. Charlotte-Mecklenburg Board of Education*, a 1971 case upholding an activist remedy—in this instance, busing. Following a generation of conservative legal scholarship that cited *Swann* only to score it as evidence of the court's overreaching, Bredemeier cited *Swann* as proof of the court's "broad powers to remedy constitutional violations" (pp. 28–29).

15. Interestingly, this was a concern held by players at opposite ends of the spectrum in the voucher drama: Clint Bolick and Grover-appointed Parental Choice examiner John Witte (conversation with John Witte, October 17, 1993).

16. See Daniel McGroarty, "Education's Long March," *Policy Review*, Summer 1994, pp. 57–58.

17. Brief in Support of Defendant's Motion, September 26, 1994, p. 8; p. 9.

18. See Affidavit of Allen C. Hoye, principal of Emmaus Lutheran School, the designated choice of a fifth *Miller* parent, Valerie Barrett, for her children Reigne Brown and Rahbilu Barrett.

19. *Miller* reply brief, p. 8.

20. DPI brief, pp. 11–13. What is interesting—other than the Benson brief's firm belief in its power to literally divine the divinity of private individuals' intentions—is the curious equation this reasoning sets up between establishment-clause and free-exercise cases. According to *Lemon*, in order for *establishment* claims to survive scrutiny, the intent or aim of the law must be secular, and only *incidentally religious*. For *free-exercise* purposes, motivation must be religious in intent, and only *incidentally secular*. What it meant was that only individuals asserting religious motivation to "outwit" a secular law could pass muster under the Benson "rule": a kind of legal limbo-bar, by turns too high to get over and too low to crawl under.

21. ACLU, p. 2.

22. "The principal concern of *amici* is to preserve the integrity of the Free Exercise Clause . . . ," ACLU, p. 2.

23. ACLU, p. 15.

24. The ACLU cites the Parental Choice requirements in detail, pp. 13–15, 17.

25. Ibid., p. 16.

26. Ibid., p. 3, n. 2; p. 15.

27. DPI brief, p. 22.

28. Ibid., p. 17 and also p. 3; p. 18.

29. Ibid., p. 20.

30. *Miller* reply brief, p. 21.

31. 444 US 646, 658.

32. *Miller* reply brief, p. 25.

33. Ibid., p. 7.

34. "Polly Moves into Position," *Wall Street Journal*, December 9, 1994.

35. WCPE, letter to Wisconsin senators, December 6, 1994.

36. Reynolds, pp. 5–6; title page. Thus were the fears of Clint Bolick in this instance misplaced.

37. Ibid., pp. 13–14.

38. Ibid., pp. 3 and 11.

39. *Nyquist*, 780, quoted by Reynolds, p. 11.

40. Reynolds, p. 8, quoting *Nyquist*, 413 US at 788.

41. See Reynolds, p. 8.

42. *Nyquist*, p. 2, n. 4, quoting Chief Justice Burger in *Walz v. Tax Commission* (1970).

43. *Miller* appeal, pp. 28 and 33.

44. Landmark Legal Foundation, press statement, March 15, 1995.

45. Benson, pp. 21–22, emphasis added.

46. "Thompson Undaunted by School Choice Ruling," *Milwaukee Sentinel*, March 16, 1995, emphasis added.

Chapter 10: Accentuate the Negative

1. Witte served as executive director of the 1985 "Better Public Schools" study (see Chapter 1). While denied any opportunity to review Witte's data, two evaluators have assessed his First Year Report: George Mitchell, for the Wisconsin Policy Research Institute (1992), and Professor Paul Peterson of Harvard University, in a section of his chapter in *Seeds of Crisis: Public Schooling in Milwaukee Since 1920*, ed. John L. Rury and Frank A. Cassell (1993).

2. An earlier version of this chapter, evaluating Witte's first three reports, appeared as "School Choice Slandered," in *The Public Interest*, Fall 1994. Since that time, Harvard's Paul Peterson has issued his own review of Witte's findings (February 1995) and the Wisconsin State Legislative Audit Bureau has published its five-year audit of the Milwaukee Parental Choice Program (February 1995), as directed by the original statute. Howard L. Fuller and Sammis B. White's July 1995 report, "Expanded School Choice in Milwaukee" (WPRI, vol. 8, no. 5), provides additional statistical profiles of Milwaukee's private sectarian schools.

3. Carnegie Foundation for the Advancement of Teaching, "School Choice; A Special Report," released October 26, 1992, pp. 22, 81, and 82.

4. NEA/TSTA, "Our Public Schools: The Best Choice for Texas," May 1994, pp. 29–30, 34, 26.

5. Telephone interview, April 21, 1993.

6. The echo effect continues. July 15, 1995—two weeks after the Wisconsin legislature voted to expand Parental Choice to religious schools and two weeks before Governor Thompson signed the bill into law—the *Milwaukee Journal Sentinel* bannered a "Harvard University study" under the headline "Choice Programs Showing Little Success, Study Says." Within days, Susan Mitchell of the Wisconsin Policy Research Institute reported that the "Harvard study" contained "no new information and no 'Harvard research.' Actually, the 'Harvard research' . . . appears to consist solely of previously reported information from John Witte, a professor at UW-Madison, not Harvard" (S. Mitchell, "When Is a Harvard Study Not a Harvard Study?" July 1995). Follow-on news stories reporting the phantom Harvard study's negative findings on school choice ran in the *Los Angeles Times* and the *Washington Post*.

7. *Choice and Control in American Education*, vol. 1, ed. John F. Witte and William Clune, p. 43.

8. "Where We Stand: Looking at Chubb and Moe's Numbers: Sleight-of-Hand Logic," *New York Times*, November 18, 1990. Shanker cites Witte's criticism of John Chubb and Terry Moe's influential *Politics, Markets and America's Schools* (1990), the bête noire of the antichoice forces.

9. G. Mitchell, p. 23.

10. Witte, First Year Report (hereafter referred to as Witte I), p. 21; pp. v, 22–23. One paragraph later, Witte opines that attrition could have also been attributed to the impact of *Davis v. Grover:* "Because parents were uncertain whether the program would continue, when an alternative permanent arrangement became available, they took it."

11. All data are drawn from the text or tables in Witte's reports. To date, no researcher has succeeded in gaining access to the data from which Witte draws his conclusions. Clint Bolick has come to the aid of Harvard's Paul Peterson, requesting that DPI assert its authority over public information gathered at its behest or face a mandamus action ordering it to do so under Wisconsin's Open Records Act (letter, Clint Bolick to Steven B. Dold, Assistant State Superintendent, Wisconsin DPI, January 4, 1995).

12. Witte I, 18, n. 14.

13. Telephone interview, Sue Freeze, DPI, August 31, 1993.

14. Carnegie, p. 78. Grover, quoted in Economic Policy Institute, *School Choice: Examining the Evidence*, p. 251. (More evidence of the echo cham-

ber effect: the foreword to the EPI book was provided by Ernest Boyer, editor of the Carnegie Report.) TSTA/NEA, p. 29.

15. Discussion with Witte at the UCLA Graduate School of Education Conference, October 17, 1993. Telephone interview with Peterson, March 17, 1994. Peterson in *Seeds of Crisis*, p. 295.

16. SER–Jobs's drag on attrition continued in Choice's second year. Again, buried in a footnote, Witte reports SER's completion rate for the second year at 23 of 38—15 attritions of the 44 total for all Choice schools (Witte, Second Year Report, 12.12). Witte reports the second-year rate as 9.3 percent (ibid., p. 20). Excluding SER–Jobs, MPCP's second-year attrition drops to 5.5 percent. As for the Third Year Report, a Witte footnote reveals the "noncompletion" rate for what was by then two "alternative" high schools as a total of 33 out of 46, or 71.7 percent (p. 19, n. 11). The Fourth Year Report, again in a footnote, puts the noncompletion rate for the two "At Risk" schools at 21 out of 67, or 31.3 percent (p. 13, n. 13).

17. Staff Report #3, October 1985, p. 10.

18. Peterson, pp. 27–29, emphasis added.

19. Witte III, p. vi.

20. Ibid., p. 27, emphasis added. Peterson, citing 1992 census data, puts the average urban mobility in perspective: 18 percent of African-American and 20 percent of Latino residents of Midwestern central-city households reported having moved in the previous year. National figures for female-headed households show even higher mobility: 30 percent for African-American central-city families with children between six and seventeen, and 43 percent in families with children younger than six. For Latinos, the numbers were 32 percent and 52 percent (Peterson, pp. 30–31). While moving cannot be equated with changing schools in every instance, these statistics suggest that attrition from Central City Choice schools is in fact remarkably low.

21. Witte III, pp. v and 29, emphasis added. As Peterson (1995) notes, in the Fourth Year Report, "Witte drops the charge that choice schools cannot retain their students" (p. 7).

22. Ibid., p. 26, emphasis added. The 1995 Wisconsin Legislative Audit Bureau report uses attrition numbers which, while differing somewhat, seem to mirror Witte's own; the LAB avoids, however, Witte's invidious interpretation of Choice attrition. According to the LAB: "the average annual rate of attrition . . . for those who have not completed the highest grade offered has been 30.3 percent" (p. 27). "[T]here appears to be no reason

to believe they [the reasons Choice students leave the program] differ significantly from those that cause public school students to change schools" (p. 28).

Witte, in his Fourth Year Report, after observing that "Attrition from the program is not inconsequential, although there appears to be a clear downward trend," goes on to note: "Thus excluding the first year when Juanita Virgil went bankrupt, attrition during the year was less than MPS in all subsequent years based on students leaving from September to June" (p. 21).

23. Carnegie, p. 78. See the Texas State Teachers Association report (1994), p. 29. Also see Peter W. Cookson, Jr., in his 1994 book, *School Choice*: "In the first year only 341 students participated in the program, *and many of them ended up dropping out*" (p. 67, emphasis added). In terms of statistical spin, Cookson's account—which leaves the impression that the students not only left the program but dropped out of school—does Carnegie one better.

24. Witte II, p. iv; pp. 6–7, 10; Witte III, p. 5.

25. Witte IV, Table 5d.

26. These are 1990–93 averages; see Witte IV, Table 5d.

27. Of all Choice families, 76 percent are headed by a nonmarried parent, compared to 65 percent of low-income MPS families and 49 percent of all MPS families. See Witte IV, Table 5c, and LAB, pp. 24–25.

28. Based on Witte's four-year figures in Tables 5c and 5d, the ratio would be 2.1 children per parent for Choice, 1.95 for all MPS families, and 2.4 for the low-income MPS sample. See also Peterson, p. 21.

29. At the time of the publication of the Carnegie Report. For the first four years of the program, the average family income of Choice families was $11,630 (LAB, p. 25).

30. Carnegie, p. 20, emphasis added.

31. Witte IV, pp. v and 26. See also Witte III, pp. v, 28, and 29. Shanker, "Where We Stand," *New York Times*, January 31, 1994.

32. Witte I, Appendix A, emphasis added.

33. Witte II, p. 13, emphasis added. Witte III, p. 20. For whatever reason, Witte makes a slight amendment to this statement in his Fourth Year Report: "Because cohort scores do not report on the same students from year to year, the *most* accurate measure of achievement gains and losses are [*sic*] change scores" (IV, p. 14, emphasis added).

34. Witte I, pp. iv and 23.

35. Ibid., p. 18.

36. Ibid., n. 15.

37. Ibid., p. 19, emphasis added.

38. November 24, 1991.

39. Witte II, pp. v, 17; 21; 22.

40. Witte II, p. v.

41. Witte also begins what will become a pattern of quietly responding to critical reviews of his work without explicitly engaging the criticism. See George Mitchell's critique of Witte's First Year comparison of Choice students to the MPS average rather than the low-income MPS sample—an invidious and indefensible comparison Witte never again attempts.

42. Witte III, p. 20; IV, p. 14.

43. Witte III, p. 20, emphasis added. On the matter of selective reporting of Witte's findings, the TSTA/NEA report deserves special recognition. It cites Year Three reading scores—which show two straight years of decline for Choice students—and erroneously reports "modest gains" for public school students, which Witte notes registered a small decline in Year Three. For math, TSTA/NEA prefers the Year Two scores that show Choice students "remained static," rather than Year Three, which shows a significant *gain* for *Choice students* and a significant *decline* for *public school students*. In its introduction, TSTA/NEA states flatly that in Milwaukee, Choice students' "test scores have actually declined" (p. 2).

44. Witte III, p. 23.

45. Witte IV, pp. 14, 26.

46. Ibid., p. 15.

47. Ibid., Tables 11a–d. The all-MPS sample achieved a 44.2 Math NCE in the first year of Witte's study. The *highest* Math NCE attained by the low-income MPS sample was 42.2—very near the level to which Choice students *declined* in the fourth year (42.0).

48. Compare Witte IV's Figure 2b to Tables 11a–d. Peterson, for his part, discerns a political agenda behind Witte's graphs: In his view, this departure from previous practice "suggest[s] that Witte expects these inappropriate comparisons to be influential with public officials, who may not be well informed on the intricacies of evaluation research" (p. 13).

49. Witte IV, pp. 9, 10, emphasis in original.

50. Ibid., p. 18, emphasis added.

51. Ibid., pp. 15, 18, 28, emphasis added.

52. Paul E. Peterson, "A Critique of the Witte Evaluation of Milwaukee's School Choice Program," Harvard University Occasional Paper 95-2, February 1995, pp. i, 18.

53. Witte IV, Table 5b.

54. Peterson, p. 22.

55. Witte I, p. 8.

56. Here, LAB highlights what Witte does not: "The group of choice students is different for each of the four comparison periods" (Table 6, p. 29, note). LAB's notation accompanies the change score table reproduced from Witte's Fourth Year Report.

57. As the LAB audit observes, the group of Choice students, with new students joining each year, was being measured against MPS students "among whom the youngest were in the 4th Grade by 1994–95" (p. 30). In fact, just 39.4 percent of all Choice students enrolled in the program's fourth year had test scores from two years to permit a change assessment (p. 28).

58. LAB, pp. 4, 28, 30, 21.

59. Witte III, p. 8, n. 7, and p. 23.

60. Witte I, p. 8. In his Third Year Report (p. 23), Witte notes the young age of most Choice students, and even implies that the tendency of scores to decrease as a child moves up in grade—the "grade effect"—*inflates* Choice scores. Yet Witte's easy assurance does not counter the "test trauma" that often skews first-test performance.

61. LAB, Table 5, p. 26.

62. Witte IV, p. 9, n. 8.

63. LAB, p. 31. Witte took issue with the conclusion of the LAB audit, "strenuously object[ing]" to a conclusion he claimed would aid and abet "supporters of choice who wish to see this program extended to religious schools and eventually to all private schools in the state" (John F. Witte, Response to the LAB, press release, February 7, 1995).

64. Ibid., and see p. 5.

65. See G. Mitchell, p. 38.

66. Witte III, Appendix C, "Technical Notes and Analysis." Also see Witte II, Table 14, and pp. 8, 13.

67. Once again, the sudden "correction" took place only after the "refusenik" students were discovered lurking in his footnotes (see Daniel McGroarty, "School Choice Slandered," op. cit., pp. 105–6). At that time, after the release of Witte's Third Year Report, I wrote:

    "What this data might show is anyone's guess. Still, it is odd that the one comparison Witte treated as determinative in a letter written at the time of his appointment is nowhere evident in his reports.

    "The mystery will remain for the foreseeable future, because Witte is only now beginning to allow access to his data. Citing confidentiality constraints, he refused—in spite of Wisconsin's Open Records Act—to allow other evaluators to examine his data; only recently has he agreed to turn it over to the state entity that commissioned his study. Reviewers of Witte's work have been entirely dependent on the charts and tables he includes at the back of his reports. And as we have seen, some of the most interesting statistics are submerged in footnotes, and some charts vanish from one report to the next."

68. Witte IV, p. 24. The LAB essentially accepts Witte's explanation, reporting: "The students who were not selected by participating schools were tracked, but their number was too small to provide a meaningful comparison until the fourth year" (p. 29).

69. See the first set of Choice student change scores, Witte II, Table 17a.

70. The small size of the refusenik response—around 200—to Witte's annual surveys cannot account for his reticence; this is still two and a half times the size of the Choice change score subgroup, and in any event, has no bearing on the fact that Witte had access to refuseniks' prior test scores in MPS (see Witte IV, p. 24).

71. See Witte IV, Table 20. In the text, Witte mentions that Choice students' and refuseniks' reading change scores are quite close (–0.88 compared to –0.44), which has the virtue of implying that Choice students actually do marginally *worse* than refuseniks. The table shows that there is an even better indicator of how similar the two groups may be by Witte's measure: Choice math change scores are 0.18, while refuseniks' are –0.01. This margin, .19, is closer than the 0.44 differential in reading—and actually offers more support for Witte's point; using it in the text, however, might suggest Choice students enjoy a slight advantage.

72. Witte IV, p. 27. Even Witte's lone chart raises more questions than it answers: Hispanic students are significantly higher as a percentage of Choice students than of refuseniks (a fact that squares with the increased school capacity at the new Bruce-Guadalupe school building). This should, however, depress Choice reading scores; does Witte control for this? Refuseniks are also more likely to be older, given that fewer seats have been available in Choice schools' higher grades. Has Witte attempted to control for age? Finally, some refuseniks remain in MPS while others find their way to private schools. Does Witte separate out one from the other, or does he allow readers to assume any putative advantage in refusenik achievement to be confused with superior MPS performance? All in all, Witte's text tends to treat the refuseniks as synonymous with the MPS control.

73. MPS Report Card, 1993–94. Fuller and White's review of the 1994 MPS graduation statistics reveals a hidden "inflator," courtesy of students who come to MPS high schools from *private* middle schools: 69 percent of the private middle school alumni graduated from MPS, compared to 41 percent of all students who attended MPS middle schools and high schools. The authors report: "[MPS] students were 68% more likely to graduate if they had attended a private school or non-MPS public school prior to high school" (Fuller and White, WPRI, 1995, p. 18).

Chapter 11: Eliminate the Positive

1. Witte IV, Table 5b.

2. Ibid., Table 5a and p. 6.

3. Albert Shanker, "The Milwaukee Story," *American Educator*, Fall 1991, p. 14.

4. Robert Lowe, "The Hollow Promise of School Vouchers," *False Choices*, 1992 (reprinted as the "Perils of School Vouchers" in *Rethinking Schools, An Agenda for Change*, 1995), pp. 3–4.

5. Witte I, p. 14.

6. Witte III, pp. v and 18.

7. Albert Shanker, "Where We Stand," September 29, 1991.

8. *Rethinking Schools* Editorial Board, "Why We Are Publishing *False Choices*," *False Choices* 1992, p. 2.

9. Robert Lowe, op. cit., pp. 4–5.

10. Witte II, p. 8; III, p. 8; IV, pp. vi and 28.

11. Witte I, p. iv. See also IV, pp. 9–10.

12. Robert Lowe, op. cit., pp. 28–29.

13. Witte III, p. 24; I, pp. 3, 9; II, p. 19; III, p. 25; IV, p. 20; III, pp. 4, 29.

    Paul Peterson caps his account of Witte's grudging recommendation that the Choice program be continued, albeit in its original, limited scope, with a translation into plain English: "In other words, the program is not so bad that the legislature should deny Witte and his team an opportunity to continue their research" (Peterson, p. 5).

14. Witte III, p. 25; IV, p. 20. Even without a chart, Witte seems to sense that reporting these numbers in any form is a telltale sign of program success. Accordingly, he attempts a pinprick in footnote 22: "These numbers are obviously subject to response bias in favor of the program. It is impossible to measure the magnitude of that bias. The approval rate is very high even with a reasonable estimate of bias."

15. Albert Shanker, "Where We Stand," *New York Times*, January 31, 1994.

Epilogue: Class Notes

1. Scott Stephens, "Voucher Backers Hail Plan's Start," *Cleveland Plain Dealer*, November 17, 1995. According to the news account, while 1,200 families had already applied for vouchers prior to the official launch of the program, "a loose coalition of teachers unions, public school boards and civil libertarians" is devising a legal challenge.

2. Scott Stephens, "Voucher Supporters State Case," *Cleveland Plain Dealer*, February 1, 1995.

3. "Choice Breakthrough," *Wall Street Journal*, June 30, 1995.

4. Interview, July 9, 1995.

5. Three organizations track the status of voucher legislation nationwide: The Institute for Justice and the Center for Education Reform, both in Washington, D.C., and the Blum Center for Parental Freedom in Education at Marquette University, Milwaukee.

6. "Grassroots: Vouchers Surface Yet Again," *NEA Today*, December 1995.

7. Daynel Hooker, "79% of MPS Seniors Fail Math Exam," *Milwaukee Journal Sentinel,* June 28, 1995.

8. WEAC and WFT counsel were among the additional attorneys for the plaintiffs. *MTEA et al. v. Benson,* Dane County Circuit Court, 95CV1997.

9. The ACLU was joined by Americans United for Separation of Church and State. Dane County Circuit Court, 95CV1982.

10. Interview, July 9, 1995.

11. Richard P. Jones, "Court Temporarily Bars Religious School Choice," *Milwaukee Journal Sentinel,* August 26, 1995. Curtis Lawrence and Daynel L. Hooker, "Injunction Forces Some Parents to Change Their Plans Quickly," ibid.

    WCPE's Lee was one of a number of antichoice activists who championed the public schools—for everyone else's children. When Lee's son entered kindergarten, Lee enrolled him in the private University School, average tuition $8,640. By contrast, the average income in the census tract including the neighborhood around Urban Day school is $8,792 *per household.* See Daniel McGroarty, "Teacher Knows Best," *National Review,* September 25, 1995.

12. The *Milwaukee Journal* and *Milwaukee Sentinel* merged in the spring of 1995.

13. Peter Applebome, "Milwaukee Is Forcing the Debate on Vouchers for Church Schools," *New York Times,* September 1, 1995.

14. Carol Innerst, "School-Choice Pioneers Vying for Credit as Court Case Nears," *Washington Times,* September 6, 1995. Williams alleged in the same interview: "My attorney and my parents are being completely ignored." She had engaged Landmark Legal's Mark Bredemeier to represent her.

15. Interview, November 22, 1995.

Bibliography

American Civil Liberties Union et al., Amicus Curiae Brief, *Miller et al. v. Benson*, 93-C-1063. September 26, 1994.

American Civil Liberties Union of Wisconsin Foundation. In the Matter of Eligibility of Messmer High School for the Milwaukee Parental Choice Program. Amicus Curiae Brief, March 17, 1993.

Applied Population Laboratory, University of Wisconsin–Madison. *Census Data Survey.* May 1995.

Baez, Tony. *Final Report: An Independent Evaluation of MPS Alternative and Partnership Schools.* University of Wisconsin–Milwaukee, Center for Urban Community Development, August 1993.

Carnegie Foundation for the Advancement of Teaching. "School Choice: A Special Report," October 26, 1992.

Carter, Stephen L. *The Culture of Disbelief: How American Law and Politics Trivialize Religious Devotion.* New York: Basic Books, 1993.

Chaney, Felmers O., v. Herbert J. Grover et al., 90-1200-OA, Supreme Court of Wisconsin, May 26, 1990.

Chubb, John, and Terry Moe. *Politics, Markets, and America's Schools.* Washington, D.C.: Brookings Institution, 1990.

Cookson, Peter W. Jr. *School Choice: The Struggle for the Soul of American Education.* New Haven, Conn.: Yale University Press, 1994.

Council of the Great City Schools. "National Urban Education Goals: Baseline Indicators, 1990–91." Washington, D.C., 1992.

Davis, Lonzetta, et al. v. Herbert J. Grover et al., 90CV2576. Dane County Trial Court.

Davis v. Grover, N90-1807-LV. Wisconsin Court of Appeals, District IV.

Davis v. Grover, 480 NW 2nd. Wisconsin (State Supreme Court) 1992.

Doyle, Denis P. *Where the Connoisseurs Send Their Children to School: An Analysis of 1990 Census Data to Determine Where School Teachers Send Their Children to School.* Washington, D.C.: Center for Education Reform, May 1995.

"Enrollment Options Program," Bill AB 995/119.23 1989–90. Wisconsin Legislative Session.

"False Choices: Why School Vouchers Threaten Our Children's Future." Milwaukee: *Rethinking Schools*, special issue, September 1992.

Fischer, Michael. "Fiscal Accountability in Milwaukee's Public Elementary Schools: 'Where Does the Money Go?'" Wisconsin Policy Research Institute Report 3, no. 4 (September 1990).

Fuller, Howard L., and Sammis B. White. "Expanded School Choice in Milwaukee," Wisconsin Policy Research Institute Report 8, no. 5 (July 1995).

Grogan, Thomas R. Hearing Examiner. In the Matter of Eligibility of Messmer High School for the Milwaukee Parental Choice Program. May 7, 1993.

Hanushek, Eric A. "The Economics of Schooling: Production and Efficiency in Public Schools," *Journal of Economic Literature* 24 (September 1986).

Hanushek, Eric A. "Impact of Differential Expenditures on School Performance," *Education Researcher* 18, no. 4 (May 1989).

Kozol, Jonathan. *Savage Inequalities.* New York: HarperCollins, 1991.

Levine, David, Robert Lowe, Bob Peterson, and Rita Tenorio, eds. *Rethinking Schools: An Agenda for Change.* New York: New Press, 1995.

MacGuire, James. *Beyond Partisan Politics: A Response to the Carnegie Report on Choice.* New York: Center for Social Thought, 1993.

McGroarty, Daniel. "A Prayer for Better Education." *Wall Street Journal,* October 1, 1993.

McGroarty, Daniel. "Education's Long March." *Policy Review* 69 (Summer 1994).

McGroarty, Daniel. "School Choice Slandered." *Public Interest* no. 117 (Fall 1994).

Miller, Marquelle, et al. v. John T. Benson, Superintendent of Public Instruction. Memorandum of Points and Authorities in Support of Plaintiffs' Motion for Summary Judgment, 93-C-1063. August 25, 1994.

Miller et al. v. Benson, Brief in Support of Defendant's Motion. . . . 93-C-1063. September 26, 1994.

Miller et al. v. Benson, Brief for Appellants. June 2, 1995. 95-1867.

Milwaukee Public Schools (MPS) Department of Labor Relations. Arbitration Summaries.

Milwaukee Public Schools (MPS) Report Card, 1993–94.

Milwaukee Public Schools (MPS) Report Card, 1994–95.

Milwaukee Teachers Education Association (MTEA) Incorporation documents, State of Wisconsin, 1993.

Mitchell, George. "The Milwaukee Parental Choice Program." Wisconsin Policy Research Institute Report 5, no. 5 (November 1992).

Mitchell, Susan. "Why MPS Doesn't Work: Barriers to Reform in the Milwaukee Public Schools." Wisconsin Policy Research Institute Report 7, no. 1 (January 1994).

Munro, Douglas P. "How to Find Out Where the Money Goes in the Public Schools." Heritage Foundation, 955/S, August 10, 1993.

National Center for Education Statistics, U.S. Department of Education. *The Condition of Education, 1992.* NCES 92-096.

National Center for Education Statistics, U.S. Department of Education. *Digest of Education Statistics, 1993.* NCES 93-292.

National Commission on Excellence in Education. *A Nation at Risk.* Washington, D.C., 1983.

Norquist, John O. "The Future of Our Cities." *Wisconsin Interest 1*, no. 1 (Winter 1992).

Parent Guide, Milwaukee Parental Choice Program, 1995–96.

Peterson, Paul E. "A Critique of the Witte Evaluation of Milwaukee's School Choice Program." Harvard University Occasional Paper 95-2, February 1995.

Public Safety Report, City of Milwaukee, 1993.

Rasell, Edith, and Richard Rothstein, eds. *School Choice: Examining the Evidence.* Washington, D.C.: Economic Policy Institute, 1993.

Rury, John L., and Frank A. Cassell, eds. *Seeds of Crisis: Public Schooling in Milwaukee Since 1920.* Madison: University of Wisconsin Press, 1993.

Shanker, Albert. Where We Stand: "The Agenda for Privatization." September 29, 1991.

———. Where We Stand: "All Smiles." January 30, 1994.

———. "The Milwaukee Story." *American Educator,* Fall 1991.

———. Where We Stand: "Sleight-of-Hand Logic." Novermber 18, 1990.

Smith, Kevin B., and Kenneth J. Meier. *The Case Against School Choice: Politics, Markets and Fools.* New York: M. E. Sharpe, 1995.

State of Wisconsin Legislative Audit Bureau. An Evaluation of Milwaukee Parental Choice Program, February 1995, 95-3.

Study Commission on the Quality of Education in the Metropolitan Milwaukee Public Schools, State of Wisconsin. "Better Public Schools." October 1985.

Sykes, Charles. "Fuller's Choice." *Wisconsin Interest* 1, no. 1 (Winter/Spring 1992).

———. "The Future That Works." *Crisis,* January 1993.

Texas State Teachers Association/National Education Association. "Our Public Schools: The Best Choice for Texas." Austin, Texas, May 1994.

Tribe, Laurence H. *American Constitutional Law,* 2nd ed. Mineola, N.Y.: Foundation Press, 1988.

Underwood, Julie K., and Deborah A. Verstegen, eds. *The Impacts of Litigation and Legislation on Public School Finance.* New York: Harper & Row, 1990.

Witte, John F. *First Year Report, Milwaukee Parental Choice Program.* University of Wisconsin–Madison, November 1991.

———. *Metropolitan Milwaukee Dropout Report #3.* Better Public Schools Appendices, State of Wisconsin, October 1985.

Witte, John F., Andrea B. Bailey, and Christopher A. Thorn. *Second Year Report, Milwaukee Parental Choice Program.* University of Wisconsin–Madison, December 1992.

———. *Third Year Report, Milwaukee Parental Choice Program.* University of Wisconsin–Madison, December 1993.

Witte, John F., and William Clune, eds. *Choice and Control in American Education,* vol. 1. New York: Falmer, 1990.

Witte, John F., Christopher A. Thorn, Kim M. Pritchard, and Michele Claibourn. *Fourth Year Report, Milwaukee Parental Choice Program.* University of Wisconsin–Madison, December 1994.

Wooster, Martin Morse. *Angry Classrooms, Vacant Minds.* San Francisco: Pacific Research Institute, 1994.

U.S. SUPREME COURT CASES

Mueller v. Allen, 463 US 388 (1983).

Witters v. Department of Services for the Blind, 474 US 481 (1986).

Zobrest v. Catalina Foothills School District, 113 S.Ct. 2462 (1993).

Public Education v. Nyquist, 413 US 756 (1973).

Lemon v. Kurtzman, 403 US 602 (1971).

Pierce v. Society of Sisters, 268 US 510 (1925).

Swann v. Charlotte-Mecklenberg Board of Education, 402 US 1 (1971).

Walz v. Tax Commission, 397 US 664 (1970).

Committee for Public Education and Liberty v. Regan, 444 US 646 (1980).

Acknowledgments

The business of writing a book begets many debts. I wish to thank the Bradley Foundation and, in particular, Bill Schambra for his constant encouragement and keen insight. I wish to thank Robert Hawkins of the Institute for Contemporary Studies for his unfailing support, Cameron Humphries for his able research assistance, and, among the many people in Milwaukee too numerous to mention, I must single out George and Susan Mitchell for sharing with me their expertise on school policy and school politics. In preparing the manuscript for publication, I benefited immensely from the assistance of editor Steven Martin and his team at Prima Publishing, as well as Kevin Heverin, Tracy Clagett, and their colleagues at ICS Press.

I wish also to thank Jim Pinkerton, Jeff Salmon, Charles Kolb, and Bill Kristol, whose advice and interest along the way kept me on course, and my parents, whose combined fifty years of service in public schools was a daily lesson in the importance of education.

Finally, I am grateful to the parents in Milwaukee who interrupted their schedules to tell me their stories, and who welcomed me into their homes to discuss the serious business of their children's education.

Many people helped improve these pages. Any errors, omissions or failures of understanding are mine alone.

Index

ABOUT THE AUTHOR

Daniel McGroarty is a Lynde and Harry Bradley Fellow with the Institute for Contemporary Studies, a public policy think tank located in San Francisco. His work on education reform and politics has appeared in *The Wall Street Journal*, *The Public Interest*, *National Review*, and *Policy Review*. He is also a senior director of the White House Writers Group, a Washington, D.C.–based communications consulting firm. During the Bush administration, Mr. McGroarty served as special assistant to the president and deputy director of White House speechwriting. He lives in Annandale, Virginia.

ABOUT THE INSTITUTE FOR CONTEMPORARY STUDIES

The Institute for Contemporary Studies (ICS) is a nonprofit public policy research organization founded in 1974. To fulfill its mission of promoting self-governing and entrepreneurial ways of life around the world, ICS sponsors innovative work on fundamental issues, including those of governance and leadership, social policy, entrepreneurial activity, and international development. ICS Press is dedicated to furthering the understanding of these issues among scholars, policy makers, and the wider community of citizens. The Press has published more than a hundred scholarly books, which include the writings of seven Nobel laureates and have been influential in setting the nation's policy agenda.